BODYGUARDING:
A COMPLETE MANUAL
Revised and Expanded
Second Edition

by Burt Rapp
and
Tony Lesce

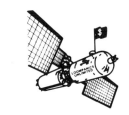

Loompanics Unlimited
Port Townsend, Washington

Bodyguarding: A Complete Manual
  Revised and Expanded Second Edition
© 1995 by Burt Rapp and Tony Lesce

Published by:
Loompanics Unlimited
PO Box 1197
Port Townsend, WA 98368

Loompanics Unlimited is a division of Loompanics Enterprises, Inc.

ISBN 1-55950-124-3
Library of Congress Catalog Card Number 95-76636

Contents

Introduction

Since the first edition of this book appeared, there have been changes in both the world situation and in protective equipment and techniques. This second edition is revised and enlarged to provide the reader with an up-to-date picture.

We've heard a lot about bodyguarding during the last few decades. It becomes a prominent topic whenever there's an assassination attempt, successful or not. There's nevertheless a great gap between what bodyguarding really is and what the public is told that it is. The extensively videotaped attempt on President Reagan's life showed police and Secret Service guards scrambling around with revolvers and even one with an UZI submachine gun, but firepower is not all there is to it. In fact, the agents involved in that incident didn't fire a single shot.

On one hand, we see films and articles about the U.S. Secret Service, the fairly professional corps of federal officers who have guarded the president and other federal officials since the turn of the century. Until 1963, they used to boast truthfully that they had never lost a president.

We also get our dose of myths along with the news. One myth is that a Secret Service agent said that anyone can kill the president if he's willing to give up his life in the attempt. Any government official who would say that would be badly mistaken, as presidential assassins do not usually die trying. During the past 40 years, we've seen Lee Harvey Oswald survive the killing of President Kennedy, only to be shot to death several days later by Jack Ruby. Two women who tried to shoot President Gerald Ford in 1975 were taken alive, and stood trial. John Hinckley, who wounded President Reagan in 1981, was captured on the scene by Secret Service agents who swarmed over him, and he is now in a psychiatric hospital. The only exception came when Collazo and Torresola made an attempt on President Truman.[1]

Another myth we sometimes find is that there are certain "professional secrets" and tricks which only the "pro" knows, and which he's reluctant to disclose to the uninitiated.[2] Myth-makers also adopt a secretive air for "security" reasons. There are actually no "secrets" that the "pros" know that anyone with a high school education and common sense can't understand.

We are also faced with the myth that the bodyguard is a physically powerful person. It's very wrong to think that effectiveness in this field goes directly with physical size or strength. An example came during the assassination of Robert Kennedy. An ex-football player, Roosevelt Grier, was Bobby Kennedy's bodyguard the night he was shot to death in Los Angeles. However skilled he was in football, he was not a professional bodyguard, and he failed to prevent the shooting.

Bodyguards suffer from an image problem, as do members of certain other occupations. One popular view of a bodyguard is the stereotyped "hulk" or "goon" with a strong back and weak mind. In real life, the retarded giant is usually the least effective type of bodyguard. It takes brains to be an effective bodyguard today, because of the diversity of tasks the bodyguard must master. The bodyguard must also be versatile enough to fit into various social milieus.

One way of overcoming a degraded image is to use more flattering terms. Many bodyguards today prefer to call themselves "executive protection specialists." This term sounds more "professional" and leaves behind the image of the "goon."

Today, we even see female bodyguards. Obviously, bodyguards can be male or female, and attackers also include members of both sexes. In fact, as physical size and strength are not among the most important qualities a bodyguard must have, females can be as proficient as males. However, in discussing bodyguarding topics generally, we won't fall into the trap of "political correctness." For simplicity's sake, we'll use the masculine pronoun with the understanding that it includes both genders, except when discussing a specific individual.

Another myth, often fostered by the client himself, is that bodyguarding is an all-or-nothing proposition. It's not true that having a bodyguard, or many of them, affords total protection. No bodyguard squad can protect the client against every possible threat all of the time.[3]

Well, if they can't do that, then what *can* they do? What bodyguards can do is greatly reduce the risk to the client. An unprotected client is an easy (or "soft") target to a lone assailant. Even one bodyguard makes the assailant's task much harder, and having several guards obliges any potential attacker to plan very carefully, and employ a large squad of conspirators to carry out an assault.

Let's get into the question of bodyguard effectiveness a little more deeply. There are at least two viewpoints on this, and we can learn something from each one.

One viewpoint is that the presence of bodyguards seems to deter the attackers. They tend to turn their efforts towards "softer" targets. Some evidence of this comes from overseas. Among the attacks in other countries, there has been a shift in attacks from hardened American companies to softer foreign-owned ones.[4]

Other evidence points in the opposite direction. Kidnap teams have grown about 50% in size in recent years. This is almost surely in response to the increase in protective forces. At the same time, there's been an increase in female membership in kidnap groups, and an increase in the use of full-auto weapons.[5]

We can reconcile these viewpoints by stating that protection is relative. A certain level of protection will be a safeguard against a certain level of threat. Almost inevitably, if the threat is severe enough, no level of protection will suffice. If "they" really want to get you, they will. Fortunately, most of us aren't that important, and don't have such formidable enemies.

However, the number of types of threats has increased. We now see "stalkers," who pursue entertainers and other people. Stalkers get media attention when they stalk high-profile citizens, such as public figures, actresses and rock stars, but relatively obscure people are stalked and sometimes harmed by ex-spouses or ex-lovers.

The popular media present an overly glamorized view of the techniques used by bodyguards. They emphasize gunplay and car chases, when in reality the major part of the bodyguard's work is demanding but non-violent. This book presents the story the way it really is. The simple fact is that if there's a violent encounter, the bodyguard has already failed at the most important part of his job.

What This Book Will Do For You

1. This book will be entertaining. Although this is a serious book, it is entertaining, because that's the best way to get and to hold your attention, especially if you're reading it for a serious purpose. Within these pages are the art and science of executive protection, delivered from several points of view. You'll gain an insight into how attackers plan and carry out their assaults. You'll see it as the leader of an executive protection team, learning the technical and administrative problems involved in running a bodyguard operation. You'll also understand it from the viewpoint of a subordinate, gaining an insight into how your assignment fits into the big picture. Most importantly, you'll see it through the eyes of a client, who depends on others to keep him safe. You'll find it interesting from the first page to the last, and I hope that you'll absorb the lessons contained herein.

2. This book will lay out for you the main methods used by government agencies charged with protection of their political leaders, as well as those used by private bodyguards. The U.S. Secret Service doesn't have a monopoly on protective techniques, and certain foreign agencies display a great degree of skill. For example, the Presidential Protection Corps of the French Sureté had to protect President de Gaulle against a well-organized band of professional military men, the Organization de L'Armee Secrete (O.A.S.), who made numerous attempts on him during his career. No American president has been so persistently threatened by such a skilled organization.

    By contrast, the British have only a few plainclothes detectives assigned to the Prime Minister and the Royal Family. These are part of Scotland Yard's Special Branch, and their main concern in recent years has been the Provisional Wing of the Irish Republican Army — the "Provos."

    This section will be of greatest help if you intend to be or are already working in the field.

3. You'll learn how to be your own bodyguard. This is the part that's most sorely neglected by the media, and by the professional training centers. You don't have to be President or Secretary of State to feel threatened. Just ride the New York subway on the way to your job in the baloney factory and you'll face more danger than the U. S. President does in a year. Really.

In another light, you'll learn what's realistic if you expect to employ bodyguards to protect you. You'll learn what qualities to seek out in a bodyguard. There are some who will present themselves with what seem to be excellent backgrounds and credentials, but who actually are not very qualified for the type of work involved. You'll find out why an ex-Marine or retired police officer is usually not the best choice.

Can you reasonably expect to hire someone who will risk and perhaps lay down his life for you for about $30,000 a year? If not, what then? You need to know the answers, and you'll find many of them within these pages.

Notes:

1. *Report of the Warren Commission on the Assassination of President Kennedy, New York Times* edition, p. 481. This incident occurred on November 1, 1950, when President Truman was living in Blair House, across Pennsylvania Avenue from the White House, while the White House was undergoing renovation. This was one of the few blazing shoot-outs to take place in the history of bodyguarding.

Two Puerto Rican nationalists, Oscar Collazo and Griselio Torresola, tried to break in by force in a frontal assault on Blair House. On guard in front of Blair House were three White House Police officers and one Secret Service agent. Collazo shot one White House Policeman, and engaged in a gunfight with another and a Secret Service agent. Out of ammunition, he sat down on the steps of Blair House to reload his pistol. The shoot-out was short and sharp, and took place entirely in front of Blair House, because the gunmen never made it inside. The attackers killed one White House Policeman, and wounded two others. The mortally wounded White House Policeman, Leslie Coffelt, opened fire before expiring and scored one hit, killing Tor-

resola with a bullet in the head. Collazo was wounded by the other agents.

A significant aspect of this attack was what it revealed about the "defense in depth" that the Secret Service mounts around the president. Inside the front door of Blair House was another Secret Service agent, Stewart Stout, armed with a submachine gun. His job was to hold his position and stop any attackers who penetrated into the house. Upstairs, in the hallway in front of the bedroom where President Truman was taking a nap at the time, were more agents.

2. *Dead Clients Don't Pay*, Leroy Thompson, Boulder, CO, Paladin Press, 1984, p. 11.
3. *Terrorism and Personal Protection*, Brian Jenkins, editor, NY, Butterworth Publishers, 1985, p. 319.
4. *Terrorism and Personal Protection*, Brian Jenkins, editor, NY, Butterworth Publishers, 1985, p. 187. See also page 11 in the same volume. One important point is that these are only trends, and may reverse themselves in the future. One possible cause of a large-scale change would be a strong increase in anti-American sentiment.
5. *Terrorism and Personal Protection*, Brian Jenkins, editor, NY, Butterworth Publishers, 1985, p. 17. The connection between the increase in protective forces and the corresponding increase in the size of kidnap groups seems clear. The increased use of automatic weapons also seems to have a cause-and-effect relationship to the need to overwhelm the protective forces. The number of women in these groups seems to be related to other factors, however, which are beyond the scope of this book.

1

Protective Theory

Professional bodyguards agree upon some points, and differ widely regarding others. Sometimes this is the result of ignorance and an "unprofessional" attitude. One excellent example is the person who advertises himself as a bodyguard, but whose only qualifications are a private investigator's license and a career attending martial arts schools.

Let's review the major issues quickly:

All experts agree that avoidance is better than confrontation. The safety of the client is the first priority, and the best way of assuring this is by keeping him out of harm's way, not by having him witness a confrontation which endangers him.

Generally, the best way to protect the client is to anticipate trouble and take steps to avoid it. This demands an effort at gathering information about the client, possible enemies and potential threats.

Keeping a low profile is basic to executive protection, but it's not always possible. Much depends upon the client. If the protectee is a politician or entertainer, or both (such as Ronald Reagan), it's impossible to maintain a low profile. A business executive, by contrast, is much less likely to be recognized or to attract attention unless his lifestyle is very conspicuous. A diplomat or businessman in a foreign post usually stands out from the crowd.

"Target hardening" means building up defensive screens to make the client less vulnerable. Hardening includes all defensive measures, such as alarms, fences, locks, bodyguards, etc.

How much hardening is necessary? Your client will want to know this, because most defensive measures, such as an armored car, cost money. Also, no defensive system provides absolute protection, because in this business nothing is 100% guaranteed. Experience has shown that some attackers, when faced with a hardened target, will choose a "softer" one.[1] This suggests an obvious answer to the question: "How much?"

A level of protection higher than other potential targets in the area will deter some attackers and persuade them to try an easier target. The conspicuous exceptions are when your target is so high-profile that attackers decide to make an attempt, whatever the cost, or when they don't mind dying in the attempt.

Defense in depth is another of the basic concepts. Everyone agrees on this one, but few have the means to carry it out. For best results, there should be several layers of defense. The outer layers are screens, to shield the client and his bodyguard from routine nuisances and casual threats. Closer to the client are the hard defensive shells, such as a squad of bodyguards.

A controversial point is whether the client should take part in his own defense. The traditional view, held by the U.S. Secret Service and most government-sponsored protective agencies, is that the client should cooperate passively, and "leave it to us." In other words, do what he's told and not worry.

This viewpoint holds up when there are enough manpower and other resources to provide several concentric shells of protection. The VIP doesn't have to do anything but walk and talk while screens of bodyguards look after his safety.

In most situations, the bodyguard screen is thin indeed. Many who need bodyguards can afford only one or two, which inevitably leaves gaps in the defenses. In the worst instance, the bodyguard can be disabled in an attack, which leaves the client on his own. It's worth the effort for the client to take an active role in his defense, even to the point of being armed. In a desperate situation, his being able to "back up" the bodyguard can make the difference between life and death.

One obvious point, which is not controversial but is still not widely understood, is that the bodyguard's first priority is the client's safety, not apprehending a criminal. The bodyguard's job is to stay with and evacuate the protectee from the danger zone, not to

Bodyguarding

6

make an arrest. The executive protection agent engages in combat only as a last resort, if there's no other way to assure the client's safety. As we'll see, this can be a pitfall for the ex-cop or former military person, conditioned as he is to taking aggressive action to apprehend the perpetrator.

Another important but unglamorous task is gathering information. Most of the "intelligence" required consists of mundane details, such as finding the best route for travel, the location of nearby hospitals, etc. There's no brilliant undercover work, just hard work.

Part of the task is building up a network of personal contacts. It helps to know the local police, and extending the network of contacts to other locales frequented by the client will sometimes bring rewards.

Now that we've got the whys under our belts, let's look at the nuts and bolts of executive protection.

Notes:

1. *You're The Target*, Shackley, Theodore G., Oatman, Robert L., and Finney, Richard A., New World Publishing, Ltd., 1989, pp. 99-100.

2

Threat Assessment

This pompous-sounding term has a real and definite meaning, but it's much easier to understand than we might conclude from the sound of the words. Basically, we have to understand what sort of threats are on the horizon, and how vulnerable the protectee is to these threats.

The worst way to assess possible threats is to take scare headlines seriously. The recent Gulf War provided a good example. The media had their usual feeding frenzy predicting an increase in terrorism in the wake of Iraq's invasion of Kuwait in August, 1990, and the American opposition to that move. "Retired CIA agents and other experts predicted the worst was yet to come."[1]

This is a familiar scene. TV networks can always round up a few "experts" to discuss a trend or event, and to suggest a threatening future. Bad news sells, and the news media show that they know this very well in their continual campaign to produce audiences for their advertisers.

The facts, however, don't always fit. In 1991, there were 113 terrorist attacks in Europe and the Middle East directed against Americans, contrasted with 193 in Asia and Latin America. Still, American companies panicked, and reduced foreign travel by their executives, while students abroad returned home.[2]

Before that, the shooting down of an Iranian Airbus by the U.S.S. Vincennes in 1988 produced alarmist predictions of terrorist attacks against Americans and American businesses, but again, this didn't happen.

Statistics don't necessarily tell the true story, although this volume cites statistics from several sources. One conspicuous example is the definition of "terrorist attack." The U.S. State Department counts an attack as a "terrorist attack" only when it involves citizens of more than one country. When British executive Kenneth Marston was killed in Lyons, France, the State Department counted that as an incident. When fellow Germans killed Karl-Heinz Beckurts and French at-

tackers killed Renault chairman Georges Besse, these did not count in the State Department tally.[3]

Business Risks International is a private firm that collects data on threats to corporations and their personnel, and has compiled a database dating back to the early 1970s. BRI's figures show that over eight times the State Department's tally of terrorist incidents actually took place throughout the world. BRI's total of corporate assassinations, bombings and other attacks for 1989 is 4,422.[4]

RISKNET, operated by the Ackerman Group, provides up to date threat information by wire to subscribers. Covering 80 countries, the *Executive Digest* is one service, and Ackermans *Airline Guide* evaluates threats to air carriers. These are available from:

The Ackerman Group, Inc.
1666 Kennedy Causeway, Suite 700
Miami Beach, FL 33141
Phone: (305) 865-0072
Fax: (305) 865-0218

How, then, can we get a realistic assessment of danger to the client? First, let's look at threats from the perspective of the protectee. There are two rules of thumb:

1. The type of threat often varies with the type of protectee. The high-profile public figure, such as the screen actor, rock star or politician is likely to attract crowds of well wishers, autograph hunters, fans and "nutcakes." The well known person is far more likely to be injured by the crush of a crowd than maliciously attacked. The danger from the crowd is ever-present, but lurking in the background, almost unperceived, is the small but more serious danger of a calculated and deadly attack by a stalker. The murders of performers Sharon Tate and John Lennon are two examples of what can happen. A deadly raid at home by a cultist gang results in mass murder. Crowds often serve as

screens for the few people who pose deadly threats. Some may actually use the audiences as concealment while they "stalk" their targets, as did Arthur Bremer while following George Wallace's political campaign around the country. As we'll see, stalkers are dangerous to both public and private figures.

In 1981, singer Linda Ronstadt found her home trashed, and a note stated, "You next time." That her brother Peter was chief of police in Tucson, Arizona, was little help, because Linda lived in Malibu, California. The next year, actress Theresa Saldana was stabbed ten times while unlocking her car, by a man who'd been stalking her. Her attacker believed he had a divine mission to kill her.[5]

The low-profile client is unlikely to attract crowds, mainly because he's unknown to most people. The corporate executive does not get the sort of publicity that an actor or politician does. Except for certain extreme situations, such as a labor crisis, his face is not going to be on the front page of a newspaper. This sort of client's likely to attract only the dedicated and malevolent attacker, intent upon kidnapping or killing him.

There are a few exceptions. The novelist Salman Rushdie, author of *The Satanic Verses*, found himself condemned to death by Moslem fundamentalists because his novel allegedly blasphemed their religion. He's been in hiding, protected by British police bodyguards, since the threat, and some bookstores declined to carry his book because their managers were afraid of violence.

Law professor Anita Hill kept a low-profile existence until her involvement in the Clarence Thomas hearings. Once the news broke, she began using bodyguards, including "student volunteers and campus security guards."[6]

Rodney King was unknown before the nationally publicized incident with Los Angeles police officers, but since he's come into prominence, he's received threats, and now wears body armor and travels with bodyguards.

Another exception is the individual with a personal enemy, such as a former lover, boyfriend or spouse. Court orders do not stop a determined stalker. Although California passed an anti-stalker law in 1990, its effectiveness is uncertain because of the difficulty of identifying the clever stalker. In these cases, the threat may be so severe that the individual hires a bodyguard.

Yet another exception depends upon the time and place. Being a journalist in Colombia is dangerous to one's health. A "huge car bomb" detonated in front of Bogotá's *El Espectador* newspaper, killing one person, injuring 80 people, and causing severe physical damage.[7]

Jose Salgar, co-publisher of *El Espectador*, has had his life threatened, and drives to work by various routes to avoid assassination, while police guard his doors. His wife and two children are under constant police guard, because of the well known predilection of Colombian drug cartel killers to target families. The newspaper is under military guard, with ropes and other barriers surrounding the building as protection against attacks. In 1986, then publisher Guillermo Cano was machine-gunned and killed by cartel killers. The following year, the home of columnist Maria Jimena Duzan was blown up.[8]

Still another exception was Sharon Rodgers, wife of the captain of the U.S.S. Vincennes, the cruiser that shot down the Iranian airliner by mistake. A bomb exploded under her Toyota van as she stopped for a red light. She was unhurt, and immediately jumped out, but metal fragments had pierced the roof, and the blast and fire destroyed the van. Several threatening calls had preceded this incident, and Captain Rodgers and his wife obtained police protection and went into hiding.[9]

2. The client's lifestyle not only determines the sort of attacker he attracts, but has much to do with his vulnerability. The rock star or political leader must make public appearances because these are his stock-in-trade. Appearances expose him to danger by giving threatening persons opportunities to strike at him. A controversial or abrasive talk-show host offends many people who would otherwise not notice him, and a few of these may actually vent their dislike in violence. The talk-show host exposes himself to his audience, and follows a predictable path each day commuting to the studio.

By contrast, the low-profile protectee can live in the shadows, unknown to the public at large and under no pressure to make his whereabouts and movements known. This low-profile existence is an important protective technique.

Threat Types

There are only a few general types of threats, which is fortunate because they're serious enough.

Impersonal Threats

This category covers fire, natural disasters and other general types of threats which are not purposeful actions instigated by individuals. It may seem surprising that a bodyguard has to concern himself with the prospect of a fire, but his responsibility is total. One example is the concern of the Secret Service for the safety of President Nixon when a fire broke out at San Clemente in 1970.[10]

Another impersonal threat is air travel on airlines with poor safety records, or in areas with deficient air traffic control or safety procedures. One example is Russia, cited by the International Airline Passengers Association in its April, 1994, newsletter. Of course, the few airlines providing service into Russia denied the report, but a security advisor must take all factors into consideration.[11]

Personal Attacks

These include attacks by firearms, bombs, poison, arson and other violent methods, as well as kidnapping. While it's wasteful to plan for countering the most unlikely methods of attack, it's good to keep in mind that some attackers have access to rather exotic weapons such as rocket launchers. Whether these are likely to come into use depends a lot on the importance of the client and prevailing local conditions. A protectee in Beirut, for example, may find a rocket coming through his window. Anyone trying to kill the mayor of Middletown, U.S.A., is most likely to do it with a handgun.

Political unrest sometimes involves violence, especially in the Middle East. The March, 1994, elections in Turkey were preceded by a series of bombing and shooting attacks on campaign offices. Four people, including a 12-year-old girl, died as a result. Many others were wounded, both by bombs and gunfire.[12]

Israel, of course, is always in turmoil, and travelers to that country are in danger of being caught in the cross-fire, literally. The danger is acute in public places. After the February 25, 1994, machine-gunning of Moslems in a Hebron mosque by a Jewish fanatic, there were a spate of revenge attacks. One was a suicide car bomb that exploded at a city bus stop near three high schools in Afula, in northern Galilee. The bomb killed eight and wounded 45, including many students.[13]

When a bomb went off inside a bus in the Hadera Station, it killed six and injured 28, including 18 soldiers. Another bomb had been left inside the station, timed to go off 90 minutes later.[14]

One authority points out the danger involved for an American executive meeting with a Jewish industrialist in a locale under attack by Islamics, as the American may be dragged into someone else's scrap. In October, 1993, two Americans were shot dead in Cairo. Possibly relevant was the fact that their company was conducting contract negotiations with the Egyptian government for the construction of a pipeline.[15]

Threat Levels

Let's lay out the types of threats in order of increasing seriousness. We'll also examine the types of people likely to be involved.

A. *Crowds.* These usually are friendly crowds, as evidenced whenever a screen actor or popular political figure makes a public appearance. The danger comes from the prospect of being trapped or trampled by the crowd. This is what gives the Secret Service anxiety whenever the president steps into a crowd to shake hands. Entertainers are very vulnerable to friendly crowds of agitated fans. A thousand of singer Tevin Campbell's fans showed up at a Southfield, Michigan store to get his autograph in March, 1994. At least two were hurt in the crush of bodies, and the singer had to barricade himself in a back room with his bodyguards.

B. *Special individuals.* Some dedicated autograph hunters and "groupies" show great ingenuity in penetrating the protective rings and coming into contact with the client. Others will make supreme efforts to meet the celebrity face to face. In one extreme case, an individual penetrated the defenses of Buckingham Palace in London and made it into the Queen's bedroom. Fortunately, he did not show aggressive behavior towards the monarch.

C. *Pranksters and nuisances.* These may be simply gate-crashers or egg-throwers, with no serious malicious intent, but some of their stunts can become dangerous. Another nuisance is the "paparazzo," the intrusive photographer who annoys notables by his presence everywhere. Some entertainers expect their bodyguards to confiscate the film or camera of any photographer who takes their picture, but in practice this is usually impossible. Pranksters pose headaches mainly because they're so numerous, and in reality there's little a bodyguard can do.

D. *Unfriendly crowds.* These come in all sizes and types. A business executive may hire bodyguards to look after him because of a picket line he must negotiate each day. An unpopular politician may face demonstrations wherever he's recognized. In certain foreign countries, Americans are very unpopular, and the few whose jobs keep them there need bodyguards to protect them.

E. *Kidnappers.* These are political or professional criminals who try to use the victim to extort ransom or certain concessions. The target may be the principal or a member of his family or staff. The ransom may be money or hard goods, such as "food for the poor." The price for the victim's safety may be the release of prisoners.

F. *Individual assassins.* These may be mentally deranged individuals, but usually they have personalities that are integrated enough to plan an assassination. For this reason, they're generally not "legally insane." In the United States, it's politically expedient to treat political assassins as insane, because this deprives them of legitimacy.

Individuals may be disgruntled or psychotic employees or vengeful ex-employees. There have been recent instances of employees shooting up the workplace and killing supervisors and other employees.[16] The site may be anywhere, including a post office or a printing plant, and the lethally violent employee often shows behavioral cues before embarking on his course of action. Although there's no accurate predictor, violent employees are often "loners," depressed, an intimidating type, and prone to drug or alcohol abuse. Paranoid traits and constant complaining hint at the turbulence below the surface of this type of personality. Finally, a history of violence is a definite warning sign.[17]

Fortunately, there's a growing legal and practical basis for taking workplace threats seriously. Section 5 of the 1970 Occupational Safety and Health Act (OSHA) mandates employers to respond to threats. A company's security director today is very likely to maintain a continuing study of potentially disruptive or violent employees, and conduct periodic re-evaluations. This has become critical in some firms, because of the stress caused by "down-sizing," a policy likely to foster many bitter feelings. The bodyguard often can depend on advance information from the security manager regarding possible threats to his principal.[18]

Individual assassins usually have little in resources. Unlike violent groups, they don't have rocket-propelled grenades, missiles and other sophisticated hardware. Bremer and Hinckley are two recent American examples, and they carried out their attacks with snub-nosed revolvers. The plans of lone assassins cannot be complex, and therefore often fail for lack of information,

equipment or "back-up." In short, they're less formidable threats than organized terrorists.

Now let's look at the other side of the coin. Because individuals work alone, the bodyguard usually has no warning of the attempt until it's actually under way. These individuals don't confide their plans to others, which eliminates the risk of informers and leaks.

G. *Hostile groups and organizations.* These are usually the most severe threats. They're tightly organized, well-dedicated groups, often consisting of former military types. Civilian groups have intensive training programs, and they develop well-trained attackers who will disregard their own safety for the sake of fulfilling their missions. The killers of Egypt's President Sadat provide a good example.

On October 6, 1981, Sadat was reviewing a military parade under supposedly tight security from his American-trained bodyguards. Security officers had checked to ensure that none of the soldiers in the parade carried live ammunition, and metal detectors screened guests admitted to the reviewing stand. Suddenly, four uniformed soldiers burst from the procession and attacked the reviewing stand with grenades and automatic fire. Spraying the crowd to force security men to duck for cover, they killed five and wounded 28. They then focused in on Sadat, hitting him in the neck, chest, thigh and knee. The chest wounds proved fatal.

Another example of a group was the O.A.S., the French group that narrowly missed killing de Gaulle several times.[19] This group was tightly organized, but had been penetrated by informers who at times were able to warn the authorities of threats to de Gaulle's life. At other times, the attackers' sheer bad luck, or good planning on the part of de Gaulle's bodyguards saved him.

An example of a lone agent who forms part of a group is the driver who took a truck loaded with explosives into the U.S. Marine compound in Beirut in 1983, killing well over 200 Marines as well as himself (or herself — we'll never know) in the explosion. It's a serious error to believe that our opponents are not as dedicated and brave as ourselves and our allies, or are unwilling to sacrifice their lives for a cause.

We're not going to spend any more time studying these groups and meticulously describing every terrorist gang or potentially hostile political group. Suffice it to say that there's an alphabet soup of groups such as

PLO, PFLP, etc., in the world, and that information about them is often inaccurate when published and always becomes obsolete quickly. Publicly available hard information about these groups is sparse, and often hedged with weasel words such as "estimated," which is often a euphemism for "wild guess." As a practical matter, a bodyguard can't immediately ascertain the identity or political connections of an attacker, and in the urgency of the moment, he doesn't care.

Fortunately, the United States has not suffered much from terrorist groups of foreign origin. Terrorism generally declined in the early 1990s, but there's no guarantee this trend will continue. European groups work mainly in Europe. Mid-Eastern groups don't need to venture far afield because their main enemy, Israel, is in their back yard. Latin American groups fight against their own governments. They will, however, menace American diplomats and businessmen who come to their territory. Americans have been killed and kidnapped in Europe, the Mid-East and Latin America.

Rarely do these groups export violence to mainland America. The World Trade Center bombing was a conspicuous exception. The Irish Republican Army has agents in the United States, but only to raise funds for the movement. Armenian terrorists have assassinated the Turkish consuls in Los Angeles and Boston. An Israeli diplomat was shot to death in Washington, D.C., during the early 1980s. Rabbi Meir Kahane, himself a terrorist leader, was shot to death in New York City.

There are also violence-prone domestic groups, such as the animal rights extremists, anti-abortion extremists, anti-Arab extremists, Aryan Nations, Black Liberation Army, environmental extremists, Jewish Defense League, Native American extremists, and other groups with a record of violence. Occasionally, labor unions engage in violence, but they typically direct it against strike-breakers, not company executives or owners. When coal miners went on strike against Pittston Coal in Virginia, West Virginia and Kentucky, a car bomb exploded in front of a coal company in Virginia.[20]

Attacks involving only property damage can provide early warning. A band of eco-terrorists toppled power poles one night in California, depriving about 95,000 people of electric power.[21] As we'll see in the discussion of animal-rights and anti-abortion groups, property attacks can be precursors to personal attacks.

Many groups, such as the animal-rights and environmental extremists, have concentrated on destroying property, not lives, but some use fire-bombs and ex-plosives that are threats to life if anyone's unlucky enough to be on the scene when they explode.

In 1985, the Animal Liberation Front (ALF) caused $500,000 damage at a University of California laboratory in Riverside, releasing 450 animals in the process. Eight months later, the ALF attacked a University of Oregon laboratory, releasing animals and destroying expensive equipment, including a $10,000 microscope. In April, 1987, a fire set by the ALF destroyed a laboratory at the University of California at Davis. The ALF also attacked laboratories at the University of Arizona in Tucson.[22]

Not all of these attacks involved only property damage. Arson on a Danish ferry killed two people. Police disarmed a bomb placed in a car owned by the CEO of a British construction company. Attackers threatened fur shop employees with guns while they damaged furs.[23]

There is an international animal liberation under-ground. Members have not only committed sabotage, but have come out into the open to harass hunters. This is one more thing to keep in mind if your client is involved with any company that uses animals or animal products, or if he hunts.

Southern racists bombed the Bethel Baptist Church in Birmingham, Alabama in 1967, killing four black children. The Order, a right-wing group, bombed a porno theater in Seattle on April 22, 1984, but without fatalities. There have been various assassinations, such as that of Martin Luther King, Jr., and various attempts, such as that against Vernon Jordan in 1980. Alan Berg, a Denver talk-show host who made a point of being obnoxious, was shot to death in 1984. Right- and left-wing groups, such as the Symbionese Liberation Army, and the Posse Comitatus, have been involved in shoot-outs with lawmen.

Some right-wing militant groups compile "enemies" lists, which are actually potential target lists. There have been at least two groups operating computer bulletin boards soliciting information, such as names, addresses, employment, associates, etc., about political enemies. These databases provide basic information for setting up a "hit." This is roughly comparable to anti-abortion groups' putting up of "Wanted" posters depicting doctors who perform abortions, listing their home addresses and telephone numbers.

Anti-abortion groups have come into prominence because of picketing abortion clinics, harassing abortionists and their clients, and their avowed goal of driving abortionists out of business. One abortionist stated that foes have poured barbecue sauce on his car and punctured its tires, made phone calls to his mother, picketed his home and broken his girlfriend's car windows. Others have received threatening phone calls, and one doctor found gunshots coming through his windows.[24] A few of the anti-abortionists have gone further than picketing abortion clinics and hassling their employees. The shooting of Dr. David Gunn (note the irony of that name) several years ago highlighted the vulnerability of physicians who perform abortions, and the aftermath gave an example of how not to handle such an incident.

The mainstream media loudly condemned the violent act, using it as a way to discredit abortion opponents. This had an effect they perhaps didn't foresee: copycat crimes. Another shooting followed within a year, and in July, 1994, there was a double killing in Florida. Paul Hill, a shotgun-carrying abortion opponent, shot a doctor and his escort-bodyguard to death in Pensacola, despite their wearing of body armor. He simply aimed for the head, and the media carried this vital detail as well, thereby providing anyone else contemplating killing abortionists with practical advice on how to succeed.

These precedents, plus the copycat effect, make it clear that doctors who perform abortions are in more danger today than before. Halting protests by court orders has resulted in mass arrests, such as those outside a Wichita, Kansas clinic that performed third-trimester abortions.[25] Another factor has been the partly successful effort of pro-abortion organizations to have their opponents declared criminal conspiracies, because this drives opponents underground and stiffens their resolve.

The only redeeming factor with hostile groups is that they cannot maintain total secrecy as can a lone assassin. They cannot keep as low a profile because they're constantly involved in recruiting, training and allied activities, so that some information about them leaks out. Some organizations have legal branches engaged in legitimate political activities. Sometimes it's possible to plant an informer among them, or to "turn" a captured member. In other instances, their efforts to procure weapons and supplies, such as explosives, expose them to discovery by law enforcement officers, and their possession of illegal weapons permits criminal prosecutions.

The Fake Group

Another type of threat is the individual masquerading as a group. On December, 16, 1989, a bomb delivered by mail killed federal judge Robert Vance at his Mountain Brook, Alabama, home. A bomb delivered in Savannah, Georgia, killed Robert E. Robinson, a civil-rights lawyer. Law enforcement officers disarmed another mail bomb sent to the Eleventh Circuit Court of Appeals in Atlanta, Georgia and one addressed to N.A.A.C.P. president Willye Dennis in Jacksonville, Florida.[26]

A few days later, a letter arrived at a TV station in Atlanta, purportedly from "Americans For A Competent Federal Judicial System," threatening more bombings. There was no evidence that such a group of persons existed, and the speculation was that only one person was involved, a "young, intelligent working class white man seething over a legal system he believes unfairly favors minorities."[27]

Single individuals are hard to catch, and when they're part of what appears to be a grass-roots effort, one attack can be the precursor of many others. In the case of the Southern bomber, it's easy to see that the bomber may have many sympathizers, and some imitators.[28]

From this, it's easy to see that almost anyone can adopt a grandiose name and pretend to be a group. It's also clear that a one man effort isn't necessarily less dangerous. A bomb can be as effective as a mass attack, which is why it's wise not to ignore a single person.

How Vulnerable is the Client?

In assessing the likelihood of a client's being attacked, the security specialist has to consider a number of related aspects. One is his client's character and occupation. Usually, this is obvious, and is the reason the client hired him. The next is the level of attacks in the locale. While some attacks are truly unpredictable, there usually are cues for the alert protection specialist. Sometimes these clues are so obvious that everyone's aware of them. A spate of killings or kidnappings, for example, usually brings a rush of clients to the offices of local security agencies.

It's important not to fall into the trap of dismissing the potential attacker as incompetent. While it's politically correct among government and security circles to describe attackers as "loners," "misfits" and "losers," this doesn't help the protective agent because it tends to minimize the threat. One authority cites "German sociologists and psychologists" who stated that terrorists tend to come from broken families and have not done well educationally or vocationally.[29] This isn't very helpful, because obviously the terrorists are doing well enough in their field to cause the government severe concern. Wealth, advanced education and emotional well being aren't prerequisites for pulling the trigger.

Other factors, such as special training, enhance the danger from individuals and groups. Reserve and retired Israeli military officers have found work training private groups. Several Israeli instructors trained "ranchers" to defend themselves against guerrillas. However, the "ranchers" were employees of the landowner, a member of the Medellin drug cartel.[30]

Physical location is a critical factor in assessing a client's vulnerability. A business executive in the United States has less to fear than one who travels to Peru, for example, where "Shining Path" guerrillas have killed foreigners representing what they abhor. The movement began its campaign of violence, including attacks against government officials and foreigners, in July, 1980. Despite the 1992 arrest and sentencing of Abimael Guzman, Shining Path's leader, the movement has experienced a resurgence, and is carrying out raids and bombings much as before.[31]

As an example of flexibility and adaptability, the Shining Path movement is outstanding. Formerly a strictly revolutionary political movement, Shining Path struck an alliance with illegal drug traffickers when American Drug Enforcement Administration agents and U.S. Army Special Forces troopers moved into remote Peruvian areas in an attempt to try to eradicate drug running.[32]

Sri Lanka turned out to be unsafe for tourists because of a long lived Tamil separatist movement. A series of bombs specifically aimed at hurting the country's tourist industry detonated in April, 1994. One bomb went off at a zoo, and three more inside hotels. A fifth bomb went off prematurely, killing the bomber, on railroad tracks near a resort area.[33]

Early Warning

Despite the unreliability of hard information about specific threats, there are early warning signs that the alert bodyguard can spot:

Local Threat Patterns

A series of recent attacks on other people with the same characteristics (entertainer, businessman, etc.) as your protectee makes it obvious that a threat exists. A problem arises when moving to a new locale, such as a foreign country. Preparation should include contacting the U.S. State Department's Citizens' Emergency Center, 2202 "C" Street NW, Room 4811, Washington, DC 20520. The phone number is: (202) 647-5225. This agency may not always provide all necessary information because of security restrictions, but it's a start.

Another State Department source is the Overseas Security Advisory Council, phone number (703) 204-6185.

A good source of information on local threats abroad is the U.S. embassy or consulate, which provides information to American citizens in need. The diplomatic security officer can advise of recent threats or attacks, dangerous areas, local government contacts (such as police administrators, private security agents and services), local laws covering security checks and possession of weapons. As we'll see, contacting the local police chief can secure tangible help in many countries, and often the deciding factor is how much money is available to reward him for his efforts.

Crank and Hate Mail

Many public and semi-public individuals receive crank mail, most of it from people who pose no threat. Newspaper editors and writers receive crank mail as a matter of course, and in almost every case the letter-writer is harmless. Crank mail may advocate arcane and crackpot economic or scientific theories, or be sarcastic and insulting, but unless there is an expressed or implied threat it's not worth investigating, considering the limited resources generally available to a private protective team.

The difference between crank and hate mail lies in the expressed or implied threat to the individual, not the bizarre nature of the contents. Protectees may receive hate mail, especially if they're public figures. Low-profile protectees, such as executives of medium-sized corporations, receive less attention from both cranks and serious threats.

Fan mail to entertainers also requires scrutiny. Michael J. Fox received over 6,000 threatening letters from a female "fan," Tina Marie Ledbetter. When she sent rabbit turds to Fox in the mail, Ledbetter was apprehended. However, this did not totally remove the potential danger, because Ledbetter's sentence was three years' probation.[34]

Screening crank mail, and identifying letters containing serious threats, is more of an art than a science. The U.S. Secret Service closely examines all crank mail received by the president, and tries to identify and locate authors for further investigation. The Secret Service can do this because it has more resources than any private protective organization, and can call upon the services of any police agency in the country while protecting the U.S. president. The private agent, who may have only himself and an assistant, can't be as thorough, and must discriminate carefully.

It's important to know the difference between fan mail and crank or hate mail. Ordinary fan mail is fairly innocuous, but when it contains sexual fantasies and unrealistic ideas it requires further scrutiny. Some crank letter writers begin with simple fan letters and progress to messages filled with hate and violence.[35]

The danger signs are:

Statements referring to violence, such as, "You ought to be shot." More direct and emphatic statements, such as, "I am going to shoot you," are reason for taking the author very seriously. The critical point is the use of the pronoun, which implies commitment to a course of action.

Statements with psychotic content, such as wild ideas of persecution, often denote an individual who may be both inclined towards, and capable of, carrying out his ideas. Accusations that the principal is listening to the writer with electronic devices, or is shooting silver arrows through his head, are reasons for taking these letters seriously.

Statements dealing with sex, especially the writer's sexual fantasies regarding the protectee, are also suspect. Entertainers receive this sort of mail regularly, but one female correctional officer received a series of cards and letters from a man who wrote extensively about his sexual fantasies involving her.[36] Sexual fantasies may be very bizarre, involving verbal and physical sadism, and even sex with animals and corpses.

There are courses in linguistic analysis available, and these provide insights into analyzing crank letters and separating them into threatening and harmless categories. A linguistic consultant can provide insights into the person who wrote a questionable letter.

One such consultant is:

Avinoam Sapir, President
Laboratory For Scientific Interrogation
P.O. Box 17286
Phoenix, AZ 85011
Phone: (602) 279-3113
Fax: (602) 277-7502

Stalking

Although by nature assassins stalk their victims, a special category of threats called "stalkers" has come to be indentified. These keep track of their intended victims, and may actually follow them during their travels. The term "stalker" is conventionally used only for individuals, but we should recognize that a professional terrorist or kidnapping group also stalks its targets. With more personnel and talent available, groups can be more effective in stalking, and because individual members take turns keeping the target under observation, they're less likely to make themselves conspicuous to the target or his bodyguards.

Some of these individuals can be very dangerous. They often depend on sheer audacity and aggressiveness to carry them through. Psychiatrist Park Dietz stated that psychologically disturbed people have made as many attacks on celebrities since 1968 as during the previous 175 years.[37] Some of the celebrities stalked and attacked are Sean Penn, Tom Selleck, Sharon Gless, and Stephanie Zimbalist. Mark Chapman shot and killed John Lennon outside his home in New York City.

Stalkers have sometimes been stopped before they could attack the celebrity, and have even killed others who got in the way. Nathan Trupp shot and killed two Universal Studios security guards while trying to reach Michael Landon, whom he felt was a Nazi. Ken Gause wrote threatening letters to Johnny Carson for two years, then showed up at the NBC studio, where he was arrested.

There are two types of individual stalkers, according to one authority.[38] One is the psychopathic personality, usually male, who is the more common type of stalker. This type of stalker is out for revenge, and is logical enough to organize a well-planned campaign against his victim. He's likely to begin with a program of harassment, sending his victim spurious deliveries, having utilities canceled or suspended, vandalizing property, then finally directly attacking his target.

The psychotic stalker isn't out for revenge. Instead, he has the delusion that he loves his target, or that his target loves him. He'll often begin with telephone calls, during which he professes his love. He may follow up by sending gifts, and try to approach his target physically. When he sees that the object of his love doesn't reciprocate, he may become violent.

The problem with psychological discussions of stalkers is that the experts can't accurately predict what a particular caller or letter writer may do. The best they can do is offer advice to take every one seriously. Taking every crank caller seriously is one thing, but implementing adequate follow-up measures is another. The private bodyguard cannot conduct a full-scale investigation of every possible threat if there are many.

The other side of the coin is that the bodyguard's client is likely to receive far less "kook" mail and calls than the U.S. president or a celebrity. A former wife stalked by her ex-husband has only one concern, and the bodyguard can usually obtain a photograph of the stalker and watch for him. In other cases, it may be possible to trace the stalker, photograph him, and distribute prints to all members of the protective team.

Some entertainers are the objects of hate because of the roles they play. Michael Moriarty received a lot of hate mail from Jews after his role of SS General "Dorf." He was not unique. Morgan Brittany received threats after killing Bobby Ewing on the TV series *Dallas*.[39]

Further direct measures are likely to be ineffective. As we've seen, the law can't adequately protect against stalkers. It's difficult to arrest and prosecute someone who has, as yet, committed no crime. Court orders of protection have repeatedly failed, because the determined stalker ignores them.[40] The psychopathic stalker who sends unwanted deliveries, magazine subscriptions, etc., covers his tracks well, and in practice it's hard to prosecute him.

Stalking Tactics

The physical stalker actually follows his target, moving with him from one locale to another. The electronic stalker uses computerized databases to track his victim, learn his home address and trace his movements. The electronic stalker may also record all TV news appearances and documentaries of his target, and repeated playbacks can help the stalker identify the target's protective agents.

Physical stalkers often take the time to observe security precautions and wait for an opportunity to attack. Arthur Bremer was the watershed case, and after his attack on Alabama Governor Wallace, Secret Service agents discovered him in photos of crowds taken at widely-separated places.

Countering Stalkers

Although the bodyguard team is too busy watching over the client during public appearances to take crowd photographs, another assistant or member of the entourage can do it. One logical choice is the public information officer, who should carry a camera with him and photograph crowds during all appearances. Protective agents should review all prints and try to spot people who appear in crowds at widely-separated locales.

Black and white prints should be at least 11″ x 14″ to show fine detail. Slides should be Kodachrome or Fuji Velvia, both very sharp films that allow huge enlargements.

Finding the same face in photos taken at different places is perhaps the only reliable indicator of a stalker. Some bodyguards, including those of the U.S. Secret Service, think that they can spot dangerous persons by their behavior or facial expressions. However, the photos of Arthur Bremer show a smiling face that doesn't appear out of place or threatening.

Bodyguards protecting entertainers face a special problem with stalkers, though. It's practically impossible to distinguish them from fans who follow their stars around to obtain autographs, or even just to look at them. Many, many fans just want to touch their stars, as entertainers' bodyguards know, and it's hard to pick out the individual with harmful intent from a crowd of excited fans. Photographers present another problem. The "paparazzi" who stalk entertainers to take their photographs for the tabloid press are annoyances, but not deadly threats. However, a camera with a long lens is a perfect cover for someone with more harmful intent. Entertainers cannot hide from their public, which makes protecting them perhaps even more difficult than protecting the president.

As an example of the problems involved, Mark Chapman behaved exactly like a fan. The afternoon of the day he shot him, he asked John Lennon to autograph an album for him. Later, he returned with a gun, still carrying the album.

The Bottom Line

Usually, threat assessment is a matter of using eyes, ears and common sense. There's nothing arcane about perceiving and understanding threats. Likewise, preparing to cope with them is mostly common sense, fortified by some technical skills. We'll study in detail how attackers prepare their plans in the next chapter.

Notes:

1. Nudell, Mayer, "Trends for Terrorism in the Nineties," *Security Management,* June, 1992, p. 28.
2. *Ibid.,* p. 28.
3. Kovsky, Steve, "Corporate Terrorism: A New Global Threat," *Management Review,* October, 1990, v79, n10, pp. 39-43.
4. *Ibid.,* pp. 39-43.
5. Gross, Linden, "Celebrity Stalkers: When Fans Become Fanatics," *Cosmopolitan,* September, 1990, v209, n3, pp. 264-268.
6. Pesci, Carolyn, "Hill Finds She's the Center of Attention," *USA Today,* October 9, 1991, News p. 2A.
7. "Blandishments and Bombs," *Time,* September 11, 1989, Nation, p. 23.
8. Gutkin, Steve, "Bogota: Newspaper Bloodied But Unbowed," *USA Today,* February 14, 1990, News p. 6A.
9. "Bombs Across the Ocean?," *Time,* March 20, 1989, Nation, p. 26. One after effect of this was that the administration of the private school where Mrs. Rogers taught asked her not to return because of possible danger to pupils. From this, it's easy to see how a terrorist threat can disrupt a person's life.
10. *Protecting the President,* Dennis V.N. McCarthy with Phillip W. Smith, New York, Wm. Morrow & Company, 1985, pp. 36-42.
   See also: *Secret Service Chief,* U.E. Baughman and Leonard Wallace Robinson, NY, Harper and Row, 1962, pp. 1-2. During the Roosevelt era, FDR's Secret Service guards had to plan their whole protective effort around the President's disability, because Roosevelt was unable to flee a threat or even cooperate more than passively in evacuating a dangerous scene.
11. Kramer, Gene, US, "Airlines Call Fear of Flying to Russia Unjustified," Associated Press, April 13, 1994.
12. "Bombings Hit Election Offices with Elections Approaching," Associated Press, March 25, 1994.
13. Laub, Karin, "Car Bombed in Revenge for Hebron Massacre," Associated Press, April 6, 1994.
14. MacFarquhar, Neil, "Israelis Noticed Bag Just Before it Exploded," Associated Press, April 13, 1994.
15. Boim, Israel, and Smith, Karen, "Detecting Weak Links in Executive Armor," *Security Management,* vol. 38, no 2, February, 1994, pp. 50-55.
16. *Prime Target,* Bruce L. Danto, M. D., Philadelphia, The Charles Press, 1990, pp. 82-93.
17. Walton, J. Branch, "Dealing With Dangerous Employees," *Security Management,* September, 1993, pp. 81-84.
18. Johnson, Dennis L., "A Team Approach to Threat Assessment," *Security Management,* September, 1994, pp. 73-83.
19. *The Day of the Jackal,* Frederick Forsyth, NY, Viking Press, 1971, pp. 3-13. This is a novel, but it begins with an account of a real life event to lay the background for the fictional account that follows. In 1963, a group of O.A.S. members laid an ambush for President de Gaulle at Petit-Clamart, in a Parisian suburb. The attempt almost succeeded.
20. *Time,* July 24, 1989, Business Notes, p. 41.
21. Kovsky, Steve, "Corporate Terrorism: A New Global Threat," *Management Review,* October, 1990, v79, n10, pp. 39-43.
22. Burke, Robert R., and Hall, Gwendolyn F., "The Roar Over Animal Rights," *Security Management,* September, 1990, v34, n9, pp. 132-140.
23. *Ibid.*
24. Hall, Mimi, "Abortion Foes Target Doctors; Goal is to Ruin Business," *USA Today,* February 5, 1992, News p. 3A.
25. Usdansky, Margaret L., "Clinic Arrests Mount; Abortion Foes Target Wichita," *USA Today,* July 30, 1991, News p. 3A.
26. Carlson, Margaret, Murder by Mail, *Time,* January 1, 1990, p. 33.
27. *U. S. News and World Report,* January 8, 1990, v108, n1, p. 18.
28. "Home Brew," *The Nation,* January 22, 1990, v250, n3, pp. 75-76.
29. *You're The Target,* Shackley, Theodore G., Oatman, Robert L., and Finney, Richard A., New World Publishing, Ltd., 1989, p. 23.
30. The Israeli Connection, *Time,* September 11, 1989, Nation, p. 26.

31. Hammack, Dan W., "Understanding the Path of Terrorism", *Security Management*, January, 1993, pp. 27-30.
32. *Ibid.*, p. 29.
33. Cruez, Dexter, "Bombs Explode in Colombo Hotels, Railroad, Zoo," Associated Press, April 9, 1994.
34. Gross, Linden, "Celebrity Stalkers: When Fans Become Fanatics," *Cosmopolitan*, September, 1990, v209, n3, pp. 264-268.
35. *Prime Target*, Bruce L. Danto, M. D., Philadelphia, The Charles Press, 1990, pp. 228-229.
36. *Ibid.*, pp. 233-238.
37. Gross, Linden, "Celebrity Stalkers: When Fans Become Fanatics," *Cosmopolitan*, September, 1990, v209, n3, pp. 264-268.
38. Geberth, Vernon, "Stalkers", *Law and Order*, October, 1992, pp. 138-143.
39. Gross, Linden, "Celebrity Stalkers: When Fans Become Fanatics," *Cosmopolitan*, September, 1990, v209, n3, pp. 264-268.
40. *Ibid.*

3

Setting Up The Hit

Let's look at the protection problem from the other side of the fence, to gain an understanding of the problems facing a potential assassin or kidnapper. The statistics are not very comforting, although the undeniable fact is that kidnappings and killings are still relatively rare. More people die in traffic accidents.

Assassinations are uncommon, although we have to note that the success rate is about 50%.[1] One disquieting fact for Americans is the low level and quality of effort it takes to succeed in wounding or killing an American president or presidential candidate. Despite the high level of protection a U.S. president enjoys, he's very vulnerable. Foreign leaders are usually killed by members of a military coup, as was Egyptian President Anwar Sadat, and the professionalism of these assassins is often very high.

By contrast, those who attack American leaders are typically individuals operating without help and with few resources. They have little or no skill, are often unemployed, and are the sort of people we think of as "failures" or "losers." That the U.S. Secret Service often fails to protect against such inept people reflects poorly on this agency.

Kidnapping is another story. U.S. Government officials are rarely kidnapped. The case of General Dozier is an exception.[2] However, the threat to businessmen in foreign countries is severe. Between 1970 and 1983 there were almost 1,000 terrorist kidnappings abroad. In Italy alone there were 25 terrorist kidnappings between 1970 and 1982. Criminal gang kidnappings exceeded them, with 487 kidnappings during the same period.[3] Those who compile statistics distinguish between "terrorist" and "criminal" kidnappings, although this fine distinction doesn't make much of a difference to a protection specialist whose job it is to prevent any sort of kidnapping.

Kidnappings have been slightly less frequent lately, possibly because of increased security measures. It's easy to understand how beefed-up security can be a deterrent, and cause kidnappers to select another target that's less well protected.[4]

Diplomatic kidnappings, although not the concern of private security specialists, are fairly common. There have been 130 between 1968 and 1982.[5]

Whether the action against your client is a killing or kidnapping, there are certain predictable stages in an adversary's planning and preparation. These tend to follow a pattern, and understanding what happens and why it happens will help you to prevent your client's becoming a victim.

Selection

How does an assassin, kidnapper or terrorist decide upon a target? The first requirement is awareness, and someone who maintains a high-profile makes himself a potential target. If the target is a prominent person, he or she is a candidate for a "hit." The word "prominent" is often a euphemism for "rich," but in this regard not necessarily so. The potential target may attract media exposure because of his official status or activities. A political personage or entertainer leads a high-profile life. Captain William Nordeen, U.S. Naval Attaché to Greece, was important enough to attract assassination by lay-off bomb in June, 1988. Often, the damage is self-inflicted because the publicity that high-profile people seek attracts attackers as well as voters or fans. Publicity, such as a potential target's location or travel plans, provides valuable intelligence for attackers.

An executive can be unnecessarily exposed by his company's public relations office. A news release often accompanies a promotion or change of assignment. An article in a newspaper's business section can tip off a potential attacker that your client has just been appointed branch manager of the local office of the XYZ Company. Your client may be the newly appointed director of an abortion clinic. Anything that magnifies your client's importance can attract unwanted attention.

We've already mentioned target hardening in a previous chapter. The more defensive measures in place, the more likely they are to deter an attack.

Reconnaissance

To arrange a killing or kidnapping, the attacker must learn where his victim will be, and at what time. He must also know of any protective measures employed by the target. Many attackers are sophisticated enough to understand that they can't simply approach their target impulsively and carry out an off-the-cuff plan. There's usually a long period of scouting and preparation.[6]

In one sense, protecting the target is counter-productive because the more protection provided for the target, the more conspicuous he becomes. A single car isn't as high-profile as a motorcade, especially one with a motorcycle escort.

Some of the techniques used are direct surveillance and phony phone calls. A member of the group telephones the target's home or office to determine if he's in, or when he's expected. When Action Direct, a French terrorist group, assassinated General Rene Audran, the French Defense Ministry's official who controlled arms sales, they put the telephone to good use. A woman with a thick German accent telephoned his home one evening to ask when the general was expected, and his daughter replied that he'd be home from work shortly. When the general drove up soon thereafter, assailants pumped eight bullets into his head.[7]

Indirect reconnaissance, which includes using information from public sources, plays a large role in target selection and surveillance. Many prominent targets aren't fully aware of how much important information about them is easily available.

A Belgian terrorist group denied in a communiqué that they had access to secret NATO documents to plan their attacks. They said their main sources of information were "the telephone directory and the naked eye."[8]

One organization that attracted attention as a possible source of information about multi-national corporations for terrorists was the Transnational Institute of Amsterdam.[9] This doesn't seem very likely, though, because the amount of publicly available information about businesses of any size is vast.

There's no need for a specialized information-gathering bureau. Many potential targets are prominent because their names appear in newspaper and magazine articles. We regularly see features such as the "Fortune 500" list, and newspapers often print annual lists of the country's richest people. Business magazines run profiles on notable business leaders, often with photographs which show an attacker what his target looks like. Many profiles reveal copious personal information which can be used to help plan an attack.[10]

Many libraries have *Thomas Register, Standard and Poor's,* or *Moody's* reference volumes, and these provide detailed information about companies, products, finances, and the names of the corporate officers. These supplement information which is available in magazines.

Direct surveillance on foot works well where there's a lot of foot traffic around the target's home or office. The people who do the close-in reconnaissance can vary. These days, nobody uses large and swarthy men in trench coats. Inconspicuous men, women, and even children scout the area. A woman walking a baby carriage will not usually arouse suspicion, and for that reason makes an excellent surveillant. Street repair crews and family groupings are other covers for surveillance. This is what complicates the bodyguard's task hopelessly, because literally anyone could be a surveillant, and this leads to a paranoid attitude.

Detecting surveillance serves as an early warning of an impending attack. Discrimination lies in detecting an increase in possible surveillance measures, such as mysterious phone calls and people loitering outside.

There have been instances of attackers "stalking" their targets. One was Arthur Bremer. On the move, a surveillance vehicle of common and undistinguished appearance is useful. Using informers among the target's entourage is also a valuable technique. A maid or cook may be reporting the target's activities to the attacking group.

In the United States, a commonly available method is to employ a private investigative agency to scrutinize a non-governmental target. Obviously, a private investigator would be suspicious of an assignment to shadow the president or Secretary of State. A private party, though, is another matter. This requires a cover story, and one is that the target is having an extramarital affair. This pretext is unlikely to arouse suspicion, as marital infidelity is widespread in this country. Because of the American private investigative pattern of operating, the client will receive written reports detailing the daily activities of the target.

One of the most important aspects an attacker will want to cover is the protective screen around the target, because eliminating the bodyguards is the first task. In many instances, the bodyguards reveal themselves because of their appearance or demeanor. From the attacker's viewpoint, the bodyguard becomes obvious when he:

- Scans all around him constantly. His eyes are always moving.
- Wears mirror sunglasses to conceal his eye movements.
- Wears a distinctive lapel pin.
- Carries an earphone with a wire leading down to the radio in his clothing.
- Wears excessively heavy clothing to conceal a weapon or otherwise dresses inappropriately for the surroundings.
- Wears a single-breasted suit, the best kind for quickly drawing a handgun.
- Never has his hands encumbered carrying anything, except possibly an attaché case with a submachine gun inside.
- Seems unusually large and muscular.
- Remains close to the target without being an obvious family member or business associate.
- Is where a bodyguard would be, such as the right front seat of a limo or in a follow-up vehicle.
- Appears out of place for either a clear or indefinable reason.

Carrying it Out

The attacker will choose a time, place, weapon, approach, method of attack, and often a method of escape. Unless he plans a sacrificial attack, escape is as important as the approach. In kidnappings, escape is the first priority, because without escape, there is no success. Only bombing, with a remote control or booby-trap device, offers the attacker the chance of avoiding grave personal risk.

The personal attack will always be a variant of the ambush, taking advantage of surprise, to kill or kidnap the victim. It can happen on foot or using a vehicle. The attackers try to eliminate the bodyguard first, to clear the way to the target. In both the Schleyer and Moro kidnappings, which we'll examine later, the attackers eliminated several bodyguards before snatching their victims.

The attack is usually close-in. Sometimes the choice of weapon dictates this. A knife, though rarely employed, is a contact weapon. Handguns are usually short-range weapons, with the chances of a hit greater at very short ranges. One practical matter to consider is that the attackers are not necessarily expert marksmen.

Rifles aren't commonly used, but submachine guns are becoming more popular. The main reason for using submachine guns is that heavy firepower helps neutralize the bodyguards.

Bombs are always potential threats, and their use depends very heavily upon locale and culture. Some attackers are addicted to bombs, and have made them traditional. Others never use them, preferring firearms. Bombs are indiscriminate, while firearms are more selective. The choice often depends more on personality and outlook than on pure tactics. Poison and radioactive substances are not known as common assassination weapons. This may be merely a case of such methods passing undetected and deaths being attributed to natural causes.

To end on a pessimistic note, if the attackers are competent, plan well and begin an attack, they'll succeed despite anything you can do. They'll plan to use enough force to overcome the defenses. Both Hans-Martin Schleyer and Aldo Moro had several bodyguards, including some in a follow-up car, yet the attacks succeeded. Kenneth Bishop, a Texaco executive in Colombia, was kidnapped and his two bodyguards killed by gunfire. British Ambassador Geoffrey Jackson was ambushed and kidnapped by Tupamaro guerrillas in Montevideo, Uruguay, in January, 1971. A van pulled out in front of Jackson's embassy limousine, ramming the left front fender. Other attackers gained access to the car while a covering force opened fire at Jackson's follow-up car with its bodyguards, injuring one of them. The kidnappers drove Jackson away into captivity in his own car.[11]

Unless the attacker is a lone agent, his chances of success and escape are good. It's usually the singular, deranged and alienated killer who becomes vulnerable to capture.

Notes:

1. *On Assassination*, H. H. A. Cooper, Boulder, CO, Paladin Press, 1984, p. 121.
2. *Terrorism and Personal Protection*, Brian Jenkins, editor, NY, Butterworth Publishers, 1985, pp. 80-82.

22

3. *Ibid.*, p. xxi.
4. *Ibid.*, p. 11.
5. *Ibid.*, p. 25.
6. *Executive Protection Manual*, Reber, Jan, and Shaw, Paul, Schiller Park IL, MTI Teleprograms, 1976, p. 139.
7. *You're The Target*, Shackley, Theodore G., Oatman, Robert L., and Finney, Richard A., New World Publishing, Ltd., 1989, p. 25.
8. *Ibid.*, p. 25.
9. *Ibid.*, p. 47.
10. *The Executive Protection Bible*, Martha J. Braunig, Basalt, CO, Executive Protection International, 1992, p. 27.
11. *You're The Target*, Shackley, Theodore G., Oatman, Robert L., and Finney, Richard A., New World Publishing, Ltd., 1989, pp. 58-59.

4

Training
The Bodyguard

There's no substitute for complete training. There are many skills involved in bodyguarding, and it's impossible to pick them all up in one quick course. Many executives and other potential clients, as well as aspiring bodyguards, don't truly know what makes for a good protective effort, partly because they get their ideas from television. Let's discuss combat skills first.

There's no consensus regarding the skills required. Most agree, for example, that a bodyguard should be proficient with weapons and in unarmed combat, but hardly anyone will agree on exactly which weapons a bodyguard should use. In the field of unarmed combat, there are more "schools" of martial arts than anyone can know, and the police and armed services have their favorite methods of unarmed defense.

There are actually three kinds of martial arts: exhibition, sport and survival martial arts. Only the last is oriented to the street. The others are useful for physical conditioning or as good, clean fun, but the techniques they teach will get you killed if you have to fight for your life. The police and military employ utilitarian techniques which aren't as elegant as those in Hollywood martial arts movies, but they're effective.

Apart from the violent arts, there are other skills that can be useful. You and your clients will have to decide which apply in each case. Be aware that these skills will probably be far more important, and more frequently needed, than combat arts.

Should the bodyguard be skilled in cardio-pulmonary resuscitation? Obviously, the client with a heart problem will feel more confident if his protectors have skill in CPR. Should he have a paramedic certification? If not, what about a "First Responder" course, which is designed for quick stabilization of the victim while other help is on the way? There are widely differing opinions on this, and they often vary with the needs and capacities of the protectee's organization. If the protectee has his own doctor to travel with him, as do the American and French presidents, medical training for the bodyguards is much less important than otherwise.

Evasive driving is a widely advertised skill, but does every bodyguard need it? Obviously the chauffeur does, but he may not be included in the security staff if the planning is short-sighted.

Among the more mundane skills needed may be fluency in a foreign language. If the client travels abroad, skill in the local language can literally be a life-saver. Being able to explain yourself to a police officer or a doctor can be very important.

Should the bodyguard be skilled in EOD (Explosive Ordnance Disposal)? Usually not, because there are specialists for this task. The bodyguard's job is to get his client away from danger, not try to disarm a bomb himself. He should, however, be able to recognize bombs and other dangerous devices. If the client lives in a remote area where the needed experts are not readily available, EOD skill may come in handy.

Electronic security is another questionable field. The bodyguard may feel more professional if he knows how to "de-bug" a room, but while he's doing that, he's not guarding his client. The bodyguard's unlikely to be as skilled at "de-bugging" as the specialist, and this task is best left to the expert.

Where Is Training Available?

There are as many opinions on this as there are regarding the types of instruction needed. Let's examine "store-front" karate schools and the like. Next, we'll look at "shooting schools," which purport to teach self-defense gunnery.

Self-defense Schools

As we've seen, karate schools tend to train students for competition, not defense against a deadly threat. They also concentrate on developing style, rather than quick, economical and disabling blows and holds. The skill of some instructors is questionable.

Most protective agents, like most police officers, are not martial arts experts. They don't need to be. Any effective defensive martial arts course should be short and simple, aimed towards the novice student. The course must be short, to train the student in basic empty hand defense in an economical amount of time. It should also be simple, because it takes longer to learn complex tactics, and they're harder to execute under stress.

Shooting Schools

The "shooting schools," which have received much publicity during the last few years, are mostly geared to competition. This is despite their being advertised as schools where citizens can learn defensive shooting. The unfortunate fact is that most are not oriented to the type of shooting required for defensive purposes, despite their advertising claims.

They tend to use the weapons and techniques which work well in competition, ignoring the important real world considerations. Two examples will suffice, to give you an idea of what to avoid:

1. Many shooting schools advocate the Colt Government Model, in caliber .45ACP. This handgun is obsolete and not easily concealable, no matter what the arguments about "stopping power" may be. No matter which "shooting guru" advocates this pistol, the professional bodyguard will find this clunker less useful than a more up-to-date weapon such as the SIG P226. For concealment, the professional bodyguard is likely to choose a compact model such as the Walther PP or the SIG P230.

2. Shooting schools tend to teach the two handed grip. This technique works in the artificial conditions of shooting matches, and students learn faster when they can use both hands. In the real world the bodyguard who can shoot only while using both hands is seriously handicapped. The reason is that one hand is often taken up with something else, such as opening a door, pushing an assailant away, etc.

Police Academies

Another source of training is a police academy. In fact, many retired police officers take on work as bodyguards. The problems with this approach are the subject of another chapter.

The Secret Service and other Federal Agencies

The United States Secret Service provides some of the best training in this country for those interested in protective work. However, the Service doesn't run a school for those who merely want to take a course. Retired Secret Service agents often find work as bodyguards and as directors of security, supervising a corps of bodyguards. The Secret Service does run some sporadic courses for senior police executives who have a responsibility for protective details.

There's one serious problem with Secret Service training. It's geared towards the agency with a large budget, not the small, shoe-string local agency or the private protective agent. As mentioned elsewhere in this book, the U.S. Secret Service has a huge budget compared to most police departments and private corporate security budgets. Their protective agents are always part of large details, and customarily call upon local agencies to provide extra support when needed. They're geared to massive, high-profile protective efforts. This is why their training isn't the best for the bodyguard who has to operate with limited resources.[1]

Another federal police force which graduates some competent bodyguards is the U.S. Marshal's Service. For about two decades, the Marshal's Service has been operating the "Federal Witness Protection Program" for the benefit and protection of those who testify against the "mob."[2]

The military provides some basic familiarity with weapons, and because of the recent publicity that certain elite units such as the SAS and Delta Force have gotten, some think that these units are ideal sources for bodyguards. Not so.

The Military

The military, like the police, tend to inculcate an overly aggressive attitude. The military, however, carry it to an extreme. A gung-ho, do-or-die mentality is suitable for assaulting a defended beach or fortification, but it's wrong for executive protection. Discretion is truly the better part of valor in bodyguarding. This is why the bodyguard who can retreat to safety with his client is more valuable than the one who prefers to stand and fight while his client is killed in the cross-fire.

Even the elite units tend to take this aggressive attitude. Units such as the SAS specialize in crisis actions. When they go in, as in the Iranian Embassy incident in London in 1980, they're primed to kill. Their best hope is to hit the terrorists and not shoot any hostages. Because of this, they're well suited to protecting a VIP in a war zone, but not in ordinary situations. Nevertheless, former members of the SAS and other specialist units find work as bodyguards, trading upon their reputations.

Specialized Military Schools

A few military men get specialized training in executive protection. One such group is the detail of U.S. Marines assigned to bodyguard the ambassadors in their respective countries. Not every Marine on embassy guard detail gets such an assignment, but those who do get special training and gain valuable experience.

Private Academies

A number of academies specializing in training bodyguards have sprung up in this country during the last couple of decades. Most of them keep very low profiles as far as the public is concerned. For example, how many people have heard of the Executive Protection Institute in Berryville, Virginia?

Some of the schools which provide instruction in executive protection are listed below. These are not the only ones, but they're among the top echelon in competence.

Ackerman Group, Inc.
1666 Kennedy Causeway
Miami Beach, FL 33141
Phone: (305) 865-0072
Fax: (305) 865-0218

The Ackerman Group trains both bodyguards and executives in security awareness and protective techniques.

Executive Security International
225 Teal Court
Aspen, CO 81611
Phone: (800) 874-0888
Phone: (303) 925-3630
Attn: Bob Duggan

ESI offers a wide variety of courses linked to executive protection, covering protective techniques, terrorism, defensive shooting, electronic security, bomb defense, executive protection driving and other allied topics. A home study course is available. Other courses offered are intelligence gathering, and a maritime and yacht security program. An Associate Degree Program is also available.

Executive Protection Institute
Rt. Two, Box 3645
Berryville, VA 22611
Phone: (703) 955-1128
Fax: (703) 955-1130
Attn: Richard Kobetz, Director

EPI offers courses on executive protection, including defensive driving, practical protective combat shooting, risk management, emergency medical assistance, building searches, movements and escort missions, advance surveys, corporate aircraft security, workplace violence and other allied topics. EPI offers separate courses in various cities, including Ft. Lauderdale, New York City, New Orleans, and as far west as Dallas and Chicago.

Kobetz and his training academy have a splendid reputation among the professionals. The staff is top-notch, including many professionals from both private and government agencies. College credits for these courses are available from nearby Shenandoah University.

IPS
4854 Old National Highway, Suite 210
Atlanta, GA 30337
Phone: (800) 235-4723
(404) 766-1545

This school offers courses directed towards the executive, such as a two day Executive Family Awareness Course, which covers kidnapping, hostage survival, surveillance detection, travel security, evasive driving and home defense. The Executive and Family Protection Course covers executive protection methodology, case studies, evacuation, bombs, threat assessment, searching vehicles, advance methods, firearms proficiency, survival driving and hostage survival.

Rosson & Associates
203 Idyllwild Drive
San Jacinto, CA 92583
Phone: (909) 654-2893

This school is physically located in Nuevo, Mexico, about 25 miles south of Tijuana. It provides training for bodyguards, with a special crash course for protectees. This three-day course, covering martial arts, evasive driving, situation awareness, weapons safety, marksmanship, safe travel, anti-carjacking, home security, family protection and medical trauma/CPR, was priced at $1,050 in 1994. This includes weapons and ammunition, but not lodging. Rosson & Associates also provide training at the customer's facility, by special arrangement.

Scotti School
10 High Street, Ste. 15
Medford, MA 02155
Phone: (800) 343-0046
Phone: (617) 395-9156
Fax: (617) 391-8252
Attn: Tony Scotti

Executive Safety & International Terrorism

This school's Executive Protection Course trains both drivers and bodyguards, and the school's clients include over 40% of the top 100 in the Fortune 500 list. Scotti conducts courses and seminars "on location" in this country and Latin America, Europe, S.E. Asia, and the Mid-East. This school's president, Anthony Scotti, teaches defensive driving at the Executive Protection Institute, but Scotti's school also has full bore courses in executive protection. These courses employ a varied staff, including a former Secret Service agent and a pri-

vate bodyguard. Scotti has scheduled seminars in various parts of the country for 1995.

Tony Scotti is the author of *Executive Safety & International Terrorism* and a videotape on defensive driving for the bodyguard, "Counterambush Driving Skills and Evasive Techniques." Another of his books is *Driving Techniques for the Professional and Non-professional*, which is a revision of his 1988 book *Police Driving Techniques*. All are available from The Scotti School.

Consultants

In special situations, it may become necessary to call in a consultant to help with extraordinary circumstances. Some consultants do provide special services, while others provide only expertise and advice.

Many of the organizations listed here provide services in more than one category. Some of the schools, for example, also provide consultation for clients.

Best Security Consultants, Inc.
3881 Holl Way
Eagle, ID 83616
Phone: (208) 939-0149
Attn: Mike Best

Best Security Consultants is operated by a former U.S. Secret Service agent who teaches executive protection techniques. Among the services Mike Best provides are security surveys and recommending executive protection agents.

Control Risks Ltd.
4330 East West Highway
Bethesda, MD 20814
Phone: (301) 654-2075

Nuevevidas International
P.O. Box 25571
Dallas, TX 75225
Phone: (214) 437- 3999
Attn: H.H. A. "Tony" Cooper

This company provides consulting services and conducts courses in terrorism, executive protection, hostage survival and corporate aircraft security. Cooper is a noted counter-terrorism expert.

Protection Development International Corp.
180 Vander Street
P.O. Box 2048
Corona, CA 91720
Phone: (714) 734-7531

Media Sources

There are many books and videotapes available on topics connected with protective techniques. A list of books appears at the end of this volume. A few videos portray various self-defense and survival techniques. These can supplement hands-on training, but are in no way a substitute for actual practice. The experienced protective agent with street martial arts skill can glean some new material from videos, and can modify his techniques in the light of new knowledge, but it's unwise to try to learn street martial arts only from watching videos.

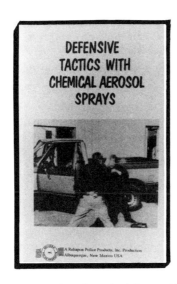

Defensive Tactics With Chemical Aerosol Sprays

An important video for the agent who will be carrying an aerosol is the one by John Peters, of Defensive Tactics Institute. The 45-minute video has segments dealing with use of force, chemical agents, medical effects of chemical agents, gripping and spraying methods, decontamination, and personal protective methods.

Another of John Peters' tapes is *Realistic Firearms Disarming*, a guide oriented towards police officers, but with techniques applicable to many situations. The simple fact is that when an attacker is within reaching

distance, it's quicker to disarm him or to deflect the weapon with empty hand techniques than to draw a firearm from under clothing.

A.S.P.Tactical Baton is another Peters tape, dealing with carrying, drawing and using the expandable baton. Although the tape features the A.S.P. brand, the techniques are applicable to all brands.

All of these tapes are oriented towards the person without extensive martial arts training, but with some familiarity in street fighting or basic defensive tactics.

These videotapes are available from:

Defensive Tactics Institute
P.O. Box 14822
Albuquerque, NM 87111
Attn: John Peters
Phone: (800) 423-0668
Phone: (505) 291-0366
Fax: (505) 299-4976

The next two videos deal with defense against knives. *Surviving Edged Weapons* is oriented towards the police officer, and the emphasis is on creating distance and controlling the situation with a firearm. However, the tape does cover close in defense, and is worth viewing by the bodyguard.
Available from:

Calibre Press
666 Dundee Road, Suite 1607
Northbrook, IL 60062-2727
Phone: (800) 323-0037
Fax: (708) 498-6869

Surviving A Street Knife Fight deals with the down-and-dirty aspect of empty hand coping with a knife attack. This video is for the ordinary citizen and for the bodyguard, not necessarily the armed police officer. It delves into various types of knife attacks, and how to block and parry them.
Available from:

Paladin Press
P.O. Box 1307
Boulder, CO 80306
Phone: (303) 443-7250
Fax: (303) 442-8741

Master Moves is a hardcore videotape dealing with realistic street fighting, or survival martial arts, by Richard Ryan. This video emphasizes the distinction between elegant exhibition martial arts and the economical, down and dirty techniques useful on the

street. The tape is neatly divided into individual segments, each stressing one principle of survival fighting, and is very easy to understand.
Available from:

Personal Defense Systems, Inc.
P.O. Box 31129
Phoenix, AZ 85046
Phone: (602) 482-7252
Attn: Richard Ryan

Continuing Training

Once hired, the bodyguard needs to integrate with the team, unless he's a lone agent. This often takes the form of on-the-job training, catching the peripheral assignments first and gradually moving into more responsible and sensitive duties as he "breaks in."

If possible, there should be formal training sessions, with bodyguards practicing formations, immediate action drills and other protective actions. When a crisis strikes, each has his job to do, whether it be pushing the client to safety or running interference, and any hesitation or uncertainty can only work for the assailant. For this reason, training should be regular and continual, not sporadic and haphazard.

There's growing recognition of the value of keeping in good physical shape. This is valuable not only for general good health, but because attackers tend to be young and in excellent shape. In this country, no presidential attacker has been over 40. Middle-Eastern terrorists are usually well trained operatives in their teens and twenties, dedicated to their cause, and hard fighters. Unlike the police officer or bodyguard, this type of terrorist has a kamikaze outlook, and isn't thinking of going home and sitting before the TV with Mama and the kids. His only concern is the next few minutes, when he'll die carrying out his mission, thereby earning his ticket to Heaven. Some use drugs to boost their strength and endurance for the assignment. A dedicated and well trained terrorist unit can out fight an American police or bodyguard unit of equal size. Better believe it.[3] The bodyguard must keep in good shape, to help compensate for younger attackers' strength and endurance.

Another question is that of the human shield. Can a client expect his bodyguard to interpose himself to block an assassin's bullet? This depends on the situation. Some public figures can expect to find some dedicated law officers who feel that the safety of the

"chief" is more important than their own. In the private sector, however, it's far less likely. Body armor, by giving the agent a better chance for survival, helps somewhat. Whatever his original intent, the agent may have a change of heart when facing a real threat.

The key to having protective agents interpose themselves is training, even in private security operations. The purpose is "programming" the trainees to respond properly, shield the client and disregard their own safety in the face of a threat. The team leader must have training sessions at least once a week, with the team members practicing formations which have them placing themselves between the client and danger. By constant drilling and repetition, he can condition the agents to respond as desired. This training differs from the usual military training in that there's no demeaning treatment of the trainees, no insults or abuse. A protective agent has to operate on a high level, and cannot be treated as a robot.

Yet another problem is the bodyguard who can be "reached." This isn't a problem with Americans as much as it is in certain foreign countries. Some bodyguards are susceptible to bribes. Others can be reached with warnings. In some parts of the world, the local crime confederation is so powerful and all-reaching that one of them can convince the agent to "defect." The technique is to point out to him that his family's safety can't be "guaranteed" if he fails to cooperate. Cooperation means leaving his post at a given moment, to clear the way for an assassin.

Human Material

The bodyguard is a flesh-and-blood safeguard for his client. In many ways, he's expected to do an impossible job. However, in most instances he comes through for his client. The combination of personal qualities and training shows itself in superior performance.

Notes:

1. Heine, Kimberly, "Body Double: Protecting Company Executives," *Security Management*, vol. 38, no. 2, February 1994, p. 58.
2. *Methods of Disguise*, Second Edition, John Sample, Port Townsend, WA, Loompanics Unlimited, 1993, pp. 187-201.
   Also *The Alias Program*, Fred Graham, Boston, Little, Brown, & Company, 1977. These

sources, particularly the last cited one, describe the measures taken to safeguard witnesses under death sentences from organized crime. The most valuable aspect of these sources is the insight into what can go wrong with protective operations. Much can go wrong, and it's better to learn from others' mistakes than to pay the price yourself.

3. Lesce, Tony, "Can Terrorists Out-Fight American Tactical Teams?" *Police Marksman*, Jan/Feb 1989, pp. 21-24.

5
How
Government Bodyguards
Work

Government protective services have budgets that are practically unlimited in comparison to those of private corporations or individuals. They can devote a huge amount of manpower and draw upon the resources of other government agencies to protect their VIPs.

Let's look at the way the U.S. Secret Service protects the president, in order to gain an understanding of how this works. We'll benefit most from this example because we are familiar with conditions in our country and the methods they require.

Despite chronic complaints that the budget is too small, the Secret Service, like other government agencies, has a vastly swollen staff compared to private security services. Recent (1992) figures show that the U.S. Secret Service has about 4,600 employees, including the Uniformed Division, and 2,000 special agents, some of whom are assigned directly to presidential protection. Other Secret Service personnel protect the vice president, his family, former presidents, presidential candidates, visiting heads of foreign states, and other foreign visitors the president may order protected.

The number assigned to presidential protection is classified, but the exact figure is not important because it varies from day to day, depending on the nature of the task. The Secret Service has 132 field offices, in most major American cities and a few foreign countries, and the Presidential Detail draws extra manpower from them during VIP visits. The Secret Service also draws support from other federal and local agencies. From this we see that the nominal strength of the White House Detail is unimportant, and can even be misleading.

These huge resources allow very comprehensive defense of the president and his family. It's necessary because the President of the United States is not a low-profile figure. By tradition and by choice, he travels in style, turning a smiling face to citizens and voters. This makes the task of protecting him far more difficult than if he kept his movements secret and avoided public appearances, but the government has the means to protect him despite his exposed lifestyle.

Because of the vast resources, the government protective operations are laid out in concentric rings of protection, or "defense in depth." Calling them "rings" may give the impression of impenetrability, which is definitely not the case. It's more accurate to call them "protective screens," because they are somewhat porous, and in fact attackers have broken through them. However, although the outer screens are very porous, they get much tighter closer to the president.

The first line of defense is intelligence gathering. The Secret Service keeps tabs on any likely threat. This includes individuals who have threatened the president, revolutionary groups, mentally deranged people who might pose threats, and other "leads" furnished by allied government agencies.

The sources of such "intelligence" are varied. One simple and obvious one is scanning the president's "hate mail."[1] While most public figures, whether they be entertainers or local officials, get hate mail, the volume that the American president gets is enough to require a full-time effort. The mail for the White House gets a once over by secretaries, who report anything suspicious to the Secret Service agent on duty. This is done not only to detect letter bombs and other obviously dangerous devices, but to get a line on people who might be threats to the president's safety. Any letter that seems angry or threatening is turned over to the Secret Service for evaluation. An agent scans it to determine if it shows signs of mental imbalance, and if the author is stating a clear threat. It's illegal to threaten the president, and this gives the Secret Service a lever to get the authors of such letters confined.

Usually, those who are dangerous tend to write more than one letter. This is why the Secret Service keeps hate letters on file. Each letter gets a classification process, noting the type of ink, paper and writing style involved. An agent analyzes the contents, noting if the writer expresses any ideas which seem psychotic.[2]

Packages coming into the White House get special scrutiny. The full treatment includes X-raying and explosives detection by dog or electronic sniffer. Of course, packages without return addresses are always given first priority in suspicion.

On another level, any report of someone threatening the president goes into the Secret Service's investigative hopper. It might be a person overheard saying, "He should be shot!" in a bar, but there will be an investigation to determine if this person is a serious threat and warrants any further steps, including prosecution. In any event, the person's identity will wind up in the Secret Service's computer for possible further reference.

The Secret Service also gathers intelligence from other agencies. This has been greatly expanded since 1963, when the testimony before the Warren Commission showed that the FBI had not notified the Secret Service of Lee Harvey Oswald's location and activities.[3] At the time, the Secret Service also did not have the equipment to process all available information, and was looking into the prospects of obtaining an IBM computer.

Although the way in which this is done is classified, we can assume that the FBI, CIA and other government agencies keep the Secret Service's "Protective Research Section" posted on the identities and make-up of various political and quasi-political groups that may pose threats to the president. Because of the mentality of government workers, and their inclination to accept the worst case assumptions, the government keeps track of individuals and groups on the basis of two criteria: intent and ability.

A group that seems inimical to our form of government winds up in a file in the office of the FBI, CIA or other federal police agency. This happens whether they are armed or not, because they may in the future acquire weapons. An armed group, dedicated to an entirely different purpose, still rates an entry because it has the capability, although it's not directed at the White House at the moment. The net result is that many groups, such as the Posse Comitatus, KKK, etc. are on file. The political complexion doesn't matter, only the prospect of a threat.

The weakness of this system is that attackers who don't join groups, and who are discreet about their intentions, don't attract the attention of the authorities. This is why the majority of successful attackers have been "loners," those who remain apart from groups and operate as individuals.

In physical protection, the Secret Service excels. This is because of the manpower and physical resources available to it. Unlike private clients, who may get protection only when they leave their homes, or while on trips, the president and his family get 24-hour-a-day protection, wherever they may be.

At the White House, the president and his family are incomparably safer than most Americans. There are electronic fences and other intrusion detectors. The Secret Service Uniformed Division has armed guards on duty 24 hours a day, whether he's in residence or not. All arrivals pass through gates and other check-points, where uniformed guards and Secret Service agents scan them to verify their identities. There are electronic gates to detect weapons. The White House even has a nuclear-bomb shelter, although it's surely obsolete by now. The White House is well defended, with troops on call nearby in case of severe riots or other problems. Allegedly, anti-aircraft missiles are concealed nearby to cope with any attempt to attack from the air.

But comforting supposition that the White House has an effective air defense system crashed and burned with the Cessna 150 that descended on its South Lawn on September 12, 1994. The pilot, a 38-year-old "loser" who had apparently not attended kamikaze school, stole the aircraft from a nearby Maryland airport and made a suicide dive into the White House's South Portico. Apart from the physical damage, the only casualty was the myth that the White House is adequately defended.[4] The tight-lipped reaction by the U.S. Secret Service suggests that they have a lot to hide about the deficient security screen. If anti-aircraft missiles are indeed available to White House guards, they weren't on alert that night.

The subsequent shooting against the White House by a man with an assault rifle pointed up other deficiencies. It was only by luck that nobody was hit by bullets. The shooter was tackled and overpowered by nearby citizens, and turned over to White House guards.

The president's tracks are dogged by Secret Service agents. When he's in his office, agents are outside the door. Although he's relatively safe in the Oval Office, we can assume that he has a "panic button" on or under his desk to summon help if needed. It's not likely that the Secretary of State or other guests will attack the president, but the attitude of the bodyguards is "better safe than sorry." According to one unverified account, a Secret Service agent stood hidden behind curtains while FDR was having a stormy meeting with General de Gaulle during the war. Apparently, there was some concern that de Gaulle might lose his temper and harm the president.

Each time the president leaves the White House the Secret Service goes with him. More significantly, it sends agents to scout the way and make preparations. When visiting another city, agents show up days or weeks in advance to check out the security of the accommodations and coordinate with local police. The Secret Service may rent an entire hotel floor for the president and his party, and the rooms immediately above and below the president's suite. This ensures that all occupants beyond the four walls are friendly.

Part of the security arrangements will include surveying all routes, with special attention paid to motorcade routes. Agents will check out buildings along the way, and sometimes arrange for security officers to stand on the roof of each high building. The Service runs a security check on all members of the hotel staff who will either come into contact with the President or have anything to do with his food. Employees of businesses he visits, and any other people who will be in his presence, will get a security check from the Secret Service. They are issued lapel pins to wear during the visit. These pins, changed for each trip, identify those "cleared" to be in the presence of the President.[5]

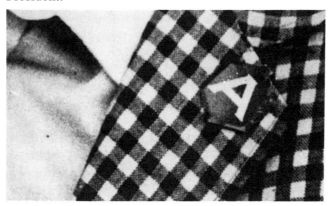

Secret Service agents and other security officers also wear lapel pins, changed every day to preclude an attempt at penetrating their screen by forging a pin. These pins are different in design from the ones issued to those merely "cleared" to be in the president's vicinity. The pins are necessary because the security

agents don't all know each other. At an airport, for example, there will be airport police, city police, members of a special police unit such as SWAT, Secret Service agents from the local office, and of course the traveling members of the White House Detail. Some are uniformed, while others are in civilian clothes. Complicating the security problem is the ease of buying a uniform. There has to be a means of quick recognition of anyone entitled to carry weapons near the president. This helps avoid tragic mistakes, such as security agents shooting each other in the belief they are attackers.

A myth has arisen that you can recognize the Secret Service agents around the president by their mirror-finish sunglasses. At one time, it was the fad for Secret Service agents to wear this type of sunglasses, but they've gone out of style. What they do wear, every day of the year, are their lapel pins. In many photographs of the president, lapel pins are visible on some of the people facing the camera. Agents around the President also carry radios with earpieces, remaining in constant contact with the command post. The combination of lapel pins and earpieces identifies them as Secret Service agents.

The presidential limousine is armored, of course. This has been a standard practice since the Kennedy assassination. Presidents have had armored cars before this. When WWII began, President Roosevelt used Al Capone's armored car, which had been seized by the government, until a new one could be custom built for him.

All of the president's transportation is secured before he boards. His limousine remains under tight security in the White House garage. The Marine Corps keeps at least two well guarded helicopters available for his use. His personal aircraft, "Air Force One," is in a secure area at Andrews Air Force Base. There are regular searches for bombs and other harmful devices, including "bugs," by Secret Service agents. Electronic security is an important concern of the White House Detail.

The president's chauffeur is a Secret Service agent, and an agent sits next to the chauffeur, "riding shotgun." A Secret Service follow-up car stays right behind the president's vehicle every foot of the route. This car carries extra agents, some of them seated and others riding on extra wide running boards. These agents jump off and jog alongside the president's car when it slows down, as in a parade. Their task is to stop anyone from running out and reaching the president's car, and to deflect any objects thrown at the vehicle. Most of the objects are bouquets, but there are occasional heavy objects that could cause injury. There's also the small possibility that a flying object might be a grenade, and the agents take no chances. They deflect everything they can see and reach.

The practice has varied from year to year, but in many instances Secret Service agents will ride on running boards built onto the presidential limousine. This is partly to screen him from potential assassins, and partly to give agents a rest from jogging alongside. When there are no running boards on the presidential vehicle, as happened at the time of the Kennedy assassination, the agents drop back and get on the follow-up car when the procession speeds up or when they're tired. Another agent drops off the follow-up car to take the place of the one being relieved.

The follow-up car serves two other functions: it's a back up in case the presidential vehicle breaks down, and it carries heavy weapons in case they're needed. While the U.S. president's Secret Service agents are certainly high-profile bodyguards as a deterrent, they have to maintain a certain decorum and avoid giving the impression of being thugs. They all carry handguns, usually in belt holsters, and as we saw in the tape of the Reagan incident, at least one carries a submachine gun in a briefcase. In case heavier weapons are needed, the follow-up car has a full complement, including rifles and shotguns. We can assume that the Secret Service follows the principle of being ready for any contingency, and also stocks the follow-up car with tear gas and masks, in order to cope with a riot.

In certain instances, there will be more than one follow-up car. This depends on the Secret Service's perception of potential threats. During one period, when the rumor flew that a Libyan "hit team" had entered the United States to kill the president, a Chevrolet Suburban station wagon filled with men in jumpsuits was seen following the presidential car. Agents from this team made an appearance on TV news tapes during 1992, when a riot began during one of President Bush's visits to Latin America. Agents wearing jumpsuits and carrying shoulder weapons jumped out and formed a protective cordon around the presidential party. Another follow-up car has the duty of blocking pursuit in case the president's inner ring of bodyguards has to evacuate him in the face of a threat.

In a motorcade, and during any public appearance, there are sometimes Secret Service agents and local officers mingling with the crowd. This is double insurance, because an assassin can draw a weapon concealed by the crowd, and remain unnoticed until he uses it. This is exactly what happened in the attempt on President Reagan.[6] McCarthy, the agent who was first to tackle Hinckley, stated that he saw the pistol when the third shot had gone off, and rushed to subdue Hinckley. Hinckley still managed to empty his revolver at the Reagan party, hitting four people, before being buried under a swarm of bodies.

The attempt on President Reagan revealed one weakness of depending on local police. Photographs of the scene just before John Hinckley opened fire showed District of Columbia Police officer Thomas Delehanty looking at the President emerging from the hotel. Instead of keeping his eyes on the crowd, which would have given him a chance to spot and perhaps stop Hinckley, he allowed himself to be distracted.

Protection in Other Countries

Let's take a very quick look at the scene in a couple of other countries, in order to note the differences in style of the governmental protective agencies. In Britain, where police are traditionally unarmed, the protection is much more low key. The protective responsibility falls upon Scotland Yard's Special Branch, the combination political/secret/counter-espionage police. British bodyguards are armed, but there are fewer of them. There always have been. Even during WWII, Winston Churchill had one main bodyguard and one assistant, both Scotland Yard officers. The recent activities by the IRA have resulted in a stepping-up of precautions, but they're still not up to the American scale. A small staff of bodyguards looks after the Prime Minister and selected government leaders. Still, they have their failures. John Taylor, a Member of Parliament from Ulster, was shot while approaching his car. His bodyguard was too far away to intervene.[7]

President de Gaulle of France led a charmed life, or else he had a supremely efficient corps of bodyguards. His protective detail consisted of four men under the command of Commissaire Jacques Ducret.[8] These four were his immediate entourage, but there was also a police chauffeur and other forces, such as a motorcycle escort, available when needed.

There were at least 30 attempts made on the life of de Gaulle. Most of these were by the O.A.S., as described elsewhere. Because of their military backgrounds and access to weapons, these were surely the most dangerous "hit-men" on Earth at the time. Few recent organizations, despite some spectacular successes, can match their record.

The counter-effort included much more than de Gaulle's four close protection officers. The Presidential Protection Corps was able to obtain cooperation from the French Intelligence Service, the armed services, and various branches of the police. At the time, there was an active war against the O.A.S., with kidnappings and counter-assassinations by French government agents. The intelligence service had a certain "Section 5," the "Action Service," a squad of toughs who carried the war home to the O.A.S. It took several years, but this massive effort finally broke the back of the O.A.S. This was a struggle of a sort unknown in America.

Governments have resources unavailable to private citizens, even chairmen of multinational corporations. Bodyguards for heads of state can call upon the army, navy, and air force for support, as well as local police agencies. This is why the private bodyguard can learn only so much from the ways in which government bodyguards go about their tasks.

Notes:

1. *Secret Service Chief*, U.E. Baughman and Leonard Wallace Robinson, NY, Popular Library, 1963, pp. 41-53.
2. "Report of the Warren Commission on the Assassination of President Kennedy," *New York Times* edition, pp. 44.
3. *Ibid.*, pp. 50-51.
4. Liu, Melinda, and Waller, Douglas, "Terror on the South Lawn," *Newsweek*, September 26, 1994, p. 42.
5. Personal experience of the author, who performed a minor function for President Ford on one of his visits.
6. *Protecting the President*, Dennis V.N. McCarthy, NY, William Morrow & Company, 1985, p. 16.
7. *Police Tactics in Armed Operations*, Colin Greenwood, Boulder, CO, Paladin Press, 1979, p. 269.
8. "Commissaire" is a French police rank that translates as "commissar" and is roughly equivalent to the American "inspector" (NYPD) or "commander" (LAPD). This is not to be confused with the San Francisco rank of "inspector" which, as in the French police terminology, means "detective."

6

The
Police
Bodyguard

Police officers are sometimes assigned to bodyguard duty, protecting the mayor, governor or visiting VIPs. Others work as bodyguards part-time, moonlighting to earn extra money. Still others take up this work after retirement, obtaining licenses as private investigators. The contacts officers make during their careers are often helpful in finding work after retirement.

Officers on bodyguard duty while on the job may be assigned temporarily to assist the U.S. Secret Service or other federal security agency when the president, vice president, or other high official comes to town. Others may draw a semi-permanent assignment to guard the mayor, governor or other local office holder.

Executive protection requires a drastic change of attitude for the police officer. His priorities change because of the nature of the assignment. The police officer typically is trained to take direct action to resolve a crisis, up to and including arrest. As a bodyguard, his main task is to assure his principal's safety, not make an arrest. This conflicts with his training and experience, and some officers never make the transition successfully.

One police sergeant, a member of a local department with an inept chief, was totally indoctrinated in his department's philosophy, which could be summed up as "kick ass and take names." Although he had moonlighted as a bodyguard for some local wealthy people and visiting entertainers, he had only one approach to meeting a threat: to make an immediate arrest. He felt that this was the quickest way to stop the danger, and could not see that in some situations this would expose his protectee to greater danger.[1]

In one sense, this attitude was understandable, because the only threats he'd faced in his protective work were from people we could characterize as "punks," not serious offenders. He'd never faced a determined attack which would require evacuation of the protectee as first priority. Importantly, he'd never had any formal training in protective techniques. Like many law officers, he thought that his status as a policeman gave him expertise in any and all aspects of law enforcement.

The attitude required to be a successful bodyguard is a more passive one than most police officers are accustomed to showing. A bodyguard noticing someone suspicious cannot confront him and say, "Hey, asshole, let's see some ID." By its very nature, police work is not a low-profile occupation, and officers who assume executive protective duties must re-orient themselves.

This point is well documented in recent history. The films of the Kennedy assassination and of the attack on President Reagan show the Secret Service agents evacuating the protectee immediately, leaving the outer screen of agents and local police officers to deal with the assailant. In the attacks on President Ford by Sara Jane Moore and "Squeaky" Fromme, peripheral agents and police officers overpowered the assailants while the close protection officers evacuated Ford at once. In none of these incidents did the bodyguards fire a single shot.

The French police bodyguards protecting President de Gaulle during the attack at Petit-Clamart did not shoot back at the attackers, who were equipped with full-auto weapons. They instead relied on speed and evasion to get their principal to safety.

Working with the Secret Service

The U.S. Secret Service protects the president, his family, the vice president, president-elect, presidential candidates, and their families. It also protects the widow of a president until she remarries, and his children, until they reach majority. The president may also order the Secret Service to protect foreign visitors, such as heads of state.

In the White House, the Secret Service provides all of the protection the president needs. When he travels, however, the Secret Service relies heavily on cooperation and support from local agencies.

When a federal protectee arrives in the area, the local police never have to concern themselves with close-in protection. Their task is to provide the outer rings of security. Some of the duties include surveillance, traffic and crowd control, and outer perimeter support. Other tasks may include setting up and manning barricades and reviewing stands. This practice fits best with the organization and orientation of local police departments. They're assigned to do what they do best. In case of a threat, the Secret Service agents closest to the protectee move him to safety while the agents and local police in the outer perimeters neutralize the threat and make the apprehension. In some cases, the threat can seem serious, although there's no intent to harm the principal. An example is when a badly driven automobile rammed President Ford's limousine. There were no injuries, and this would have been merely another fender-bender traffic accident if it had happened to anyone else.

The nuts and bolts of the method of operation is that the Secret Service's advance agent holds a meeting with local police before the arrival of the VIP. This meeting deals with traffic control, motorcade assistance, duty posts, barricades and other crowd control measures, the schedule and routing, etc. Secret Service agents plan routes and drive over them several times, looking for potential danger spots and noting the distances involved and the time needed to cover the routes. The advance agents note nearby hospitals, and lay out the shortest routes to them. The driver of the protectee's car must have this information, although in practice a local police car usually heads the procession and will lead the way to emergency facilities if needed.[2]

Other support the Secret Service solicits from the local agency is manpower and specialized units to assure building security. The police will contribute manpower for searching buildings to be visited or occupied by the protectee, and in some instances will use their own explosives detection dogs. The local department often also provides support from their "bomb squad" if needed to dispose of explosive devices.

Officers assigned to protective duty during the visit of a federal protectee will find it boring and unrewarding. Typically, the Secret Service instructs local officers to face away from the dignitary, in order to watch the crowd. Officers within sight of the protectee will usually be assigned to crowd control or checkpoints at entrances to buildings.

Another important point the Secret Service agents cover is to solicit information from the local police department's intelligence officers regarding people who might be threats to the protectee. In cases of special concern, the Secret Service will ask the local agency to arrange discreet surveillance of particularly worrisome people during the protectee's visit.

During these VIP visits, the police continue to operate through their own command structure, using their own communication equipment. They sometimes operate in parallel, as when Secret Service agents are teamed with local officers in perimeter roles. In such cases, each has his own radio and works through his agency's communication net.

Protecting Local Officials

In contrast to the subordinate role taken by police cooperating with federal protective officers, those looking after local officials such as the mayor or governor take a much more active role, and have to both plan and carry out the protective measures themselves. The local officer does not have the generous and seemingly unlimited budget of the federal agents, and consequently must make do with much less.

The local officer is not likely to have undergone special schooling for the assignment, as do Secret Service agents. Study of protective methods forms part of each Secret Service agent's basic training, and agents take refresher courses when assigned to protective duties. Local officers typically have police academy training and in-service training, but little or none of this deals with protective duties.

Very few local officers get specialized executive protection training, partly because there are so few sources for it that are acceptable to local police agencies. The U.S. Secret Service occasionally conducts courses in executive protection for local officers, but these are not well known nor widely advertised. Consequently, few American police officers receive specialized training in executive protection from the Secret Service. The private schools that offer such instruction are usually not acceptable to police executives because they have no official status. This is unfortunate, because their staffs often are actively employed bodyguards with far more protective experience than most police officers.

This is very important. Although the U.S. Secret Service does offer courses, their orientation is towards their method of operating. The Secret Service instructors tend to teach how to work protective details with large numbers of officers and extensive resources. The Secret Service budget is generous, and allows the Service to buy lavish and expensive equipment and to hire almost all the agents it needs. Local departments have to make do with much less, as do private bodyguards, and need instruction on how to conduct protective operations on a shoestring.

An assignment to a protective detail results in about the same method of familiarization as being assigned to homicide or narcotics. The officer will be introduced as a junior member of the detail, and expected to "learn the ropes" by following the instruction and examples of the commander or senior members. The odds are very great that the senior members will have learned their duties the same way.

The most important point for the local officer to understand is that, once he's assigned responsibility for protecting a VIP, his priorities change. As we've seen, some officers have trouble handling this, which is why no officer should be assigned as leader of the protective detail until he's served a period of "apprenticeship" in a subordinate role to become accustomed to the different way of working and the different mentality required.

The head of the protective detail must understand that his main task is avoidance, not confrontation. A confrontation is justifiable only when absolutely necessary to negate an attack or to clear an escape route. Even then, the confrontation should be as short as possible, because the main priority is escape. One of the team leader's most important responsibilities is to ensure that each new member of the team understands this thoroughly.

Some recruits will not accept this. In every organization we can find glory hunters. These are especially unsuitable for protective work, because their concentration on seeking high-profile arrests and dangerous assignments can get their principal killed.

The officer serving as bodyguard can no longer take the same attitude towards "street crime" that he previously held. If he sees a crime committed in his presence, he must not take action unless it threatens his protectee. A nearby disturbance will only be a distraction, taking him away from his principal if he decides to intervene. Worse, it may be a purposeful diversion, to attract his attention and perhaps get him to move away from his protectee, leaving the way clear for an attack. Malcolm X's bodyguards moved away from him towards a staged disturbance, leaving their protectee wide open for the kill.

An important difference between protecting a federal VIP and a local one is that the local official is likely to be somewhat less well known, and tends to maintain a much lower profile. He or she may be known in the immediate community, but away from home is not as easily recognized as nationally-prominent figures.

This is valuable in that it attracts much less attention, and the local police officer's job is to help keep it that way. It would be inappropriate to use a specially equipped limousine that attracts attention on the street. Although the mayor of New York City rates a limousine, local officials in other parts of the country are better off not following his example.

Protective officers have to deal with threats and potential threats, and one source of information is to examine the "hate mail" which officials tend to receive. In this regard, the U.S. Secret Service also scans the hate mail which federal officials receive. Most of it isn't truly threatening, just in bad taste, but some dangerous individuals start out by writing letters, then graduate to planning attacks. The mail can provide early warning signs of such dangers.

The local officer may be only a part-time bodyguard, picking up the official at his home in the morning and escorting him throughout the day. Often, the budget or the official won't allow round-the-clock protection. Some local officials want protection only on public occasions, such as when campaigning or attending functions with large numbers of people.

The police officer traveling officially with his protectee can expect cooperation from other local officers in practically all parts of the United States. His carrying of a concealed firearm will not cause him problems, even in jurisdictions with strict firearms laws, because of the "courtesy" that police officers traditionally have extended each other. In foreign countries, though, it won't be that simple. Many foreign police agencies simply don't recognize that an American officer has any jurisdiction at all, and will not even allow a protective officer the status of his limited duty. As for carrying a firearm, this can lead to prosecution in some instances.

Our government has reciprocal arrangements with certain foreign countries to allow U.S. Secret Service agents with the president and other American dignitaries to carry firearms abroad. Likewise, foreign dignitaries' bodyguards may carry sidearms while escorting their protectees inside the United States. One example of this was a bodyguard traveling with Saudi Arabia's Prince Bandar, who was openly carrying a holstered pistol.[3]

It's best to make advance arrangements with foreign government officials to assure the smoothing over of potential problems. With the proper diplomatic approach, the foreign police agency may provide armed officers to supplement the protectee's team. This supposedly makes it unnecessary for the protectee's officers to bring their weapons into the country. This isn't a perfect solution, but is better than leaving the protectee's agents totally unarmed and defenseless.

The Retired Officer

This requires the most drastic change in orientation. The individual no longer has any official status, and many of the courtesies he might have expected from fellow officers are no longer assured. In other jurisdictions, he's simply a civilian, with no special status at all. In foreign countries, he doesn't even have a quasi-official position, and can face serious problems in protecting his client.

It may be surprising, but this is often the case in Great Britain. If the foreign visitor is a government dignitary, his protective officers will have much more latitude than if he's a private person. Foreign diplomats and their agents have diplomatic status, and can "carry" without fear of search and arrest. Private protective agents must go unarmed, or risk breaking the law. Even private British agents must go unarmed, as British law does not allow carry permits for private investigators and agents.

Sometimes the retired officer can work as a bodyguard without any formalities, but in other jurisdictions there are some strict official requirements. He may have to obtain a private investigator's license and/or a concealed firearms permit. Although the requirements vary with the jurisdiction, being a retired police officer usually

lubricates the way towards obtaining this official paperwork.

Notes:

1. Personal acquaintance of the author. This officer later became a local justice of the peace, and later chief deputy under another sheriff.
2. Lesce, Tony, "The Police Officer as Bodyguard," *Police Marksman*, July/August, 1984, pp. 8-22.
3. Grapevine, *Time*, August 21, 1989, Nation, p. 26.

7
The
Human Factor

What sort of people make good bodyguards? What sort of people make good protectees? These are very important questions because they affect the relationship between the bodyguard and his client, and they affect the strength of the operation. Many executives and other potential clients as well as aspiring bodyguards, don't truly know what makes for a good protective effort, partly because they get their ideas from television.

The Protectee

Let's begin by studying the normal problems in protecting a client. The bodyguard must adapt his schedule to his client's, but the client sometimes has to accept changes too. It may be prudent to give up late-night walks, for example. The principal must also give up the idea that he can stroll away from the office or home without notifying anyone. The bodyguard will become his shadow.

The family may also be part of this picture, especially in a foreign country. All members will have to understand their roles in establishing security.

Minor children often need special bodyguards. One good rule to follow here is to assign only guards who have children of their own. Some feel that women are especially suitable for guarding children.

Some protectees, without meaning to be difficult, give their bodyguards headaches. One well known example was President Harry Truman. He typically took a walk before breakfast, leaving the White House gate with the Secret Service scrambling after him.[1] The Secret Service White House Detail found it a problem to keep the president safe on the sidewalk, especially as they could not escort him with any heavy armament showing. One adaptive technique they used was to have a car with armed agents following a few yards behind Truman.

President Roosevelt was usually confined to a wheelchair, which meant that the Secret Service had to see to it that there were special ramps built for him wherever he went.[2]

Eisenhower gave his protectors difficult moments. His trip to Korea was one which taxed the Secret Service bodyguards to their utmost, and his liking for golf meant that he exposed himself to a sniper attack while he was playing. The Secret Service had to mount a strong perimeter security operation around the golf course while the president was playing.

The protectee should recognize that there is a potential or actual threat, and that the bodyguard will help him cope with it. He should not expect the bodyguard to carry the entire burden, and any bodyguard who claims he can is being dishonest. There's a certain minimal cooperation needed from the principal, and without it there will be unnecessary gaps in security.

The Bodyguard: Human Factors

What qualities does a bodyguard need? Brute strength is not necessarily the main quality, although it has its place in certain limited situations. Rock stars may need big bruisers whose knuckles drag the ground to "protect" them from their fans. Their value is mainly as deterrents to cope with low-grade threats. They'd be totally outclassed by any serious threat. We've already seen how Roosevelt Grier failed to keep Robert Kennedy from being shot to death.

Intelligence is important, but not necessarily an intellectual and bookish intelligence. The sort of intelligence needed for executive protection is best described as "street smarts." Equally important is a calm, "together" personality. The protective agent should be realistic, not romantic. He should be aggressive, but not excessively so. Anyone who is "trigger-happy" may commit a wrongful shooting. Anyone with a tendency to use "hand talk" may assault someone without justification, and a subsequent lawsuit is likely. This is where the "kick ass and take names" attitudes of some former police officers can be a handicap. The bodyguard must have great patience, and a high tolerance for boredom. He's going to be faced with many dull hours and many unexciting days. He'll need the ability to stay awake and alert when nothing's happening. He'll also need a single-minded devotion to priorities, and the ability to avoid being sidetracked.

It's also important to avoid the dangers of mind set and complacency. One criticism made of the Secret Service reaction during the Kennedy assassination was that they had become complacent. This perhaps accounted for their generally slow response, although in fairness we should note that certain individual agents, such as Clint Hill, responded very quickly. Hill ran from the follow-up car to the president's limousine, grabbing Mrs. Kennedy and pushing her back onto the seat.

The bodyguard should be able to blend into the milieu, not be conspicuous. There are two important reasons for this.

The first has to do with the client. He's concerned with public relations, and doesn't want the presence of a person with "thug" written all over him. If the executive protection agent has to accompany his principal into a conference room, he must seem to belong. Anyone with bulging muscles and a baleful glare will seem out of place. A lowbrow will also not inspire confidence from the protectee. Good grooming and table manners are as important, in this context, as other skills.[3]

The second is that in any serious attack, the bodyguard is the target. Eliminate him and the rest is easy. The bodyguard who stands out from the crowd makes himself a more conspicuous target. Why make it easy for the attackers?

Complicating this picture is gossip by the client's family and associates.[4] Gossip can travel far enough to pin-point the bodyguard for an attacker, and this can be fatal.

One more factor is the bodyguard's integrity. If you're politically active, you may feel uncomfortable with a bodyguard who is politically opposed to you. India's Prime Minister, Indira Ghandi, was shot to death by two of her Sikh bodyguards in 1984. Although

the conspirators were hanged in 1989, this did not bring back Mrs. Ghandi.[5]

Another example took place in Tunis, Tunisia, in January, 1991. A bodyguard working for Salah Khalef opened fire and killed Khalef, as well as PLO Security Chief Hayel Abdel-Hamid and Abu Mohammed Al-Omari, Khalef's personal bodyguard. Khalef had been the planner of the Munich slaying of Israeli Olympic athletes, which led to speculation that Israel had been behind the shooting.[6] Whoever was behind it, Israel or another faction, Khalef was still the victim of a treacherous bodyguard.

Another example of inadequate protection was Luis Colosio, the Mexican presidential candidate who was shot to death in Tijuana on March 23, 1994. Although major candidates are entitled to police protection in Mexico, Colosio did not have the best. Some of his guards had been dismissed from the Tijuana police force for misconduct. Several were arrested after the shooting, but later released for lack of evidence.[7]

Seeking a Bodyguard

If you're shopping around for a bodyguard, don't just pick up the yellow pages and start leafing through them. There's no category for "bodyguard," anyway. You'd have to seek them out under "investigators" or "detectives." Some private detective agencies have display ads in the yellow pages listing their services, which can include polygraph tests and routine surveillances.

If you're going to interview prospective bodyguards, you'll want to seek out certain qualities. When the applicant walks into the room, note his demeanor. Is he swaggering, trying hard to project a "macho" image? If so, he's definitely not the man for you. He's either very immature or playing you for a fool, trying to impress you with bravado.

What's his background? What sort of education and training has he had? Has he had military service? Police experience? Service with a specialized agency such as the U.S. Secret Service? The training given by these different services differs sharply in relevance to executive protection.

If he starts telling you about how he attended many karate schools and is now an instructor, don't waste any more time. He's absolutely the wrong type.

Has he had any special training in executive protection? Some private academies offer this training, which can be valuable or not, depending on the academy. On the other hand, the operative a private detective agency sends over might have limited or irrelevant experience.

What specific experience has he had? Check references! In the private as well as public sectors, novices start at the fringes, and gradually move to positions of greater responsibility as they learn their jobs. Whatever formal training your applicant has had, several years' practical experience in executive protection is extremely valuable because it tells you two things:

1. He's had the opportunity to learn his job by doing.
2. He's been good enough at it to last.

Don't let a prospective bodyguard sidestep the question of practical experience by telling you that he's bound not to speak about previous assignments. Legitimate bodyguards and agencies provide references. However, some applicants may cite "secrecy agreements" or "national security" to avoid providing specific experience in protective work. If you buy this explanation, and don't insist on specific details, you're taking a chance. Again, check references!

What is his attitude? What does he see his role to be? If he starts talking about defending you against all sorts of lurid threats, keep looking. You want someone who will concentrate on keeping you out of trouble, not someone looking for a brawl.

Does he seem reckless? If so, be cautious. He might be letting you in for an expensive lawsuit.

How much money does he want? One tip-off is if he's asking much below the prevailing rate. He might be inept and desperate for a job. Another problem can arise with the bodyguard who expects too much. Don't be shy about asking him what justifies the money he's asking. This can open up a view into an overly-inflated ego.

The prevailing rates vary with the region of the country. Here are some rough guides:

$20 to $50 per hour for one agent on a daily basis. Rates will drop somewhat for extended periods. The range will then be $15 to $30 per hour.

Hollywood has some of the highest rates, which is no surprise. A first-class bodyguard goes for about $75 per hour, eight-hour minimum, but the agency throws in a limo. Each additional agent will cost $60 per hour. Expenses are extra.[8]

A bodyguard working for an agency earns from $7 to $20 per hour, depending on level of skill. This suggests that if you need protection for an extended period, you'd be better off hiring your guards directly. This will save you money, but will bring other problems, such as administration, insurance and the other legal ramifications. See the chapter on legal aspects.

When interviewing the bodyguard, don't worry at all about why he left his last employment, unless it's because his client was killed. If it was because of a personality clash, which often happens, you may not get the straight story from his former employer.

One of the best ways to judge an applicant is by personal references. This doesn't mean letters written by people you don't know. This means word-of-mouth references by friends and/or acquaintances who have employed him and found his services satisfactory. Personal references are valuable, because you can then find out about possible problems such as lateness, a drinking problem, etc.

Many bodyguards or agencies are very reluctant to give out information about their clients, which can be an obstacle when asking them for references. If they do provide references, you can be sure that the deck is stacked, because they would not mention anyone who found their services unsatisfactory. That's why it's best to ask among your friends, acquaintances and business contacts.

What your prospective bodyguard did before is important, because it provides clues regarding what he's likely to do for you, and whether or not he's a stable and trustworthy person. Some employers hire bodyguards with strange pasts. William Favre, himself involved in some shady businesses, hired Sammy Wamfleur as a bodyguard in 1987. He had met Wamfleur in jail in Geneva, Switzerland, while detained over copyright and trademark violations incurred while manufacturing replica Ferrari automobiles. Wamfleur, in turn, was in jail for having violated Swiss law by working as a mercenary in South Africa. Favre's new bodyguard didn't last long, however, having hired out to Libya's Colonel Muammar al-Qaddafi to blow up an Italian lighthouse. On the way to the lighthouse, Wamfleur and his partner in this operation had an accident, and the resulting explosion killed his partner. Wamfleur was arrested, but somehow was never prosecuted for his part in this affair.[9]

Are there irreconcilable differences in your viewpoints? This could be the precursor of real trouble. You may want to live a high-profile existence, for example, while he insists that you keep your profile low. One or the other must bend. If not, he won't be able to guard you to the best of his ability.

Is he willing to work long hours? This is a mundane detail, but will be exceptionally important if you travel a lot or if he's the only bodyguard you have.

Is he able to manage a team of bodyguards? The best way to judge this is by his experience. If he is a former director of executive protection for a corporation, or a former squad leader in a Marine embassy guard, you have reason to trust in his ability.

Team leaders also expect more money, but don't be reluctant to pay what's necessary. Trying to buy protection cheaply is a bad bargain. Team leaders can earn from $37,000 to $75,000 per year, again depending on the area of the country and the individual's qualifications.

It's also important to know a bit about your bodyguard's personal life. It's not a matter of making friends with him, but finding out about any vulnerabilities that may harm you. If he leads a lifestyle that requires more money than you pay him, he may be susceptible to a bribe. This doesn't mean that he can be bribed to assassinate you, but just not to show up one day, leaving the field clear for an attacker. Most likely, though, the bribe will be for information. A bodyguard has access to sensitive information about his client, and there may be parties interested enough to pay for this information.

This is why you must consider your bodyguard's lifestyle. Does he have expensive tastes? Is he paying large alimony? Does he have a large family, or unusual medical bills? Does he drink heavily or gamble? All of these can bear on his loyalty to you.

If you're speaking with the representative of a detective or security guard agency, be direct in your questions. Be aware that they most likely do uniformed protective work for businesses. This usually means protecting against shoplifters, trespassers, casual vandals and thieves. Their experience in executive protection may be slim or non-existent. The agent they assign to you won't be of much use if his only experience has been as a rent-a-cop guarding a bowling alley or supermarket.[10]

Agencies are state licensed, and part of the licensing requirement is that they carry liability insurance. This can be very important, as otherwise you'll have to carry it. You may wish to carry liability insurance beyond the agency's coverage, as well, so when interviewing an agency representative, ask about this point.

The state bureau that licenses private security agencies can be a source of information. This is one place to ask about a private agency's record regarding complaints and lawsuits filed against it. You won't always get a complete picture from this source, but it's a good place to begin.

Overall, the human factor will make it or break it. Equipment and gadgets are no better than the people who use them. Careful choosing and blending of the right people can make a winning team.

Notes:

1. *Secret Service Chief*, Baughman, U. E., and Robinson, Leonard Wallace, New York, Popular Library, 1963, pp. 64-67.
2. *Ibid.*, p. 64.
3. *Executive Protection*, Benny Mares, Boulder, CO, Paladin Press, 1994, pp. 73-80.
4. *The Executive Protection Bible*, Braunig, Martha J., Basalt, CO, Executive Protection International, 1992, p. 3.
5. Blood and Ashes, *Time*, January 16, 1989, World Notes, p. 41.
6. Marshall, Steve, and Katz, Lee Michael, "Assassin Kills Top PLO Military Strategist," *USA Today*, January 15, 1991, News p. 4A.
7. Hayward, Susana, "Why Were Bad Guys Guarding Colosio?" Associated Press, April 18, 1994.
8. Krefft, Vanda, "The Cost of Celebrity," *Woman's Day*, June 19, 1990, pp. 66-69.
9. Yates, Brock, "The Strange Case of William Favre," *Car and Driver Magazine*, December, 1989, v35, n6, pp. 77-81.
10. One executive protection agency with a good reputation is:

Vance International
10467 White Granite Drive, Suite 210
Oakton, VA 22124-2700
Phone: (703) 385-6754
Fax: (703) 359-8456
Attn: William W. Little

When Charles F. "Chuck" Vance left the U.S. Secret Service, he started up his own protective firm. Between 1984 and the present, this company has grown to over 1500 employees, and has some of the "Fortune 500" corporations as clients. Vance has several divisions providing bodyguard and other protective services, and offices in several cities, including Moscow, Russia.

8
Briefing
The
Client

When taking on a client, it's important to arrive at an understanding at the outset. You ought to inform your client about your protective services, and make him aware of the need for cooperation from him, his family and his staff. It's vital that he understand that you require certain perquisites and privileges, not as a "power trip," but to help ensure his safety.

This takes both tact and force of personality. You may be asking him to change his lifestyle somewhat, and your success in this effort will depend on the sort of person he is, the special circumstances, and your ability to get your points across.

It helps if he's scared. If the danger in his locale is significant, or if he's just lost a friend or co-worker to assassination, he'll be more cooperative than if he's been told by his boss that he's having a bodyguard assigned to him.[1]

Sometimes, security is part of the corporate culture. The Coors family, in Colorado, accepts security as a normal part of life. In the small community where most live, they're well known, and some work at the plant. All have home security systems, and the company's security department furnishes family members with protective agents when circumstances dictate.[2]

Persuading him to modify his lifestyle for the sake of a low profile may be difficult. You may run into resistance from him, but even more from his wife, if protecting her is part of your duties. Giving up a fancy limo which serves as a status symbol can be deflating to the ego. Dropping his country club membership may seem like a real sacrifice, unless your client understands that this can be a matter of life and death. He or his wife may feel that you're an intruder, especially if your assignment includes guarding them at home.

For example, you need a free run of his property where he expects you to guard him. You must have access to every room, so that you can inspect it periodically for possible gaps in security. As a practical tip, try not to perform any inspections in his presence. This avoids the embarrassment of your opening a closet or bedside drawer to reveal condoms, vibrators or X-rated tapes.

At the start, you'll need to make a security survey of his premises. Check out his home and office, and improve security where you feel it's necessary.[3] For this you need the authority to make changes without clearing every detail with him. As a basic precaution, the locks should all be changed. You may find a need to reinforce or replace some doors, windows or fences. You might advise him to have an electronic security system installed. The best way to convince your client of the need is to show how this will save him money in the long run, by saving on manpower.

You also need to be informed of his lifestyle, especially of his visitors and travel plans. If he employs an appointments secretary, this person must have close liaison with you and your staff. You need to screen any visitors not closely known to your client and his staff. Protection is a team effort, and a weakness at any point can negate the entire operation.

If he plans a trip, you need to know about it well enough in advance to make plans for his protection. Crime, political unrest and terrorism all can pose threats to your client. This means sending an "advance man" to the destination to survey the area and plan the client's security. It may irk the client to have to "clear" his travels with you in advance, but if he understands the need, he's more likely to cooperate.

A problem may arise if the local manager resents the security specialist's vetoing a trip. The "secondary effect" includes a bruised ego, and it's wise to try to pour oil on the waters for the sake of future liaisons. The way to deal with this situation is for you to make an advance trip, look over the situation, and discuss security with the local executive. The local media can be helpful in forming an impression of the country's attitude towards the United States and towards Americans. A high rate of violence, especially if directed against foreigners, is objective evidence of danger. A personal relationship with the local manager can help establish a basis for a mutually agreed decision regarding a projected visit.[4]

Your client must also understand that it will take several weeks to get the security system fully operational. Close-in protection can begin immediately, but training household and office staffs to promote security measures inevitably takes time. Installing electronic systems, checking them out and putting them to use can take weeks. Fully integrating the various facets of the system you design for him takes time, and it goes more slowly than most people like.

This is also the time to settle the question of an expense allowance. Bodyguards, especially those who travel with the client, have definite expenses, and the client must cover them. A worthwhile practice is to issue the bodyguard his own credit card, to use on the client's business. Some suspicious clients may feel uncomfortable about this, but they must realize that they're trusting the bodyguard with their lives, and the issuance of a credit card isn't nearly as important as that.

A major advantage of having a credit card in the bodyguard's name is that he can make the payments when traveling. The client, if he uses his own credit card, is advertising his presence and making his movements easier to trace. This is especially important today, when credit card records provide an electronic trail of the cardholder's travels. It's possible for a person who has never seen your client to tap into a credit card company's computer and retrieve a record of every use, without your client's knowledge.[5]

One point that some clients fail to take into consideration is that the bodyguard is not a servant. This is not because bodyguards have inflated egos and don't want to be demoted to the status of a maid. It's because the bodyguard has an exacting job to do, and imposing other tasks on him can be distracting. Imagine that the client and his wife are about to start on a car trip. The wife, having forgotten her purse, asks the bodyguard to go back and get it. If he does, he's leaving the couple exposed on the street.

The bodyguard should not, above all, function as a media relations officer. His job is to remain low-profile, and being in front of reporters and their cameras negates this aspect. The bodyguard should appear to be an unimportant member of the protectee's staff, and he should refer all media questions to the actual public relations person.

Inevitably, the bodyguard will appear on videotape sometime. This isn't reason for concern, because the frenetic pace of TV news reporting allows only sound bites of the most important people. Studying videotapes of the president's public appearances will show how cameras focus on him, while the surrounding Secret Service agents appear only for fleeting moments.

The client must also understand that, although he's your boss, if an emergency occurs he must take orders from you for his safety. He must realize that if a crisis strikes, and you tell him to "take cover," he must do so unquestioningly and immediately, even if he has to dive into a mud puddle in his tuxedo.

You might explain the need this way:

"If you hear me shout 'get down' to you, do it. Don't ask me why, and don't stick your head up to see where the action is. If I yell at you to get down, it's because we're under attack. If I grab you, and push you towards a doorway, or down behind a car, go along with me. I'm trying to get you under cover. If there's any danger coming our way, remember that I'm in charge. That's what you pay me for."

There's another aspect to the relationship between the bodyguard and his clients that is important to explain at the outset. This is what some professional protective agents refer to as "sacred trust." It means discretion. The bodyguard must know how to keep secrets, even after his employment terminates. He may overhear conversations that the client prefers keeping private. He also may become aware of certain facts about his client that the client will prefer to keep in the dark.

Some public figures have various weaknesses and personal habits that would furnish ammunition to their opponents if disclosed. Some cheat on their wives. Others are alcoholics, and yet others are sex deviates. This is an important point to cover, because some protectees ditch their bodyguards when they go off on their flings. The bodyguard must impress his protectee that evading security this way can have serious consequences.[6]

The bodyguard, whatever his personal preferences and ideals, must develop a professional tolerance and discretion to serve his client's interests. The leader of a team of bodyguards must ensure that his agents are aware of this requirement. It's customary to dismiss immediately anyone who violates this trust. This happened to one bodyguard assigned to a free-wheeling

U.S. senator who telephoned a friend to disclose the senator's latest fling.

Trust should continue after the assignment ends, and the bodyguard who reveals a former client's personal life attains the same sort of notoriety as the former servant who tells all. With various "kiss and tell" memoirs appearing, it's understandable that some employers are a bit nervous about former bodyguards. One bodyguard who discussed his former employer's sex life in detail made both headlines and television appearances. Rudy Gonzales, former bodyguard to Mike Tyson, had interviews discussing Tyson's sexual appetite published in the *New York Post*. Fox Television News also carried Gonzales' revelations. He discussed the number of women Tyson had "had," and how he sat in a corner of the room protecting Tyson while the boxer was enjoying sex.[7]

Sacred trust does not mean that the bodyguard must tolerate or facilitate something blatantly illegal. If the client is a child molester, for example, the bodyguard should immediately drop him as a client. Otherwise, the bodyguard will only be making himself an accomplice. This can pose serious problems with some types of clients, such as royalty, and especially Mid-East potentates. They may seek out prostitutes, in areas where there's little tolerance for this type of entertainment. Kinky sex habits are often illegal, and those who cater to this type of desire are operating outside the law. Some protectees may expect their bodyguards to procure prostitutes for them. Obviously the bodyguard is not a pimp for his client, and he should remain firm in his determination to remain uninvolved.[8]

A serious problem in this regard is illegal drugs. There's no hard-and-fast answer to this problem. If the client uses them, and is in a locale where the use of illegal drugs is not tolerated, it becomes a dangerous situation for the bodyguard and anyone closely associated with the client. On the other hand, illegal drug use by Hollywood entertainers is so commonplace that it's obvious there's a certain degree of tolerance. In such a case, the bodyguard can turn a blind eye towards his obviously stoned client, but should never play any role in obtaining drugs for his client. He should also insist that his client never ingest drugs in his presence, for a clear and obvious reason. If he doesn't see it, he cannot testify to it.[9]

Obtaining the client's cooperation is vital to the protective effort. Despite this, you may find some clients to be recalcitrant. If your client's lack of cooperation endangers him severely, it's best to drop him and advise him to hire someone else. You may not like losing a client, but it's better to lose him this way than by having him killed while in your charge. It also beats getting yourself arrested for aiding a client's illegal activity. The damage to your reputation will lose you many more potential clients.

Notes:

1. *Terrorism and Personal Protection*, Brian Jenkins, editor, NY, Butterworth Publishers, 1985, p. 321.
2. Wilson, Carolyn, "Coors Brews Security Success," *Security Management*, January, 1993, p. 50.
3. *Providing Protective Services, A Practical Guide For Police*, James A. King, San Diego, California, EPS International, 1990. pp. 127-137.
4. Nocella, Henry A., "Executive Protection: Bandaging Bruised Egos," *Security Management*, February, 1990, v34, n2, pp. 89-90.
5. *Privacy For Sale*, Jeffrey Rothfeder, NY, Simon & Schuster, 1992, p. 81.
6. Leach, Norman S., "Executive Protection: An Ironclad Defense," *Security Management*, February, 1990, v34, n2, p 84.
7. White, Carolyn, "Tyson's Sex Life Gets A Closer Look," *USA Today*, August 11, 1992, Sports, p. 2C.
8. *Executive Protection*, Mares, Benny, Boulder, CO, Paladin Press, 1994, pp. 17-18.
9. *The Executive Protection Bible*, Martha J. Braunig, Basalt, CO, Executive Protection International, 1992, pp. 13 and 15.

9

Security And Access Control Systems

Your protectee has to have a home base. He either lives somewhere, works somewhere, or both. Home base serves two purposes. One is the protectee's purpose, as a home or workplace. The other is your purpose, to enhance his physical security, thus making your job easier. A man's home is still his castle, both by common law and by tactical exigencies. For this, you need a security system of some sort. As with other protective measures, cost will largely decide what sort of system you'll have.

This chapter will be a "crash course" in the theory and hardware of a security system. This will give you enough knowledge to discuss the subject intelligently if your task is to shop around for the hardware or to design the entire system. For the nuts-and-bolts information regarding how to install the many pieces of hardware manufactured for this purpose, you'll have to hire a specialist or get the information from the manufacturers.

Security Systems: The Theory

The theory of security systems is basically similar to the general protective theory. You'll find that a skillful blending of hardware and human resources will give you an economical and effective system.

Security systems used to be limited to guards, fences and walls. The enhanced possibilities brought about by modern miniaturized electronics have resulted in sophisticated hardware that economizes on manpower.

The modern concept of a security system is based on defense in depth. The first line is:

Access Control

By a system of barriers, guards, electronic gates and doors, access to a secure area is under firm control. A well-designed system will keep out random

unauthorized visitors, as well as intentional penetrators.

This shows an important terrain feature that is critical for protection. The house is on high ground, giving a good view of the surrounding area. There's little cover available for anyone who approaches. The grounds are spacious enough to provide a lot of open area to cross on the approach to the house. A chain-link fence at the perimeter (not shown) enables the bodyguards to observe anyone outside while still denying access. All told, the terrain here definitely favors the defense.

The illusion of security. This house has a wood slat fence around it, but the fence is mainly for privacy, not security. It only permits the householder to skinny-dip in his pool without embarrassment, and doesn't provide any useful deterrence to an intruder. The fence serves merely to screen anyone who approaches the house from view. An intruder can approach to within a few feet of the house, then scale the fence or throw in a gasoline bomb.

Concrete walls are not much better. They still block the householder's view, shield anyone approaching, and are easy to scale. Many tract homes are built with such a "protective wall" around them as an illusion of security.

A simple precaution, such as outside lighting, makes a great deal of difference. Most houses already have outside lights, and the cost of installation is small for those which don't. Keeping the lights turned on both deters a night intruder, and makes spotting him easier.

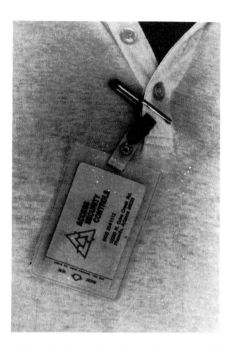

One of the basic tools of security is the I.D. and access card. This card serves two purposes. It identifies the wearer, and its magnetic printing permits opening doors to the secure area.

Cardkey Systems provides the "Reflection" video imaging and badging system which produces photo I.D. badges that are also cardkeys. The card provides access to the facilities, and serves as an identifier once inside. For extra security to guard against lost or stolen cards, an option provides for a Personal Identification Number (PIN) that the user keys in after putting his card into the slot.

Another new wrinkle in the card system is the DOOR-GARD reader that can recognize any magnetic card that conforms to ABA specifications, including VISA, MasterCard and American Express. This allows employees to use bank cards they already carry, and saves the cost of issuing cards to many employees. DOOR-GARD is supplied by International Electronics, Inc.

The electronic outer ring can be very comprehensive. Still, it's possible to penetrate this outer shell, and the next line of defense is:

Intrusion Detection

Under most circumstances, it's impossible to closely guard every foot of a perimeter, and it's also possible for a determined and skilled penetrator to bypass the system and gain access. An access control system can also fail, sometimes because of an internal breakdown, or something as mundane as a power failure. Detection of an intruder is possible by various sophisticated technical means, such as sonic and infrared sensors.

This is a motion sensor, also known as a "trembler switch." One of these, attached to anything that an intruder would be likely to touch, will close a circuit when it detects the slightest movement.

When there is an intrusion alert, the next line of defense is:

Response

Depending on the gravity of the situation, and the degree of protection needed, the response can be an alarm bell, to alert legitimate occupants that there's been an intrusion, or an alert to armed security officers or bodyguards who respond to the site of the intrusion to apprehend the penetrator. The response will necessarily vary with the threat, and a well conceived security system will have responses built in to cope with impersonal threats, such as power failures and fires.

Dogs can help responding guards locate an intruder by scent or by sound. However, dogs are not substitutes for a comprehensive security system.

Redundancy

This is an all encompassing concept in security planning, to allow for the possibilities of equipment failure, human error and unforeseen events. Despite the best planning and implementation, something can go wrong, following the well known "Murphy's Law."

Overlaying all of this is complacency, as guards become lax after years with no incidents. An engineer with a vivid sense of humor was able to gain access to a closely-guarded plant where top secret work was done. He walked around unmolested for three weeks, after pasting a photograph of Adolf Hitler over his own on his security badge.[1]

Level of Protection

There are differing opinions on this subject, partly because of differing security needs. One expert emphasizes the need for defense in depth:

"When you have several different levels of protection, a failure in one system will not result in a total failure. An intruder will run into the other systems and be detected."

A contrary point of view is this one:

"If you install a good access control system, you don't need the rest. The intruder will be stopped right there, if your system's properly designed and working."

It's possible to reconcile these differing viewpoints. There are varying needs for security. An industrial plant, for example, with the need only to protect against fire and theft, can get by with a relatively simple system that deters an intruder bent on removing valuable material. A government installation engaged in top secret work, compromise of which would have grave consequences, needs more protection. In such a case, the threats would be not only from relatively unskilled thieves interested in stealing material, but from enemy agents who would seek classified information, and, if unimpeded, might get it without removing anything or leaving a trace of their efforts.

Budget also enters into it. Whatever the situation, any security system is non-productive, in the sense that it does not add to profit. It's an overhead expense, and a private concern will seek a security system at minimal cost. A government agency, with other interests to protect, often has more money available for security, because the need is more pressing. A biological warfare research establishment, or a military command center, will enjoy many more levels of protection than will a factory making auto parts.

Your client will, because he holds the purse-strings, have the final say in the amount of money spent, and this will determine the quality and quantity of physical protection he gets. Making the best use of what's already there is one way of economizing.

Hardware

Taking each level singly, we can examine the equipment available for the purposes noted:

Physical Plant

Most American buildings are adequate for existing threat levels, but there's been a trend to construct bullet-resistant and blast-proof walls for police buildings in high risk areas in American cities. Los Angeles is a good example, and newer police stations have high walls surrounding them for protection. New York City provides another example, and the new 109th Precinct Station on Northern Boulevard, in the East Elmhurst district is typical of the new closed-in design. Corporate clients may desire this sort of protection as well, especially for facilities in volatile foreign countries.

When the State Department contracted for a new embassy in Muscat, Oman, one of the specifications was reinforced concrete blast-resistant walls for the outer facade. The main consideration appears to have been security for this Middle-Eastern embassy building. The outer wall was designed to defeat intrusion by vehicles, climbing and attack with tools. Entrances are limited, and closely controlled to restrict access, even to employees. Employees park outside, and enter through check-points. A system of sallyports and "mantraps" restricts people securely while security staff check their credentials. Public functions take place in an outer area, while Marines guard the embassy's inner sanctum. Embassy officials dealing with the public work behind armored glass in teller-like booths, for protection against assaultive visitors.[2]

Fences and barbed wire can provide an extra level of physical security. One source for barbed razor wire is:

Shomer-Tec
Box 28070
Bellingham, WA 98228
Phone: (360) 733-6214
Fax: (360) 676-5248

Access Control

Physical barriers, such as fences, walls and doors, are usually already in place, and enhancing their effectiveness involves strict control of access points. To save on manpower, many access control systems depend on electro-mechanical means, such as alphanumeric keypads, on which anyone seeking access must punch in a code to open a door.

Combination door locks, requiring the user to punch in a set of numbers, are made by Simplex Access Controls, among others. Simplex also provides locks that combine keys and combinations for extra security and versatility.

An Ademco Model 517 keypad. A combination punched into this is needed to open an electronically-guarded door. The main advantage of a keypad is that the "key" is intangible. There's no metal key to lose or steal.

A somewhat more sophisticated system is the "Cardkey," by Cardkey Systems, in which the authorized person carries a magnetically imprinted plastic card, which he inserts into the slot in a "reader" to gain access. The card can serve as an identification badge, with the company's name and logo and the individual's photo sealed in. Hughes Identification Systems makes a similar device.

Two types of keypads for different purposes. On the left a shielded keypad has five rocker switches for entering a combination unseen. This is handy when escorting visitors into the secured area. The right-hand keypad also has LEDs to announce the system status.

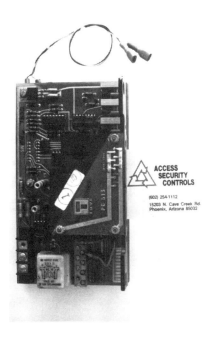

An inside view of a cardkey reader. A printed circuit board will send a signal to unlock a door if the combination is correct.

The permutations possible in such a system permit many levels of security. One model reader, for example, requires not only insertion of the card, but an individual authentication code on a keypad, to prevent access by anyone who finds a lost card. The readers can be individual readers, or have links to a central computer, to record the time and place of each authorized entry. In certain instances, there can be an "anti-passback" feature, which temporarily voids the card until it's used for exit. This feature prevents abuse of parking facilities, as one application.

A "proximity" card reader, made by Indala. This device does not have to have the card inserted to read it. This eliminates the need for a slot, and the consequent tampering to which a slot is vul-

nerable. A motorist can gain access to a restricted parking lot with minimal delay.

It's also possible to void a lost card, and to have readers at access points within a facility. This permits control of areas with different levels of security within a plant, and restriction of employees and visitors to areas to which they're authorized.

Variation on a theme. This Indala proximity card/keyring is a convenient package for the user.

One extra secure way to use a proximity card reader. The unit is behind a window, preventing access to the box. The window is protected by foil tape.

A computerized security center can have remote sensors for other purposes, such as fire and intrusion detectors, and serves as a central guard post for dispatching responders to an alarm.

Intrusion Detection

To protect large estates, there may be perimeter alarms, which are detectors of various types placed on or behind a fence. The problem with fence-mounted devices is that people casually leaning against a fence may set them off. Sensors buried underground can detect anyone walking nearby. They're not as useful as actual "intrusion detection" devices.

These are devices commonly known as "burglar alarms," and they vary in sophistication. The simplest are switches placed on doors and windows to send a signal when opened.

This device is glued to the window and tumbles out of position when the pane is broken. This change of position triggers an alarm.

Seismic switches detect ground tremors, such as footsteps. These are useful only in a remote area where there are no other causes of ground tremors. In a city, or with a road nearby, passing traffic would trigger false alarms. Seismic sensors also respond indiscriminately. A patrolling security guard will set one off as well as an intruder.

Infrared beams detect anything that breaks the beam. The limitations with infrared beams are that anyone breaking the beam, friendly or otherwise, will trigger the alarm. In addition, setting the height can be critical. A high beam will allow animals, such as guard dogs, to pass without triggering the alarm. One source for guard dogs is:

Rudy Drexler's School For Dogs, Inc.
50947 County Road 7, North
Elkhart, IN 46514
(219) 264-7519

An infrared beam set up this way has its drawbacks. This will also allow a human intruder to crawl under the beam with ease.

Inside a structure, it's possible to set up a greater variety of sensors. Beams will work better, with a lower rate of false alarms, especially if they're used on rooms normally closed off to members of the household and any guard dogs. Household pets can set off a variety of interior alarms. So can children.

One of the most common ways to protect a building from intrusion is the foil tape on the windowpane. Breaking the window interrupts the circuit and sounds the alarm.

There are also sensors placed on windows to detect the high-frequency sound of breaking glass. Other breakage detectors operate on inertia. Metal lacing in walls set off an alarm when the wire is broken.

Intrusion sensors may be defeated, or the intruder may have access to a key or the combination required to "pass" the system. A second layer of protection is in area control. These can be internal or external, and a good system often has both.

External systems detect intruders on the grounds. These are useful only if there is access control to the grounds, such as a wall or fence. Otherwise, anyone wandering by might trigger a false alarm. The basic principle of area systems is that the area under electronic surveillance must be empty. Any traffic, human or animal, can trigger a false alarm.

Ultrasonic detectors respond to movement. They project a pattern of ultrasonic beams, and any disturbance sets off the alarm. Air currents or even a pet bird loose from his cage will trigger this type of sensor.

Microwave detectors are basically small radar sets, and they also detect motion. They have greater range than ultrasonic alarms, but are also more expensive. The false alarm rate is somewhat lower.

Infrared heat detectors are probably the most reliable of all the sensors. They react to the heat level in the room, and sensitivity is adjustable. This allows an animal to enter the room without triggering the alarm.

Closed-circuit TV cameras can serve inside and outside. These are extremely reliable for use as adjuncts to an alarm system, because a human operator monitors the system and can distinguish between false alarms and significant intrusions. Some systems are designed for low-profile use, and employ a dome to hide the camera. These are often used in retail stores, but they have applications in other types of businesses as well. One manufacturer is Diamond Electronics.

Some CCTV systems have a monitor for each camera. This is cumbersome and unnecessarily expensive. More modern systems have one or two monitors and switch from one camera to another in sequence. This gives the guard fewer screens to watch, and helps concentrate his attention. A manual override is available to interrupt the automatic sequencing of cameras. This enables the guard to concentrate his attention on a particular sector if he sees anything significant.

INTEVAC EO Sensors Division makes image-intensifier modules, which are light amplifiers for CCTV cameras. This enables viewing and recording of low light scenes, such as interiors at night, and unlighted exteriors. The Intellicam low light camera provides color or black-and-white intensified images.

A VCR is important, and special time lapse recorders for unmanned recording of unoccupied areas are available. GYYR Division of Odetics supplies cameras, VCRs and digital video motion detectors for use with other equipment. An important point about using a VCR is that it provides evidence for prosecution.

We mustn't forget fire alarms. There are smoke detectors commonly available, and they should be part of any alarm system. Safeguarding the client means protecting him against all foreseeable threats, including fire.

One very low cost alarm is the "cord trap." This is a cord stretched across a doorway or corridor, with a hook at one end and a plug and socket at the other. Anyone tripping the cord will pull the plug out of the socket and trigger the alarm. Another advantage of this system is that members of the household will know about it and can avoid tripping it when moving about.

In offices and industrial plants, employee badges identify those authorized to be there. These may be combined with proximity cards for access. Visitors receive temporary badges, issued and collected by security guards at the entry. Also available are limited-time TEMPbadge visitor badges. Using these saves on personnel, because they only have to be issued. They expire by fading after a set time, or self-destruct in daylight after the visitor has left. This prevents the visitor from reusing the badge.

Finally, a "panic button" should be within the client's reach at all times. This can be a wired installation or a small portable "remote" button that sends a radio signal when pressed. Many times, the principal will be out of sight and hearing of the bodyguard, such as when interviewing or when in his bedroom or bathroom. He must have a means of summoning help quickly if needed. One special use of this is as a "holdup alarm," if the client is vulnerable to this threat.

Today, inexpensive electronic alarm kits are available starting at about one hundred dollars at Radio Shack and other outlets. While these are aimed mainly at burglars, they'll detect other intruders, and are worth installing to supplement other security measures.

Response

The sensor can trigger an audible alarm or a light on a panel. The audible bell or siren alarm is the low-end response, because it's inexpensive. This arrangement will awaken anyone within hearing, and is suitable if the protectee has a bodyguard only during the daylight hours. It will also serve for those who have a single, live-in bodyguard. Any protectee who rates 24-hour protection will have a bodyguard awake and on call at night, and this person will probably operate from a central location where an alarm panel will fit.

A full-scale alarm system will necessarily have a somewhat different design from a simple or partial one. First, each sensor will be wired to a central panel instead of being "ganged," so that the bodyguard monitoring the panel will know immediately which point of access has been breached. This allows sending a response team to the point of intrusion. The physical facility for such an installation will probably include a guard room or guard house, a place where members of the protective team who are temporarily relieved from static guard duty can relax and be available as a reserve to respond when needed.

Modern electronic systems allow economizing on manpower. It's no longer necessary to have a large force for perimeter patrol and area control. The main effort of surveillance is electronic, with human guards available as backups to respond to the site of an intrusion.

In some instances, it will be necessary to have human guards at some points. A gatehouse, for example, should be manned. This offers a further opportunity for economy. A gate guard serves mainly as a trip-wire, not as a serious protective agent. His function is as a deterrent, and to warn the guard room if anything unusual occurs. A "rent-a-cop" can serve for this purpose.

The same situation applies in many industrial installations. While it may be desirable to have a human parking lot guard, he need not be an executive protection agent, but only a normal member of the plant guard force.

A technological innovation is the "SmartPass," (manufactured by AMTECH) a proximity tag for windshield mounting. This allows a reader at the gate to sense the approach of an authorized vehicle and raise the barrier. The net effect is to speed up the flow of traffic, and this can be important in large plants.

A special remote alarm system serves to guard an unattended area. If the client is away from home and the residence stands empty for any time, it's useful to know of any attempted intrusion. A taped message sender can announce the intrusion by telephoning a predetermined number. The executive can have the device dial his office. The bodyguard may prefer that the device dial a paging service to deliver the message. This allows him to be notified even when on the move.

It's hard to over estimate the cost-effectiveness of such a system. Some alarm boxes are direct-wired to an alarm company or to a police station. This incurs the cost of leasing a telephone wire exclusively for this purpose, and is not as flexible as the automatic dialer system.

The Ademco Model 612 Automatic Tape Dialer will send a prerecorded message to a preselected number. This will serve to alert anyone away from home of an intrusion, or can be used to summon a private security system or the police. This is a very cost-effective accessory.

Probably the best method of use is to have it dial a pager. The bodyguard will want to know immediately of an intrusion, because he may decide not to bring his client home until he's had the premises checked for bugs and bombs.

Physical security systems are basically simple in concept and principle. Almost inevitably, when a leak occurs, it's the human element that has broken down. This is why the electronic alarm systems have their place, and are very valuable in saving manpower, but they depend very heavily on proper performance from the human element.

Partial List of Security Systems Manufacturers:

Ademco
165 Eileen Way
Syosset, NY 11791
(800) 645-7492

AMTECH
(Manufacturer of the SmartPass
proximity windshield tag)
17304 Preston Road
Building E100
Dallas, TX 75252
Phone: (214) 733-6600
Fax: (214) 733-6699

Cardkey Systems
101 West Cochran Street
Simi Valley, CA 93065
Phone: (805) 522-5555

European Manufacturing and Sales Office:
Cardkey Systems, Ltd.,
23 Stadium Way
Portman Road
Reading, Berkshire, RG3 6ER
England
Phone: (0734) 415 211

Checkpoint
Access Control Products Group
550 Grove Road
P.O. Box 188
Thorofare, NJ 08096
Phone: (800) 257-5540
Fax: (609) 848-0937

Chubb Electronics North America
5201 Explorer Drive
Mississaugua, Ontario M9B 2X2
Canada
Phone: (416) 620-3434
Fax: (416) 629-4970

DETEX Corporation
302 Detex Drive
New Braunfels, TX 78130
Phone: (800) 729-3839
(210) 629-2900
Fax: (210) 620-6711

Diamond Electronics
P.O. Box 200
Lancaster, OH 43130
Phone: (800) 443-6680
(614) 756-9222
Fax: (614) 756-4237

Diebold, Incorporated
P.O. Box 8230, Dept. T-79
Canton, OH 44771
Phone: (800) 999-3600

GVVR Division of Odetics
1515 South Manchester Avenue
Anaheim, CA 92802-2907
Phone: (800) 854-6853
(714) 772-1000
Service:(800) 445-9524
Fax: (800) 388-6363
(714) 776-6363

Hughes Identification Devices
14311 Chambers Road
Tustin, CA 92680
Phone: (714) 573-7294
Fax: (714) 669-5623
Attn: Diane Kehlenbeck, Marketing Manager

International Electronics, Inc.
427 Turnpike Street
Canton, MA 02021
Phone: (800) 343-9502
(800) 733-9502

INTEVAC
EO Sensors Division
601 California Avenue
Palo Alto, CA 94304
Phone: (415) 493-1800
Fax: (415) 494-6772

Litton Poly-Scientific
1213 North Main Street
Blacksburg, VA 24060
Phone: (800) 336-5917
Phone: (703) 951-4451
Fax: (703) 953-1758

Marlok Division
ILCO UNICON Corp.
2941 Indiana Avenue
Winston-Salem, NC 27105
Phone: (910) 725-1331

MDI Monitor Dynamics, Inc.
9518 Ninth Street
Rancho Cucamonga, CA 91730
Phone: (909) 944-3911
Fax: (909) 944-3229

Motorola Indala Corp.
3041 Orchard Parkway
San Jose, CA 95134-2017
Phone: (408) 383-4000
Fax: (408) 434-7057

Northern Computers, Inc.
5007 S. Howell Avenue
Milwaukee, WI 53207
Phone: (800) 323-4576
Phone: (414) 769-5980
Fax: (414) 769-5989

Simplex Access Controls
2941 Indiana Avenue
P.O. Box 4114
Winston Salem, NC 27115-4114
Phone: (800) 346-9640
(910) 725-1331
Fax: (910) 725-3269

TEMTEC, Inc. (TEMPbadge)
100 Route 59
Suffern, NY 10901-4910
Phone: (800) 628-0022
(914) 368-4040
Fax: (914) 368-4099

Westinghouse Security
Electronics
5452 Betsy Ross Drive
Santa Clara, CA 95054
Phone: (800) 624-8999

Notes:

1. Related to the author by an individual who worked in this high ecurity defense plant.
2. Arcidi, Philip, "P/A Awards Update: A Two-fold Solution."(U.S. Embassy, Muscat, Oman), *Progressive Architecture*, June 1990, v71, n6, pp. 114-122.

10

A Choice Of Firearms

It's wise to think of a weapon in the same way as an insurance policy. It's unlikely you'll need it, but it's important to have one just in case. In this light, most police officers go through their entire careers without using their firearms, except for practice and qualification. A bodyguard's even less likely to use his, unless he specializes in high risk assignments in very dangerous parts of the world.

Because executive protection is a low-profile operation, the bodyguard does not display his weapons. Those who hire executive protection agents tend to frequent offices and conference rooms, locales where gentility is the order of the day. This mandates a concealed weapon, and the most concealable firearm is the handgun.

What type of firearm should a bodyguard carry? Opinion is sharply divided. A cop or ex-cop is likely to prefer a revolver because this is the sort of firearm with which he's accustomed. Ex-military tend to prefer auto pistols, for the same reasons. IPSC shooters will almost all recommend their special, match-tuned pistols, in the mistaken belief that a competition gun is adequate for the street.

Let's look at what the U.S. Secret Service carries, because we can learn from them, especially because they don't make a fetish of tradition but always seek better tools and techniques.

The U.S. Secret Service carried revolvers for decades. Originally they were Colts, but during the last twenty or thirty years the preference was Smith & Wesson. Most S&W revolvers used by the Secret Service have been Model 19s, chambered for .357 Magnum but loaded with hot .38s, and the five-shot Chief, Model 36. These were reworked by the Secret Service's armorer before issue. Reworking consisted only of tuning and smoothing the action, because they were duty guns, not match guns. Rework definitely did not include cutting the springs to lighten the trigger pull, nor anything else to compromise reliability.

Firearms are only part of the story. The ammunition is the other half. The government buys ammunition from manufacturers according to bid, in five-million cartridge lots, and requires that the lots pass inspection before acceptance. Inspection of revolver rounds covers three vital points, among others:

The cartridges must fire reliably. A misfire can cost a life.

The empty cases must extract from the cylinder without sticking, because sticking cases impede reloading.

The muzzle flash must not be excessive. Too bright a muzzle flash can dazzle the shooter in low light.

Recently, the Secret Service has adopted the SIG pistols, which we'll discuss in detail later. This follows a general change to auto pistols among police. Auto pistols are the coming thing, although generations of cops have carried the revolver. Ammunition for autos must pass inspection similar to standards of those for revolvers.

Revolver vs. Auto

The main reason cops like revolvers is that they can draw the handgun and fire simply by pulling the trigger. This simplicity of use is important in a life-and-death situation. The older generations of auto pistols have safeties which the user must take off before he can fire. Carrying an auto pistol "cocked and locked" is simply an unnecessary complication.

The new auto pistols, such as the SIG, Beretta and Glock, have internal safeties, so that the user need only pull the trigger to fire. Most safeties include a trigger actuated firing pin block, so that the gun will fire only when the trigger is all the way back.

There are also questions of reliability. The legend is that auto pistols jam and revolvers don't. This is pure myth, because one of the reasons the U.S. Army adopted the auto pistol during the first decade of this century is that the Colt Government Model jammed less frequently than the revolvers in Army tests.

Actually, either type of pistol can malfunction if it's dirty, badly maintained or loaded with bad ammunition. The user must develop the modest skills needed to keep his firearm running properly.

Priorities

The most important quality the defensive pistol must have is reliability. This depends on both pistol and ammunition. There are some types of ammunition that are not compatible with some types of firearms. This is why anyone carrying a pistol for protection should test fire a couple of boxes of the ammunition he plans to use through it. Even one failure is cause for concern, especially because modern handguns of good quality should easily fire 100 rounds of good quality factory ammunition without any hang-ups.

The second quality important to the bodyguard is concealability. Most handguns are concealable, except for the big magnums. Concealability should not be much of a problem in most parts of the country, as we'll see.

The next most important concern is practical accuracy. The user must be able to get first shot hits at the normally short gunfighting ranges. The practical accuracy of the pistol has almost nothing to do with its inherent accuracy. An accurate target pistol may not fit a particular shooter's hand properly, thus causing him to miss when trying for a quick shot. The only way to determine practical accuracy is trial-and-error. The user must find what works for him.

Sometimes changing the grips helps somewhat, especially with revolvers. Early models of the Ruger Security-Six, for example, came with very small factory grips suited for small hands. Anyone with large hands would have to put on a set of aftermarket grips for comfort and practical accuracy.

Price and personal preference are also important. Private protection agents don't have lavish government style budgets and must often compromise on price. One way to cope is by exploring the second-hand market. Some prefer firearms which are no longer in production, because of good experiences with them. One classic model, for example, is the original H&K "squeeze-cocker," because of its slim lines and simple operation. This chapter discusses both current and discontinued models. It's worth noting that many current models are available second-hand.

Stopping Power

There's been a lot of nonsense written about "stopping power" by gun writers trying to make names for themselves. It's best to ignore the more absurd of these opinions, because they're obviously impractical. When a gun writer condemns a certain caliber as being little better than a toy, it's worth noting whether he ever volunteers to be shot with it. Also ignore the various "stopping power" formulas. Many of these are made up by gun writers who name them after themselves. These formulas have no scientific validity because they're not derived from any empirical scientific study.

The Relative Incapacitation Index figures issued by the National Institute of Justice in 1975 are a step in the right direction, although they've been widely criticized. They're still not comprehensive enough, because they don't take into account the reaction of the shootee, a drawback common to subsequent studies as well.

In March, 1986, FBI agents and two armed and dangerous suspects shot it out in Miami, Florida, leaving both suspects and two agents dead, and five agents severely injured. The FBI, not wanting to admit that their bad tactics and bad marksmanship gave the suspects the edge, chose to blame their 9mm ammunition. They worked up a new theory of bullet effectiveness, based on the premise that penetration was more important than expansion.

The FBI conducted tests to "prove" that a larger-diameter 10mm bullet would be more effective, and thus was born the short-lived "10mm Light." This fired a 180-grain jacketed hollow-point bullet at about 950 fps. However, in January, 1990, Winchester and Smith & Wesson announced the result of their collaboration in a new cartridge, the .40 Smith & Wesson. This fired the same bullet about 30 fps faster than the FBI-designed round, but in a cartridge no longer than a 9mm Luger, allowing its use in 9mm-frame autos. The new .40 S&W knocked the bottom out of the 10mm market, and the 10mm round is now dead as cheese.

Although police agencies and a variety of firearms experts embraced the new "politically correct" penetration theory, there arose a large gap between what was said and what was done. If penetration were truly important, there would be no need to develop new cartridges because the full metal jacket 9mm Luger is an excellent penetrator, as is almost any .357 Magnum loading. Even the new .40 S&W and 10mm rounds would penetrate well with full metal jackets. However, all manufacturers produced jacketed hollow-point loads. Further hedging their bets, major manufacturers also produced 155-grain JHP loads, firing at above 1100 fps. One even offered a 135-grain JHP at 1400 fps. The result is that many give lip service to the "penetration" theory, but everybody's still using hollow-points. This can be confusing if we take the contradictions seriously, but we can safely ignore them.

Since 1990, there's been a new crop of "enhanced-penetration" bullets produced by every major manufacturer, and a couple of minor ones. These bullets have a few new features, such as specially bonded jackets to reduce or eliminate jacket-core separation upon impact. The new theory is that if the bullet holds together, it'll penetrate more deeply than one that fragments. This theory ignores the desirability of creating multiple wounds, as in the case of a bullet that fragments. We see advertisements showing results of bullets fired into gelatin blocks as proof.

Unfortunately, this isn't proof of anything except performance in gelatin blocks, although some writers have made careers as "Jell-O shooters." Gelatin blocks aren't live targets, and they do not provide accurate predictions of what happens when bullets strike human or animal targets made of flesh and bone.

There's a recurring cyclic pattern with every new type of ammunition introduced. Advertisers and gun writers hail it as a super-zapper, the ultimate weapon, and this generates sales. However, laboratory "stopping power" doesn't translate into practical "stops" against suspects. After several failures on the street, it turns out that the new bullet doesn't stop every attacker, and its users begin realizing that it's only marginally better than what they'd been using before. Then someone else introduces a new ultimate weapon, and another cycle begins.

There's not much reason to be overly concerned with "stopping power" because nobody truly knows what it is. Some think that a defensive handgun should be able to stop an attacker with one shot. This is nonsense, because the site of the hit has more effect on the results than the caliber of the gun. An old gunfighting dictum states: "I'd rather be missed by a .45 than hit by a .22."

It doesn't matter what caliber or what firearm produced this result. The human body is about 90 percent water, and when a bullet produces an explosive effect such as this one in water, it will cause a severe injury to a human body. However, even a severe injury doesn't guarantee an instant "stop."

Another myth is over-penetration, a topic on which writers have wasted tons of paper and many gallons of ink. This theory states that a bullet should penetrate only so far, because otherwise it'll come out of the suspect's back and injure an innocent person. Life on the street dictates other conclusions.

The hard fact is that danger to innocent parties comes mainly from shots that miss, not shots that pass through the target and dribble out the back. Statistics from police agencies across the country show that about 75 percent of shots fired by police officers miss their targets. Felons do worse: about 90 percent of their shots miss. A missed shot, traveling at full speed, is far more dangerous to bystanders than a bullet that has lost most of its velocity while penetrating its target.

What's Right For You?

The bodyguard seeking an effective handgun must go about it in a different way than merely relying on stopping power ratings. He needs a caliber with which he feels comfortable. Its power is not very important, because if it's too powerful for him, he's overgunned and will be ineffective. In practice, most people can handle a medium caliber, such as the .38 Special or

9mm Luger, and don't need to torture themselves trying to master a magnum handgun which is probably too large to conceal.

The New York City Police Department, which experiences more shooting in its jurisdiction than any other city in the country, collected studies of 6,000 shootings over a ten-year period.[1] One of the conclusions was that "shot placement" was the single most important factor in determining the outcome. Obviously, a large-caliber hit in the foot is not going to be as disabling as a small-caliber hit in the brain cavity. When the NYPD finally put decades of tradition behind it and began converting to autos, the pistols officers were authorized to carry were the SIG P226, the Ruger P89 and the Glock 9mms.

Handgun performance dictates use. Because handguns are marginally powered firearms, there's little reason for confidence in a one shot stop, and no time to hesitate in a life-and-death crisis. Teaching shooters to fire bursts of two shots, then lower the pistol to evaluate, is a waste of time. The new thinking in defensive firearms training is to shoot until the attacker goes down and remains down.

Knowing that to be effective a bullet must hit, the astute bodyguard will find a handgun with which he can get consistent first shot hits. This may seem simple, but it depends on much more than sighting. In the close encounters that are the most likely, the light may be too dim to see the sights, or there may not be enough time. Another problem is that only one hand may be available to hold the gun because the other hand is occupied opening a door, deflecting an assailant's weapon or pushing the client to safety.

This brings us to "pointability." Some handguns point more naturally than others. Some fit a particular person's hand better than others. The pointability of a handgun is critical for a bodyguard, and it varies with the firearm and the individual. The best way to evaluate pointability, short of test-firing the gun, is to pick a small spot on the opposite wall and close the eyes. After raising the handgun to where he thinks it should point at that spot, the user opens his eyes to see how far off he is. Inevitably, he'll find that one or more pistols "point" better than others, and are better suited to his hand.

The combination of pointing quality and recoil leads us to consider "controllability." This has to do with both delivering the first shot and firing follow-up shots. This can be critically important, because rarely does one shot put an opponent down. The purveyors of

the "stopping power" myth suggest that a one-shot stop is not only possible, but *likely* with their favorite caliber. This simply isn't so, and in fact it's impossible to set up any hard-and-fast rules about handgun effectiveness. See *Shooting to Live*, Fairbairn and Sykes, Boulder, CO, Paladin Press, reprint of a 1942 book, pp. 72-80. The authors, both experienced police officers, show that there are many ifs, ands and buts with regard to the effect of a handgun bullet on a human target.

What about the effect of the new Clinton "Crime Bill," passed in 1994? This bans, among other things, new manufacture of magazines with more than 10-round capacity. Fortunately, large-capacity firearms and magazines will continue to be available on the second-hand market despite this law. Manufacturers had been working overtime to produce a backlog of large magazines before the effective date, and this has circumvented the law. Also, revolvers will not be affected, because large-caliber ones have five- or six-shot cylinders. Even .22-caliber revolvers have at most nine rounds in their cylinders.

Are 10 rounds really necessary for personal or executive protection? Are you really handicapped if your pistol carries only eight rounds? A moment's thought about conditions on the street shows that if you don't take care of the problem with the first three or four shots, you may not survive to empty your firearm at the attacker. If there are multiple attackers, as in the Schleyer and Moro kidnappings, even a squad of bodyguards may not have time to fire a shot before being killed. This is a grim prospect, but at least it shows that there's no point worrying about impossible situations.

Specific Weapons

The Heckler & Koch P-7

The Heckler & Koch P-7

The Heckler & Koch P-7 is surely the most ambitious pistol design of recent years. The P-7 is chambered for 9mm Luger cartridges, and comes in several basic models. The P-7 original version illustrated here has a single-column magazine holding 8 rounds, and a butt heel magazine release. This is the flattest of the models. The M8 version has a side lever magazine release, American-style. The magazine release is ambidextrous, and is designed to be pushed down by the thumb. The M13 version shown has a double-column magazine with a 13-round capacity.

This pistol has acquired the name of "squeeze-cocker" because it's necessary to cock it by squeezing the grip. This is a radical and unique mode of operation, and is worth discussion. The pistol stays uncocked and safe until the shooter wraps his hand around the grip and presses the cocking lever at the front of the grip inward with the last three fingers of his hand. This cocks the striker, and a trigger pressure of about 2 lbs. fires the shot. Squeezing the grip this way ensures that the shooter is exerting enough pressure to hold the pistol properly, and this is a very handy and accurate pistol to fire with only one hand.

The pistol has very few moving parts. The action is a unique gas-retarded blowback, with a piston and gas cylinder under the barrel. Gas bleeds off from the barrel to hold the slide forward until the bullet's out of the barrel and the pressure has subsided.

The chamber is fluted, which aids extracting dirty cases in adverse conditions. A flow of hot gas bleeds back along the walls of the chamber to both keep the case floating for easy extraction, and to clean out debris. This is a characteristic of Heckler & Koch firearms, and it leaves unsightly striations on the cases. This is of no importance except to a reloader. The barrel has "polygonal rifling," a system with shallow and softly-rounded lands and grooves instead of sharp ones. This system avoids engraving sharp grooves into the bullet and produces less friction in the barrel. The barrel is also easier to clean.

Firing the P-7 is a joy because of the handgun's inherent accuracy and jam-proof operation. The three-dot sighting system is very visible in low light and aids greatly in hitting targets against a dark background. The P-7 feeds all factory ammo and many reloads. Even badly made reloads failed to jam this handgun in one test.

The P-7 basic model is very compact and flat, which is important to anyone who needs to carry a concealed gun. The few protrusions mean that there's less to snag when drawing the pistol. Users like the P-7 because of its built-in safety mechanism. Releasing the grip causes the pistol to uncock itself with a loud *"clack."* This is a good feature to have as a safeguard against dropping the pistol.

This pistol has its bad side, too. Some potential users have trouble getting used to the squeeze-cocker action because it's radically different from what they've fired before. The lack of an external safety is a drawback to those accustomed to one. So is price. Even second-hand, these pistols sell for well over $600. This is probably the main reason more of them are not in use by private and government organizations.

The SIG-SAUER P-226

The SIG-SAUER P-226

The Sig-Sauer P-226 is a double-action 9mm auto pistol with 15 rounds in the standard double-column magazine, and 20 rounds in the optional extended magazine. This pistol was intended as a military service weapon, and has found acceptance among police agencies. As a member of the new group of foreign-born auto pistols challenging the American market, it's conventional enough to have found easy acceptance.

This pistol has no external safety. A trigger linked hammer block prevents firing unless the trigger is fully to the rear. A hammer decocking lever on the left side brings the hammer down to a half-cock notch. Also normally on the left side is the reversible push button magazine release.

An unusual feature of this pistol is that although it's lighter (32 oz. including empty magazine) than most others in its class, the felt recoil is milder. This may be because of the cable wound recoil spring, originally adopted because of its resistant to cold-weather failure.

Like the P-7, the SIG has very good ergonomics, which in plain language means it feels good in the hand. It "points" naturally, which makes sight acquisition at close ranges less important. Both the SIG and the P-7 have large trigger guards which permit firing the pistols while wearing gloves.

The SIG is for the person who prefers a more conventional auto pistol that is extremely reliable and simple to operate. Test firing showed that the P-226 would accept all types of factory ammunition and reloads.

The sights have an unusual dot-and-post arrangement, one which works as well as the three-dot system once the shooter's used to it. A tritium night sight system is available as an option. For those needing a larger magazine capacity, a 20-round extension magazine is still available on the second-hand market despite the Clinton "Crime Bill."

The SIG P-220

The SIG P-220

The SIG P-220 is a double-action auto pistol in .45ACP. The diameter of the cartridge dictates that only a single-column magazine is possible with this pistol, in order to fit most peoples' hands. Like the P-226, it's double-action, and has a hammer-decock lever and dot-and-post sights. Both are large-frame auto pistols, which can be a handicap for concealment. The recoil with the P-220 is heavy, although no more than with the heavier M1911. This is significant, because the P-220 weighs 31 oz. with the magazine, against the M1911's 38 oz. without the magazine.

The SIG P-225

The SIG P-225 handgun is a compact full-power model, chambering the 9mm Luger cartridge. This double-action handgun has a single-column magazine which takes 8 rounds, a double-action trigger and a firing pin block safety, as do the other SIGs. The P-225 has a smooth trigger, unlike the striated triggers of the P-220 and P-226.

This handgun weighs 30 oz. with empty magazine in place, and is flat enough to be conveniently concealable. The dot-and-post sights are similar to the other SIG sights. The magazine release is a push button on the left side. Barrel length is 3¾", and the chamber and barrel dimensions are slightly tighter than in the P-226 to get almost the same velocity out of the shorter barrel. In practice, rounds fired from this pistol are only about 25 fps slower than the same rounds out of the P-226.

The SIG P-228

The SIG P-228

The SIG P-228 is a cut down version of the P-226, or a fat version of the P-225, depending on how you see it, with a double-column magazine holding 13 rounds.

The SIG P-230

The trigger guard of this SIG P-230 pocket pistol is roomy enough to allow firing while wearing light driving gloves.

The SIG P-230 is a "pocket pistol," although the term is rarely used. It's compact and flat, fitting easily into a pocket or slim holster. This handgun is a double-action auto in caliber .380 ACP, also known as 9mm Short in Europe, and holds 8 rounds in the magazine. The factory literature claims a magazine capacity of only 7 rounds, but it's possible to squeeze an extra one in without any problem. The trigger has a smooth finish, well-suited for double-action firing.

The P-230 comes in a blue version, with steel slide and alloy frame, which weighs 19 oz. with the magazine. A stainless version weighs 24 oz. with the magazine. The pistols are mechanically similar, with the characteristic SIG hammer-decocking lever on the left side. Unlike the larger SIG models, the P-230 lacks a slide stop-lever. The slide will lock back with the last round, but it's necessary to remove the magazine or insert a loaded one to close the slide. Another difference is the magazine release, on the heel of the grip. This is unfamiliar to many Americans, but it has two advantages. It's ambidextrous, and the shooter uses his forefinger to ease the magazine out while pressing the release with his thumb. This is nice to have, in the rare case that a magazine sticks because of dirt or damage. The P-230 has a loaded chamber indicator, unlike other SIG models. The extractor protrudes when there's a cartridge in the chamber, and the shooter can detect this by feel, or by the painted red dot that is exposed.

The P-230 has the dot-and-post sighting system, and is pleasant to shoot. Strangely, the lighter alloy version has the same felt recoil as the heavier stainless model. One problem comes about if the shooter has large hands. If he doesn't grip the pistol tightly, the pistol will rock back slightly in his hand and the slide will rub the web of his thumb, which can be uncomfortable in practice. In combat, there are more serious problems deserving attention.

This is an unusually good choice for a bodyguard handgun, because of its small size and light weight. The caliber is large enough for most people to take it seriously, and in practical accuracy this pistol will deliver more than needed.

The Beretta 92SB-F

The Beretta 92SB-F handgun is the new U.S. Secret Service pistol and is also in service with the State Police Forces of Wyoming, Connecticut and Texas (the Rangers). It fires the 9mm Luger cartridge. The Model 92 is a double-action auto pistol that has a familiar look because it's fairly conventional, with its external ambidextrous safety. The safety also acts as a decocking lever and rotates the rear portion of the firing pin out of engagement.

The Beretta 92SB-F

The double-column magazine holds 15 rounds, and the magazine release button is reversible and normally located on the left side behind the trigger. Barrel length is 4.92″. The extractor has on it a red dot that protrudes slightly beyond the side of the slide when the chamber is loaded.

The Beretta Model 92 Centurion

The Beretta Centurion is, according to some opinions, the best 9mm Beretta made, because its shorter 4¼″ barrel provides a better feel than the five-incher of the standard 92SB-F.

The Glock 17 Auto Pistol

The Glock 17 Auto Pistol, with its polymer frame and 17-round magazine capacity, is worn by many American police forces, as well as carried by members of the British Special Branch Royal Protection Squad. The Glock model is also available in .40 S&W, known as the "Model 22," and the .45ACP "Model 21." The Glock's virtues are light weight and utter reliability. This is such a successful design that Smith & Wesson copied most of its features in their new Sigma pistol.

Taurus PT-58 S

The Taurus PT-58 S is a low-cost, Brazilian made pistol originally patterned on the Beretta, because Beretta sold Taurus the tooling when it discontinued Brazilian operations. This double-column, 12-round model is in caliber .380 ACP, and is compact.

Walther PP

This .32 ACP Walther Model PP (Polizei Pistole) is an oldie but goodie. With double-action and slide-mounted safety, it's both safe and accurate. Why would anyone want a protection pistol in this small caliber, though? In some countries, civilians are allowed to possess firearms only in this caliber or smaller, that's why. Anyway, it's a good shooter, and it's better to score hits with a small caliber than miss with a larger one.

Raven MP-25 and Davis Model 32

The Raven MP-25, top, and the Davis Model 32 auto pistol, bottom, are for extra concealment. Some situations just do not allow carrying a full-size pistol, and these are very reliable, low-cost pocket pistols. There have been many bitter criticisms of these small cartridges, but when that's all that's available, whatever the reason, you make the best of it.

Beretta Minx and Similar Models

Beretta has made a line of subminiature pistols chambered for the .25 ACP, .22 Long Rifle, and .22 Short, and sold under various model designations including the Minx, shown above. Some are single-action only, while others feature double-action. All have tip-up barrels, are well made, and are utterly reliable with decent ammunition. For close-in use, where the only tactic available is to empty the pistol quickly into an attacker's body, these are suitable.

Some people won't take the .22 seriously for dangerous protection work. It's a mistake to let oneself be influenced by the claims of the "big-bore" school of pistol calibers. There should be no doubt about the effectiveness of the .22 cartridge. Anyone who saw the tape of the attempt on President Reagan's life saw the devastating effect of six shots fired from a .22 caliber revolver with a 2" barrel. President Reagan was hit by a ricochet and did not immediately succumb, but the direct hits on three other men were impressive. James Brady went down with a head wound. Delehanty, the uniformed officer, was hit high in the back, and one shot put him down instantly. Timothy McCarthy, the Secret Service agent, received a solid torso hit and also went down quickly. These last two were law enforcement officers in good physical condition.

An excellent argument for choosing the .22 is ammunition cost, and its effect on proficiency. Low-cost ammo allows a lot of practice. Also, the rimfire's low recoil aids learning to shoot accurately.

Some pistols, such as this .22 Long Rifle Sterling Model 302, are too small to shoot accurately with a one hand grip. With a stiff trigger, it's essential to prop the pistol up with a forefinger to keep the barrel from dipping during aimed fire.

The Smith & Wesson Model 49

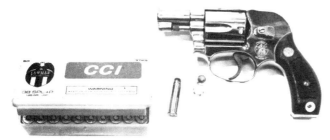

The Smith & Wesson Model 49

Some will always prefer the revolver, although the bulk of the cylinder impedes concealability. The conventional six-shot revolvers are a bit too thick for concealment in the view of many, and the five-shot versions, with their slightly narrower cylinder, have been favorites for decades.

This Smith & Wesson Model 49 is a nickel-plated version of the "Bodyguard," designed at the outset to be a pocket gun. At the time when this design appeared, the term "pocket pistol" meant exactly that, and holsters for concealment guns were unusual. This revolver has a shrouded hammer, to permit unimpeded draw and even firing from the pocket.

One problem with small-frame revolvers is that they're not designed to stand up to modern high-powered ammunition, such as the Plus-P loads. The cylinder walls are too thin, and the frame too light, to permit prolonged use of these super loads. Another problem is that the shooter will find the recoil very objectionable because of the small grips. This is why small-frame revolver users are best off using medium-power loads, such as mid-range wadcutters. These will produce a wound, yet not be so powerful as to make shooting them unpleasant or impossible. In caliber .38 Special, the mid-range wadcutter is in the same power bracket as the .380 ACP.

The Smith & Wesson Model 10 Military & Police revolver with the 2" barrel is a compromise choice. Based on a very reliable action, this cut-down version has a barrel short enough to aid concealment, but the oversize grips work against this. In this configuration, the revolver's comfortable to shoot, even with Plus-P loads, and the grip shape helps pointability.

Ammunition

The "proper" firearm and ammunition combination is often up to the individual. There are a couple of rules to follow to avoid problems. One is to test fire the gun with the particular brand of cartridges to ensure that they're compatible. Some firearms are fussy about what they'll eat.

Although jacketed hollow-point ammunition is the favorite of many, there are other choices for certain situations. One type of ammunition to consider, especially if the firearm's temperamental with hollow-point bullets, is the Dynamit Nobel Blitz-Aktion-Trauma cartridges. These are copper bullets with plastic nose caps which give the bullet the silhouette of a round-nose. This permits feeding into many pistols which hang up with other types of bullets. The nose cap blows off after firing, and the bullet becomes a hollow-point. The BAT bullet is light, and the muzzle velocity is in the range of other hollow-point bullets. For example, out of the four inch barrel of a Smith & Wesson Model 59, the BAT develops 1264 fps. This is at least 150 fps more than the "normal" 115-grain bullet. The BAT behaves like other lightweight hollow-points. It expands upon impact, although it doesn't shatter as much as composition lead- and copper-jacketed bullets.

Another type that performs well but at a considerably lower cost is the CCI Blazer. These cartridges have non-reloadable aluminum cases. Otherwise they're the same as brass case duty ammo. This makes them very cost effective.

During the early 1990s, all major manufacturers brought out new enhanced performance handgun cartridges. Winchester introduced its notorious "Black Talon," which would probably have fared much better in the public eye if Winchester had named it the "Peacekeeper." The "Golden Saber" became Remington's contribution to the hot performance market. Speer brought out the "Gold Dot," and PMC began loading the "Starfire" line of bullets into handgun rounds. Hornady produces the "XTP" series, noted for their outstanding accuracy. With all that, marksmanship is still the most important ingredient.

Another point to understand is the main reason not to use any but factory rounds. This has little to do with the quality of hand-loaded ammunition because only a fool would use bad handloads in a life-and-death crisis. The main consideration is liability. Factory rounds fail. If and when one fails in a situation leading to a lawsuit, the manufacturer has the "deep pockets," as noted in the chapter on legal considerations. The ammunition manufacturer, and not the bodyguard or his company, will most likely be the target of the suit.

Carrying extra ammunition requires a bit more thought and discretion than it does for a uniformed officer. The first point is that a bodyguard is much less likely to need extra ammo than a patrolman. If he needs to open fire, he'll need to do so urgently, and by the time he empties his pistol, the action will probably be resolved one way or the other. Still, to cover the occasional need, and for psychological security, many will want to carry extra rounds.

This is where the auto pistol stands out. It's necessary to reload revolvers with "loose change" or from bulky speedloaders.

Speedloaders are fast but cumbersome. The speedloader pouches are more for uniformed officer use than for plainclothes work. One possible exception is the Rogers Plainclothes speedloader belt pouch. This positions the speedloader with half the rounds behind the belt, reducing frontal protrusion.

An extra reload of Winchester Silvertips for this Smith & Wesson Model 10. The HKS speedloader is the best available right now. It's easily the most reliable and trouble free.

Whichever way the shooter uses to reload his revolver, he still has only five or six rounds when he finishes. Most auto pistols hold at least eight, and some a lot more. Reloading an auto pistol requires only dropping the empty magazine and inserting a fresh one. The time required doesn't vary with the number of rounds as it does when loading loose cartridges into a revolver.

Other Firearms

Although the handgun is the bodyguard's mainstay, he won't be satisfied to depend only on that if he has a choice. The justification for a handgun, with its marginal power and difficulty in aiming, is that it's light, compact and available when the bodyguard needs it. It's not the ideal weapon he'd want if he had a choice in each encounter.

Sometimes there is a choice. It's only when afoot or traveling in public conveyances that the handgun is the weapon of necessity. At home, in the office, in the car and in other limited circumstances there can be other weapons available. On the golf course, a shoulder weapon will fit into a golf bag. Indeed, the Secret Service agents protecting President Eisenhower used this technique.[2] When a motor vehicle is available, it can hold an assortment of weapons that would be too much for a man to carry.

Shotguns

A shotgun is effective at ranges up to fifty yards with buckshot and up to one hundred yards with rifled slugs. These figures are open to dispute, and the user should check out his shotgun for both accuracy and patterning before placing it into service. There really is no hard-and-fast figure for range with a shotgun, as a pellet will cause a wound if it strikes. The problem comes with shot patterning, and at longer ranges most of the shot pattern will not strike the target.

Shot pattern depends on the barrel. There are chokes and half-chokes to improve shot patterning, but these are on sporting shotguns. The fighting shotgun has a cylindrical barrel, no choke, to help shot disperse at close ranges.

The shotgun is deadly at short ranges. In this case, "short ranges" means no farther than ten yards. It's an ideal firearm for work inside and around buildings.

The 12-gauge shotgun is deadly. This gallon water jug comes apart spectacularly at a range of 10 yards. The cause is hydrostatic shock from the impact. The human body is over 90% water.

This Mossberg 500 with folding stock offers compactness and can be carried under a raincoat. With folding stock deployed, you can use well-aimed fire against more distant targets.

The two types of shotguns most often used for protective work are the pump-action and the semi-auto. Each has its admirers and detractors. It's worth noting that with modern ammunition, semi-auto shotguns practically never jam as they tended to when paper shells that would swell and soften with moisture were used.

Ammunition for the shotgun is as controversial as that for the pistol. Each swears by his favorite. One important caution for the bodyguard to keep in mind is the need to protect innocent people from wild shots and misses. The shotgun, and any firearm for that matter, can blast through interior walls to injure innocent persons in other rooms. One solution is to load with #8 or #9 birdshot. This is deadly at ten to twenty feet. At such a short range, any shotgun load will make a huge hole, called a "rat-hole," which is a wound from which the intruder is not likely to recover. At longer ranges, the birdshot pattern disperses and the small-diameter shot's velocity decays so rapidly that at thirty feet or more it won't penetrate both sides of an interior wall. This is valid only with a cylindrical bore. A choke will hold the pattern together for a longer range. This is why it's important for you to conduct your own tests on each shotgun you plan to use, to see for yourself what that particular firearm will do with the type and brand of ammunition you plan to use.

The Carbine

On rare occasions there's a need for a light shoulder weapon with longer range than either the handgun or the shotgun. If the client is on foot in a wide open area such as a beach, he may be vulnerable to a sniper. Another possible need is to protect a home. If the grounds are spacious, there will be enough range to require a carbine.

Two popular and very effective carbines are the Colt AR-15 (top) and the Ruger Mini-14 in caliber .223 at the bottom. These use the cartridge that's also known as the "5.56 NATO," and this round is commonly available in full-metal-jacket and hollow-point.

The Mini-14 is so well suited for this task that it merits a special discussion. In other fields, there's little difference between one brand and the competition. In the light rifle category, however, the Mini stands out, although its competitors will screech their disagreement. Let's examine precisely why it's an extraordinary weapon:

1. It's a developed design, with all of the bugs worked out. The Mini is descended from the Garand rifle, the famous "M-1" of WWII. This was an extraordinarily successful design that later became the M-14 rifle, in caliber .308 Winchester or 7.62 NATO. Other and more modern weapons have had their teething troubles, which in some instances have gotten their users killed.

2. The Mini has fewer moving parts than most others. This is easy to verify with a reference book such as the firearms books put out by Digest Publishing, which contain exploded views of firearms and lists of all the parts. Simplicity means less trouble. There are fewer parts to clean, jam or break.

3. The price is right. The Mini costs about half of what others in its class cost. This pays for a lot of

ammo for training. The government can afford to buy exotic and costly weapons, but private agencies cannot afford any waste.

The Mini comes with a five-round magazine as standard, but ten-, twenty-, and thirty-round magazines are available. Most are made by Ruger, but some are imported. The imported thirty-round magazines are far less costly than the Ruger clips, but some of them are of awful quality. It's best to try them out before buying. Again, note that despite the Clinton "Crime Bill," large-capacity magazines are still available.

Some would class the Mini as an "assault rifle." They can label it what they wish, but it's a very explicit recognition that this carbine is an extremely potent firearm in the hands of someone who can use it proficiently. In factory condition, and with the original wooden stock and iron sights, a mediocre shot can hit a man-size silhouette twice out of three times at three hundred yards.

Isn't the Mini too powerful to use in built-up areas? Some say it is, but let's look at an outstanding example of effective use, this time by a criminal. When eight FBI agents caught up with William Matix and Michael Platt in Miami in April, 1986, they knew they were facing hardened killers. Platt, armed with a Mini-14 semi-auto, killed two FBI agents and wounded five before succumbing to his injuries. Significantly, he did not hit a single innocent person. The gunfight took place at close range, with perhaps 30 yards separating the farthest participants.

For extra compactness, an after-market accessory is available. This is the Choate folding stock, distributed by L.L. Baston.

A folding stock does two things for the Mini. First, it reduces the overall length when folded, for easy stowage in a cramped space. It will, if necessary, fit on a sling under an overcoat. The second advantage is that the stock, when extended, provides about one inch more length. One of the few things wrong with the

Ruger factory product is the stock, which is mainly suited for people of short stature.

The folded Mini-14 is only 28 inches long. The design of the stock keeps the trigger guard free to permit firing with the stock folded. The battery powered point sight is a low-light firing aid.

The Marlin Camp Carbine shown here is chambered for the 9mm pistol cartridge, and has the added advantage of using Smith & Wesson magazines. It provides excellent accuracy somewhat beyond 100 yards, and is light and handy.

An accessory for a light carbine is an illuminated, battery-powered point sight. There are several makes, and most are good. This type of sight is a rugged non-magnifying optical sight that projects a red dot onto the target. To use it, he shooter looks through the tube. The brightness of the dot is controlled by a rheostat, and is adjustable for light conditions.

The Long-range Rifle

For certain specialized applications, a long-range, accurate rifle with excellent optics is helpful. A security agent occupying high ground can surveil the area for potential threats, and with a rifle he can engage them before they endanger the client. Often the bodyguard is at a disadvantage, numerically and tactically. Occupying high ground, such as a building rooftop, can compensate for this.

Deciding upon the "correct" caliber and rifle type for this role can inspire heated debates. Every deer or antelope hunter will mention his favorite for those long-range shots which always turn out longer in the telling than when actually measured. We can find a few ground rules, though, to help decide on a rifle.

It's still true that for accuracy the bolt-action is best. There are makers of semi-autos who claim to have developed rifles that will deliver excellent accuracy. The accuracy may be good enough for most sniping use, but is still not equal to the best bolt-actions. They also always cost a lot more.

There are several tried-and-true calibers that have delivered excellent accuracy over the years and in a variety of rifles. Some are the .30'06, .270 Winchester, .308 Winchester and .243 Winchester. This short list doesn't exhaust the possibilities. Some special magnum calibers are very accurate, but only in their own special rifles. Others are simply not commonly available, and a discussion of them belongs in a book on exotic rifles and calibers.

Modern high precision rifles are accurate enough to permit hits on human size targets at 1,000 yards or farther. Very few marksmen are good enough to be this precise. Accuracy also depends on little or no wind, because wind effect at such long ranges is severe.

Tactically, it's unwise and unnecessary to trade an attacker shot for shot at extreme ranges. It's better to go for cover and call for help. If no help is nearby, sending someone out to circle around the remote marksman will be more effective than trying to pick him off from the target area.

One choice is this Remington Model 788, in caliber .243 Winchester. The scope is a Schmidt & Bender "SNIPER," with Bullet Drop Compensator.

Another choice is the Remington Model 700 Police Sniper Special, available in calibers .223 and .308. This rifle, in .223 Remington, mounts a Bausch & Lomb Target Riflescope, and can consistently attain smaller than one-inch groups at 100 yards.

Submachine Guns

Ever since the photographs of Secret Service agent Bob Wanko standing with an UZI submachine gun at the Reagan shooting, the submachine gun's been the object of discussion and speculation. One advantage of the submachine gun is its compactness. It's a light and portable auto weapon with a high rate of fire. It's also conveniently concealable. The UZI that the Secret Service agent brandished when President Reagan was shot was normally carried in an attaché case.

Tactically, the submachine gun is for dealing with massed short-range attacks. It's simple to use for spraying an arc when a group of attackers charge. Most submachine guns also have selector switches to allow single shot use. This will probably be more useful than full-auto because in most situations, using "rock-and-roll" is simply a waste of ammunition. Conditions are different in the Middle East and other unhealthy areas of the world, but in the United States and Europe the need is for caution rather than exuberance with the trigger.

The need to avoid injuring innocents is also important. In certain other countries, it's permissible to fire recklessly into a crowd to safeguard the potentate, but any protective agent who does so in the United States or Western Europe will have to face severe consequences. In isolated areas, however, the bodyguard can open fire more freely without the worry of endangering bystanders.

In most instances, there will be innocent people around the attacker, and the Hinckley example shows this well. Hinckley fired from within a group of people who only became aware of his intent when he opened fire. Picking a lone attacker out from a crowd with short bursts from a submachine gun is very difficult.

The submachine gun also has its problems. One is that it's hard to control on full-auto. There are many people who write authoritatively about submachine guns and the excellent marksmanship possible for those who know how, but few people who actually fire submachine guns are any good with them.

One important practice is to fire in short bursts, because the submachine gun will run away with you otherwise. Some submachine guns raise their muzzles with recoil while others go off to the side. There is no submachine gun made that stays on target while firing! Anyone who claims otherwise simply hasn't fired any.

Some submachine guns deliver too much of a good thing. Long experience has shown that the submachine gun should be in caliber 9mm Luger, fire at a rate of about 600 rounds per minute, and weigh between 8 and 12 pounds. This combination provides some controllability. Some submachine gun designers have raised their rates of fire to as much as 2000 rpm, and some are too light to control at any rate of fire.

Another problem is the small capacity of all submachine guns. The typical submachine gun magazine holds about 30 rounds. At a moderate rate of 600 rpm, this gives 10 rounds per second, or 3 seconds' worth of firing. It's quick and easy to empty the magazine. This is why experienced submachine gun users "blip" the trigger. The latest models of auto weapons, such as the Beretta 93-R, have 3-shot timers built into the action to prevent inexperienced users from inadvertently running dry.

The UZI Submachine Gun

The UZI submachine gun, in folding-stock version

The UZI submachine gun is manufactured in Israel, from a design originally developed by a Czech officer shortly after WWII. It's in 9mm Luger and weighs about 9 lbs. loaded. Overall length is about 18" with the metal stock folded, and about 25" with the stock deployed. With a rate of fire of 600 rounds per minute, this is a reasonable and fairly controllable submachine gun, as firing experience confirms.

A problem with the UZI is firing single shots. The UZI fires from an open bolt. The bolt is locked back until pressing the trigger releases it, and the bolt then slides forward, stripping a cartridge from the magazine and slamming it into the breech. A stud on the bolt-face is the "firing pin." The new semi-auto UZI carbine has an extensively redesigned action, and fires from a closed bolt. This delivers much more accuracy.

The Heckler & Koch MP 5 A2

The Heckler & Koch MP 5 A2 submachine gun is in caliber 9mm Luger and with solid stock. It's German-made, and has been a success worldwide.

The Heckler & Koch MP 5 is the major law enforcement submachine gun in the world today. The model shown has a loaded weight of about 7 lbs., and is very controllable because of its roller-lock bolt design. This is despite a rate of fire of about 750 rpm. Another reason for its ease of control is that its trigger is soft and spongy, with long travel required to fire. This is strange to Americans, who are accustomed to crisp, "glass rod" triggers, but it works. It doesn't require a delicate touch to let off a short burst from an H&K submachine gun. Almost anyone can learn to do it in one session.

H&K makes a variety of submachine guns built upon the same basic model. The suppressed version is unusual. The loaded weight is about 7½ lbs., and the rate of fire is about 650 rpm. This combination, with the recoil dampening provided by the sound suppressor, results in very controllable recoil.

The suppressor doesn't make the submachine gun sound like a purring refrigerator. Suppressors don't work that way, except in Hollywood, where the revolvers have safeties on them. However, this suppressor quiets the firearm enough to make it possible to fire without ear protection.

The suppressor works by bleeding some of the gas into the silencer baffles before the bullet reaches supersonic speed. This is why the system is so effective. There isn't the usual supersonic "crack" characteristic of the 9mm Luger round. The gas bleeding into the suppressor also blows counter to the direction of recoil.

All of the H&K submachine guns have rifle-type sights of the sort found on the HK91. This makes aimed fire out to 100 yards possible, because the 9mm Luger is a 100-yard cartridge. The MP 5 fires from a closed bolt, which avoids the accuracy destroying "clank" that comes from a submachine gun firing from an open bolt, such as the UZI and the Swedish Karl Gustav.

Buying a piano doesn't make you a musician, and buying a submachine gun doesn't make you expert in its use. Only practice will do that. It takes dedication to learn to "blip" the trigger to fire in three-round bursts, but some models of the Heckler & Koch have three-round burst switches.

This 9mm Beretta Model 93-R is a true machine pistol. With a 20-round magazine, it works as an auto pistol, but has a detachable stock and folding front grip to steady it for delivery of full-auto fire.

Tritium Night Sights

A significant development in defensive firearms during the last decade has been widespread acceptance of tritium sights for shooting in poor light. Previously, there had been limited use of luminous paint on sights, electric sights, and even certain "flashlight shooting stances" devised by people who named them after themselves. Luminous paint doesn't remain bright, and electric sights are delicate and subject to battery failure. Using a flashlight draws fire, and provides an attacker with a bright aiming point. For the bodyguard, burdening the extra hand with a flashlight is cumbersome and unrealistic.

In dim light, shooting becomes difficult because it's hard to see the sights. The target may be dimly visible, but black sights blend into the background.

Only if the target's close enough to allow firing by "point-shooting" is there a good chance of getting hits. The bodyguard has to be ready to counter an attack in bright or poor light, and fire at various ranges. Self-illuminated sights are the obvious answer.

Tritium sights use radioactivity from tritium gas to make a phosphor lining the light capsule glow, providing illuminated dots that shine 24 hours a day. There's no need to turn them on at night, and the glow they produce is visible only from the rear. The amount of radioactivity involved is too little to be dangerous, and the glow of the sights does not betray the shooter's position to anyone in front.

Several suppliers provide tritium after-market sights for most makes of handguns and shoulder weapons. Trijicon provides riflescopes with tritium-illuminated crosshairs in several colors. Innovative Weaponry provides multi-colored dots for handguns to differentiate the front and rear dots. IWI also makes the "Bar-Dot" system, with a horizontal bar at the rear sight and a dot embedded in the front sight. Some firearms manufacturers offer tritium sights as factory options.

This is what the sight picture looks like with Meprolight Tritium self-illuminating sights. The dim glow is not visible to your assailant, but provides sight alignment for the shooter.

Tritium sights last at least ten years, and one manufacturer (IWI) offers a 15-year guarantee. The cost of tritium sights is moderate ($100 is a ball-park figure for handgun sights), and there are no drawbacks. One of the few valid generalizations about bodyguarding is that every bodyguard who feels the need to carry a firearm should have it equipped with tritium sights.

Select List Of Sources Of Firearms And Accessories

Arcadia Machine & Tool (firearms)
6226 Santos Diaz Street
Irwindale, CA 91702
Phone: (818) 334-6629
Fax: (818) 969-5247

Beretta USA Corp. (firearms)
17601 Indian Head Hwy
Accokeek, MD 20607
Phone: (301) 283-2191
Fax: (301) 283-0435
Attn: Brian Felter

Glock, Inc. (firearms)
6000 Highlands Parkway
Smyrna, GA 30082
Phone: (404) 432-1202
Fax: (404) 433-8719

Heckler & Koch (firearms)
21480 Pacific Blvd.
Sterling, VA 22170
Phone: (703) 450-1900
Fax: (703) 450-8160

HESCO (Meprolight tritium sights)
2821 Greenville Road
La Grange, GA 30240
Phone: (706) 884-7967
Fax: (706) 882-4683
Attn: Kerry Kinder, Sales Mgr.

Innovative Weaponry, Inc.
(P-T tritium night sights)
337 Eubank NE
Albuquerque, NM 87123
Phone: (800) 334-3573
(505) 296-4645
Fax:(505) 271-2633

L.L. Baston Co. (folding stocks and other accessories)
P.O. Box 1995, Dept. L
El Dorado, AR 71731
(800) 643-1564

SIGARMS, INC. (firearms)
Industrial Drive
Corporate Park
Exeter, NH 03883
Phone: (603) 772-2302
Fax: (603) 772-9082

Smith & Wesson (firearms)
2100 Roosevelt Ave.
Springfield, MA 01102-2208
Phone: (413) 781-8300
Fax: (413) 731-8980

Sturm, Ruger, & Co. (firearms)
57 Lacey Place
Southport, CT 06490
Phone: (203) 259-4537
Fax: (203) 259-2167

Trijicon, Inc. (Tritium night sights)
P.O. Box 2130
Farmington Hills, MI 48833
Phone: (313) 553-4960
Fax: (313) 553-6129

Notes:

1. *SOP-9, A Ten Year Study of Shootings*, New York City Police Department Firearms & Tactics Section, 1979.
2. *Secret Service Chief*, U.E. Baughman and Leonard Wallace Robinson, NY, Popular Library, 1963, pp. 133-134.

11
Carrying Weapons

In rare cases bodyguards can escort clients while brandishing firearms openly. In most situations, however, they prefer to conceal their firearms for several reasons. One is that weapons don't fit into certain locales and situations: walking down a city street, sitting in a conference room, or registering at a hotel, all demand discretion.

Another important reason is that the bodyguard doesn't want to advertise himself. Attackers want to identify the bodyguard to neutralize him, and if he stands out because he's carrying a weapon openly, he'll just make a target of himself.

Handgun Concealment

The basic principle of concealment is that the size of the firearm that will be concealable depends very heavily on how much clothing is worn. As an extreme example, it's possible to conceal a shotgun under a long and bulky coat.

The bodyguard will find that he needs several handguns to suit different seasons and climates if he wants to carry the heaviest armament possible in each situation. This isn't the best course to follow, because changing guns simply means that it's impossible to be fully proficient with each.

There's a great advantage in adopting a reliable medium-sized pistol and sticking to it. This is what the real pros do, to avoid having to change shooting habits with each handgun. A bodyguard who is very effective with a smaller weapon is more valuable than one who's a novice with each of many larger guns.

One question to answer with regard to concealment is how many guns to carry. Some advocate carrying a primary handgun, a back-up gun, a third gun, and perhaps even a knife as a last-ditch weapon. This may be good advice for a commando, but a low-profile bodyguard doesn't want to rattle and clank when he walks, and he doesn't want to be loaded down with 10 or 15 pounds of excessive weaponry. In case of a serious attack, the unpleasant truth is that he won't live long enough to use all of his weapons. Another problem is that not all holsters are equally secure. The more holsters, the more chance of something becoming unstuck. The bodyguard who spills hardware all over the floor can be severely embarrassed, and so can his client.

The bodyguard, if he needs a firearm, depends on one that he can draw quickly and bring into play without malfunctions and with no wasted motion. This means a mechanically straightforward firearm that he can fire with one hand if necessary, and normally carry in a holster that permits easy access.

There's almost always a conflict between concealment and easy access. The most deeply concealed weapons are almost inaccessible. The most easy to reach are also potentially the most exposed to view.

Wearing the handgun in the cross-draw location is almost as good, or even better, depending on individual preference. Some feel that this position enables the bodyguard to stand with his hand on the gun butt, in the "bodyguard stance,"[1] but this can be a drawback. The bodyguard sometimes is the priority target, and his use of the "bodyguard stance" alerts the attackers.

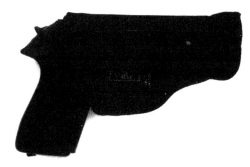

A Michaels nylon inside-the-pants holster allows quick positioning and removal at almost any place on the waist, the clip retaining it on the belt.

The most accessible place under the jacket is right over the appendix. This Kramer belt holster keeps the SIG P-230 where the right hand can reach it easily. It's worth noting that many of the most professional protective officers, the members of the U.S. Secret Service, wear their pistols in this location.

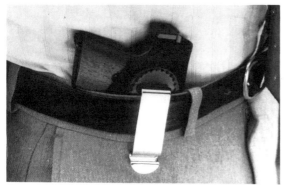

The very low profile of this Raven .25 ACP pistol leaves practically no signature when worn inside the pants.

There are problems associated with wearing the pistol elsewhere on the belt, problems that the advocates don't tell you about. Wearing the holster right on the hip helps to keep it out of sight, but the pistol doesn't blend in as well with the body contours. Even worse is wearing it in the small of the back, or over the kidney. Bending over outlines the gun under the jacket, making it obvious to even the casual observer. It's also uncomfortable when seated.

Another important question has to do with fairing. "Fairing" deals with blending the outline of the weapon in with the contours of the body. Small holsters don't provide as much fairing as do the wider "pancake" types. A holster with more material to help blend the thickness of the pistol in gradually with the body will provide more concealment, and will be slightly harder to detect during a quick frisk.

Wait a minute! The bodyguard is the one who frisks people! People don't frisk him! Not necessarily. An attacker's not likely to throw the bodyguard up

against the wall and tell him to spread his feet, but in setting up the attack he might casually brush against the bodyguard, doing what is known in the trade as a "bump frisk." It's not thorough, but it can disclose the outline of a weapon. It's only necessary to press "accidentally" on the fabric of the jacket to tighten the cloth and show the outline of the pistol grip. A fingertip touch in the crowd can disclose a hard bulge where there shouldn't be one.

This Michaels Super Belt Slide holds a SIG P-230 securely because of the safety strap. The wide paddle shape of the holster helps blend it in to the body's contours. This holster's strap attaches with Velcro and adjusts to fit different sized pistols.

The inside-the-pants holster is a clever innovation that uses the cloth of the trousers to provide fairing. Because of this design, the holster can be thin and light. The thin fabric holsters collapse upon withdrawal of the handgun. The more rigid ones remain open, but being able to re-holster with one hand isn't as much of an advantage as it might seem. If it's necessary to get rid of the gun because you need both hands for something else, there's always a pocket available, or you can tuck it in your belt.

For maximum concealment, a holster buried deeply under the clothing helps. The disadvantage is that drawing the firearm will necessarily be slow. Timing the draw from one of these holsters, concealed under the shirt but with no jacket, showed that it takes an average of three seconds to draw upon command. For a second gun, or when it's more important to conceal the handgun than to have quick access, the total concealment holsters are useful.

The shoulder holster was out of style for awhile, but it's coming back into use as the new generation discovers its virtues. The old style of shoulder holster was just a pouch that held the handgun vertically. Basically, the holster manufacturers took a belt holster and hung it from a harness. They were uncomfortable and often awkward to wear because they tended to flop with body movement. The new generation of shoulder holsters, such as this Gould & Goodrich "Presidential Series" holster, uses the horizontal carry. A thumb snap holds this Beretta Centurion securely.

The Special Weapons Products Badger is one of the most practical shoulder holsters made today. It's a faired pouch on a nylon harness, and is designed to hold the handgun in a horizontal carry, but slightly muzzle-up. Nylon is a superior material for a holster and harness worn under the jacket. Perspiration will affect leather, but nylon is resistant. Nylon is also lighter, and more easily shaped for fairing to the body's contours. The adjustable nylon and Velcro thumb-break allows fitting to many pistols, not just the SIG P-230 shown here. The Badger doesn't have a tie-down on the holster side because it doesn't need it.

The new design features that make shoulder holsters more practical are tie-down straps to keep the pouch from flopping and a counter-balancing pouch on the other side, to carry extra ammunition and accessories.

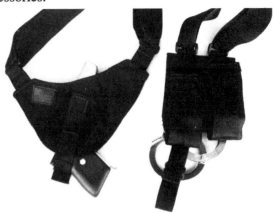

Off-duty police officers are likely to appreciate the extra features of the Badger. This configuration has a counter-balancing magazine pouch, handcuff loop and off-side tie-down. It's probably the best one at the moment.

This Badger and SIG P-230 make a good combination because the pistol is not too large or heavy for the holster, and the Badger's design does not allow it to flop under the jacket.

This Galco Executive Shoulder Holster is made for a J-Frame S&W revolver, light enough not to be awkward or unmanageable. Draw is very quick and easy, because the pistol is held in place by the close fit of the leather.

Why aren't shoulder holsters more popular? There are several good reasons. A very important one is slowness of draw. For speed, it requires one hand to pull the jacket flap open. It's very slow to insinuate one hand under the jacket and remove the handgun. A less important reason is that it's practically impossible to reholster the handgun with one hand. The other must steady the holster pouch and/or work the thumb snap. Yet another is that it's hard to carry a large-frame handgun in a shoulder holster inconspicuously, unless you're built like King Kong.

In certain areas of the country, and during the hot seasons, wearing a jacket can be extremely uncomfortable. Perhaps more importantly, it can make the bodyguard stand out, if he's the only one wearing a jacket. Conventional means of carrying the handgun aren't quite suitable. There are several ways around this problem.

One is to wear a belt holster with the shirt outside the pants. This will conceal the pistol fairly well, but unless the barrel's short, it may protrude below the hem of the shirt.

This Galco Hi-Jak holds a Beretta Model 92 Centurion firmly on the belt, under either a jacket or shirt.

An inside-the-pants holster will allow carrying a longer barreled weapon. Another problem is carrying extra magazines, handcuffs, and other gear.

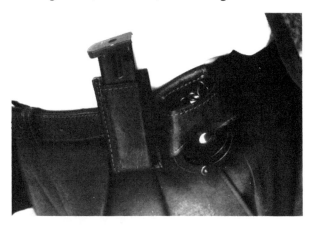

These Gould & Goodrich "Presidential Series" accessory pouches hold an extra magazine and a set of handcuffs on the belt. You can wear these on the opposite side of a belt holster, or just below a shoulder holster.

For certain situations, special designs are available. One problem a bodyguard faces is having his sidearm and other gear readily available and close to hand at all times. Belt holsters tend to drop to the floor during bathroom calls. This can be especially difficult for female agents. The Safariland "Answer" system buttons the holster and magazine carrier to the shirt, using an inner elastic belt for additional support, so that the gear does not drop with the pants.

This Safariland "Answer" system buttons onto the shirt, while a cloth-covered paddle underneath the shirt tucks into the pants.

In the hotter parts of the country, an ankle holster's the choice of many.

This Michaels ankle holster shows the construction of the typical ankle holster. The pouch and ankle band attach with Velcro. For extra support, there's a calf band and calf strap.

The ankle holster has a couple of shortcomings. One is that the wearer must wear wide or bell-bottomed trousers to help conceal the bulk of the holster. Another is that the size and weight of the pistol are severely limited. It's quite possible to carry a large-frame auto pistol on the belt, but not in an ankle holster. This sort of holster is limited to five-shot revolvers and medium-frame autos.

Note that a right-handed person would wear this on the inside of the left ankle. This position allows lifting the pants leg with the left hand and drawing with the right. A drawback is that it's necessary to bend over or kneel to draw. However, the ankle holster is very accessible for draw while seated, especially in a car. The inside position helps prevent detection of the handgun with a "bump frisk," in which the searcher slides his or her ankle alongside the wearer's.

Pocket carry appears to be gaining favor among some. The main values of pocket holsters are outline masking and ensuring that the pistol is upright when you need it.

This Galco pants pocket holster masks the outline of a small auto and allows a moderately quick draw.

There are also specialty holsters designed for inconspicuous carry while wearing light clothing. While women carry purses, men do not, and attaché cases are sometimes out of place. These specialized holsters are practical even on the beach, and are adaptable to both sexes.

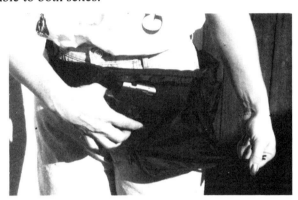

This Galco Escort comes in two sizes for handguns and several colors. The popularity of belly packs today makes this inconspicuous. Disadvantage: Drawing requires both hands. Advantages: You can carry extra ammo and other gear in the Escort's pocket.

This "Hidden Agenda" belly pack has a holster for a medium-frame auto, and loops for handcuffs, a flashlight, expandable baton, extra magazine and space for other gear.

The "Safepacker" is designed to resemble a camera pouch, purse or other innocuous container, and to shroud completely the outline of any sidearm.

Another type of carry, available for the female protective agent, is the holster purse. Galco International is one supplier, and more will be coming on the market as the number of female police officers and private agents increases.

Carrying Shoulder Weapons Inconspicuously

Keeping a low profile while carrying shoulder weapons is a problem. There have been a few systems for inconspicuous carry, but none caught on enough to remain in production.

A golf bag is useful for shoulder weapons, but would seem conspicuous except on a golf course. Folding-stock submachine guns fit into attaché cases. For carry in the trunk of a car, a specialized soft- or hard-case carrier will cushion and protect the firearm.

Select List Of Sources For Holsters And Other Carriers

Galco International
2019 West Quail Road
Phoenix, AZ 85027
Attn: Bob Hansen
Phone: (602) 258-8295
Fax: (602) 582-6854

Gould & Goodrich
P.O. Drawer 1479
Lillington, NC 27546
Phone: (800) 277-0732 or
(919) 893-2071
Attn: Phyllis Gould

Hidden Agenda (Lighthouse Uniform)
P.O. Box 19213
Seattle, WA 98109
Phone: (800) 426-5225
Attn: Steve Cohen

Kramer Handgun Leather
P.O. Box 112154
Tacoma, WA 98411
Phone: (206) 564-6652
Attn: Greg Kramer

Michaels of Oregon
P.O. Box 13010
Portland, OR 97213
Phone: (503) 255-6890
Fax: (503) 255-0746

Safariland
3120 Mission Blvd.
P.O. Box 51478
Ontario, CA 91761
Phone: (800) 347-1200
(909) 923-7300
Fax: (909) 923-7400
Attn: Norma Osborn

Shooting Systems
1075 Headquarters Park Dr.
Fenton, MO 63026-2478
Phone: (800) 325-3049
Phone: (314) 343-3575
Fax: (314) 349-3311
Attn: Len Hooper

Special Weapons Products
9033 Ninth Street
Rancho Cucamonga, CA 91730
Phone: (800) 847-0818
(909) 941-6886
Fax: (909) 941-7394

The Wilderness (Manufacturer of the Safepacker)
5130 North 19th Avenue
Suites 11 and 12
Phoenix, AZ 85015
Phone: (602) 242-4945
Attn: Ralph Holzhaus

Notes:

1. *Dead Clients Don't Pay*, Leroy Thompson, Boulder, CO, Paladin Press, 1984, p. 73.

12
Learning To Fire Accurately

The demands made upon a bodyguard can be almost beyond human ability. A police officer need not always maintain the same moment-to-moment alertness, nor need he anticipate ambush at any moment. He also rarely has to protect another person, while the bodyguard's duty is centered around the protectee. This is why developing good marksmanship, and retaining proficiency, is more important for the bodyguard than it is for most law officers.

It's vital to master the care and use of the handgun, and any other weapon employed. This goes far beyond learning how to align the sights and squeeze the trigger. It's also crucial to learn how to clear jams, reload quickly and maintain the firearm so that it performs reliably.

The bodyguard starts where others leave off. Learning the basic two-handed grip is only a first step. The bodyguard must be proficient with only one hand. He also must train to select his targets, hitting some while avoiding others, for a very clear and crisp reason: because of the nature of his work, he'll almost surely be in a crowd when danger strikes.

The Firing Stance

The usual shooting stances will not be as useful as they might seem. If he's a former police officer trained in the "officer survival" school, he'll find that he cannot automatically duck for cover when the shooting starts, because part of his duty is to stand up and shield the client with his own body. He cannot go for cover until he has his client behind his own cover. The bodyguard must also be able to fire from cramped and awkward positions, such as seated in a car. A point to consider is whether the holster he normally wears allows drawing while seated. Practice should always be from the holstered position. Unless the bodyguard works in a situation where he's allowed to walk

around with a pistol in his hand during his entire shift, he has to anticipate that he'll have to draw.

When protecting a client, it's especially worthwhile to forget all of the theory about the two-handed grip, the Weaver Stance, and the various other shooting positions. There will usually be no time to assume a certain stance if it becomes necessary to open fire, and a bodyguard who can't aim properly until he gets his second hand up there to steady the gun will be at a severe disadvantage.

The two-handed grip is useful for deliberate, aimed fire, but not the reactive fire that usually is necessary in executive protection.

If it becomes necessary to open fire, the bodyguard will have no time at all. He'll have to deflect an attack that's probably already under way, and do so from whatever position he's in at the moment. He'll probably have one hand occupied holding a car door or pushing the client down. With a close-in attack, there may not even be time to use the sights. This is where the conventional and "politically correct" method of training handgun shooters to use both hands and the sights is harmful.

A better orientation is to learn to fire with one hand, looking over the barrel or slide at the target. It's faster and more realistic, for use in situations when low light makes it hard to see the sights, or the urgency prevents acquiring a precise sight picture.[1]

Shielding the client almost dictates an erect posture instead of a gunman's crouch. Firing with one hand allows using the other hand to herd the client behind you.

Drawing The Handgun

Drawing the handgun isn't as quick or easy as it seems on a range, where shooters are primed for action, know where the targets are and don't have to react to ambiguous stimuli. In real life, a sudden noise may be a shot, backfire or a child setting off a firecracker. A bulge in a bystander's pocket could be a weapon or a camera. The prelude to drawing the handgun is always a clear progression: perceiving the possible threat, evaluating it, making a decision and taking action. These steps take time, and in practice it's uncommon for the process to take less than three seconds or more.

In practicing the quick draw, it's important to remember that smoothness counts first, not blinding speed. Getting the handgun out without hesitation or fumbling is far better than dropping it during a critical moment.[2]

Training and Practice

Once the bodyguard trainee has mastered basic handgun proficiency, he should begin firing under stress. Having him sprint one hundred yards to the targets, then draw and fire, will accustom him to the problem of getting hits with the blood pressure up and the adrenaline pumping. He can expect a sharp deterioration in his marksmanship at first, but recovery is surprisingly quick after a few tries.

The next stage is creating stress. The trainer must push the trainee hard enough to disturb his aim while firing, and scream contradictory instructions at him. This helps the trainee focus his concentration despite distractions, and learn to use his common sense. Finally, it helps him learn to keep calm when the roof is caving in.

A basic drill to help the bodyguard learn how to react in various circumstances is to have him walk back and forth along a line ten yards from a row of silhouette targets. As he's walking, someone else shouts a command, such as "Number one!" to designate the target he should engage. The bodyguard draws and fires as quickly as possible at the designated target. The trainee will quickly learn that it's possible to score hits consistently even when not in one of the approved stances, and that often it's faster to draw and extend the arm than turn his body around to face the target.

Advanced Training

Once the trainee has progressed beyond the initial stage, all firing should be in judgmental scenarios. This is because that's how it's likely to be in the real world. There's likely to be a great number of false alarms for every serious threat. The bodyguard, in reality, can't draw and fire at everyone who reaches for a handkerchief. He should not, therefore, practice this in training. Any training session which conditions him to draw and fire as soon as he sees a potential target is counterproductive. There should be a number of shoot/don't shoot targets visible, forcing the trainee to think before he acts.

An advanced exercise is to have the trainee put a paper bag over his head, while the trainer marks one of the targets with spray paint or with a photo of a weapon. The trainee then walks back and forth in front of the targets. Upon command, he removes the bag, seeks out the marked target, draws and fires. To make the exercise more realistic and challenging, the trainer may omit marking any of the targets, and instruct the trainee not to draw unless he actually sees a threat. Instead of a verbal command, the signal to start can be a blank shot from a handgun.

It's also important to practice firing at moving targets. An assailant may well be moving during an attack. Practicing firing at still targets from moving vehicles also corresponds to many real-life situations. This is especially true if the protectee travels a lot in motorcades. If he's that sort of celebrity, he'll need cover while the vehicle is moving slowly, and the ability to fire back at an attacker while hanging on to a motor vehicle with one hand is one of the skills to learn.

One of the best targets for simulating a critical and difficult shooting situation is the Speedwell "Hostage" target. This has a "bad guy" holding an innocent person in front of him as "hostage." The ability to pump several shots into a bad guy's head without hitting the hostage is worth developing. Scoring this properly requires that one hit on the hostage cancels out the entire score on the bad guy, because in real life the ensuing criminal charges and lawsuits can make the bodyguard wish he'd been someplace else.

This target is available from:

Rockwood Corporation
136 Lincoln Blvd
Middlesex, NJ 08846
Phone: (800) 243-8274
Fax: (201) 560-7475

It's good practice to learn to fire at difficult targets. Any target array which has one partly obscuring the other simulates a "hostage" situation. It's also useful for simulating a crowd with an attacker in the middle.

The final stage in training is the most difficult. The trainee walks with another person, who takes the place of the client. Upon command, the trainee must identify the threat, place his body between the threat and his client, and open fire to neutralize the target. Alternatively, he may choose to push his client behind cover before dealing with the threat. Practicing this with two-man guard teams helps develop coordination, with one guard shielding or evacuating the client while the other deals with the threat.

Learning suitable firing stances is an important stage in the bodyguard's training. Often, someone accustomed to firing one way will have to relearn the basics, because stances suitable on the target range or in law enforcement are worse than useless when the assignment is personal protection.

Notes:

1. Applegate, Rex, "Bullseyes and Silhouettes Don't Shoot Back," *Law and Order*, October, 1994, pp. 46-51.
2. *No Second Place Winner*, Bill Jordan, Shreveport, LA, privately printed, 1965, pp. 45-66.

13

Special Purpose Weapons

There are special cases in which a bodyguard needs unusual and special-purpose weapons. These are instances in which firearms are prohibited and the prohibition is enforced strictly. If it's necessary to board a commercial aircraft, you'll have a hard time bringing a firearm on board unless your protectee owns the airline. In other cases, it's more discreet to avoid firearms because of possible legal problems. In traveling abroad, clearing weapons through customs can be "Mission Impossible."

The choice used to be only between impact and edged weapons. Old-style chemical weapons and "stun guns" aren't reliable. Experience with tear gas sprays shows that they work only about 70% of the time. "Stun guns" don't paralyze reliably, and reliability is crucial.

However, the new Oleoresin Capsicum (OC) aerosols are much better, because they're more reliable. They still don't work 100 percent of the time, but neither does a firearm. We'll discuss this in detail later in the chapter.

Knives

A type of knife that's especially suited for concealment is the plastic or glass fiber knife. All weigh less than two ounces, and are between seven and eight inches long. All have lanyard holes in the end of the grip. This allows a carrying lanyard or a wrist loop. These weapons will not show up on a magnetic weapons detector. When packed in a briefcase or other carry-on luggage, these glass fiber knives are practically invisible among the other items under x-ray examination.

Some are known as "Executive Letter Openers." Another type is the "Ace of Spades" a short and stubby double-edged weapon that fits in the palm of the hand. The "Executive Ice Scraper" is a device

with a straight blade, which will produce a nasty gash.

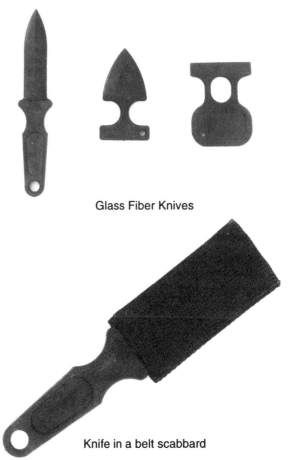

Glass Fiber Knives

Knife in a belt scabbard

Knives are simple, and have no moving parts to get out of order. Switchblades and other folders aren't good weapons, and are outside of this discussion. Because knives are contact weapons, it's necessary to be close to use them. A knife is no match for a gun. In very close quarters, however, you may have an even chance.

Knives are good for slashing or stabbing attacks. A slash at the throat can be lethal, cutting the jugular veins and the carotid arteries. A stab under the breastbone threatens the heart and major blood vessels, especially if the user swings the blade from one side to the other after insertion. The problem is that knife wounds produce slow responses, and the victims don't usually succumb quickly. The psychological effect on an attacker of seeing his blood flowing onto the floor can be devastating, however.

Carry can be in several ways. A belt scabbard is available for the "letter openers." Other ways are down the neck on a string, in a pocket, under the watch band, and tucked into the boot or sock. Other ways of carrying are in a paper bag, wallet, checkbook, purse, or briefcase.

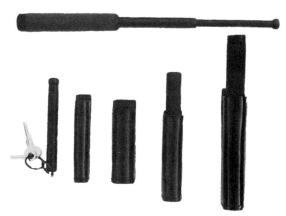

Several A.S.P. batons and their carriers. Extended lengths range from 9" to 26", from keychain types to riot-length batons. The smallest can be used both as a striking instrument and as a Kubotan. A brand new model is stainless steel, providing more mass and striking energy.

These batons have a "dead lock taper" joining adjacent sections. A flick of the wrist deploys the baton. There is a small striking knob at the end for severe blows. Striking the baton on a hard surface collapses it instantly, allowing it to be put away quickly.

Knife tucked into a sock

These are available from:

L.L. Baston Co.
P.O. Box 1995- Dept. L
El Dorado, AR 71730

Airport security checks that include body searches, on the other hand, can preclude carrying even a pocket-knife aboard.

Batons

One choice is the collapsible baton. This is a modern approach to an old problem. The A.S.P. batons collapse into small packages, fitting into small belt holsters or even pockets. This helps keep a low profile.

Executive protection often requires a discreet response to avoid creating a disturbance. Using the smallest model of baton to capture the attacker's wrist and force him to the ground is one low-profile way to use it.

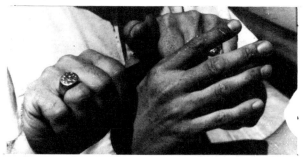

Another low-profile pain compliance hold is capturing the thumb, and going into a wrist-lock to eject a resisting subject from the premises.

The manufacturers provide training courses. These teach mainly a system of blows to joints and nerve centers. In an attack, the main idea is to maintain distance and to counter-attack with baton blows. Distance keeps the assailant from getting close enough to do harm, and also keeps him from closing in and pinning the baton hand to the body. The baton blows are basically forehand, backhand, and jabs. The targets are the elbows and knees for the forehand and backhand blows, and the abdomen for the jabs. Disarming an opponent can work, if his weapon's within reach, by striking at the attacker's weapon hand and following up with a backhand blow. Blows to the head and trachea can be quickly incapacitating and lethal if the situation calls for it.

The baton deploys with a flick of the wrist, the taper-lock holding it extended until it becomes necessary to retract it. Use of the straight baton is simple and easy to learn.

Another manufacturer is Counter-Assault Systems, (CASCO), which provides several models including a special training tool (right) to collapse batons without hitting them on the floor.

For more serious situations, a baton can be used for deadly force. It's both morally and legally justifiable to use blows to the head and neck against a person attacking with a knife or gun. Striking the

temple or the side of the neck can kill, but this may become necessary to save your client's life.

Expandable batons are available from several sources:

Armament Systems & Procedures
P.O. Box 1794
Appleton, WI 54913
Attn: Kevin Parsons
Phone: (414) 735-6242
Fax: (414) 735-6245

CASCO International, Inc.
P.O. Box 166
Gap Mountain Road
Fitzwilliam, NH 03447
Phone: (800) 232-2726
(603) 585-9422

PPCT Management Systems
500 South Illinois, Suite 3
Millstadt, IL 62260
Attn: Bruce Siddle
Phone: (618) 476-3535
Fax: (618) 476-3323

Stun Guns

Stun guns came into use during the middle 1980s, with the proliferation of small, hand-held, battery-powered devices that were more compact and generated more voltage than cattle prods. The theory behind their use was that the high-voltage, pulsing current disrupted the nervous system and rendered an opponent helpless. In practice, stun guns did not work as well as their manufacturers advertised. Street experience quickly showed that:

1. Stun guns are contact weapons, effective only if the defender is close enough to touch his attacker with the probes. In many defensive situations, it's desirable to create distance, and the stun gun limits the bodyguard's choices.
2. Stun guns generate sparks, dangerous in a flammable atmosphere. This is what happened during a spectacular incident in New York City in August, 1990, when police used a stun gun on a violent suspect they had first sprayed with a flammable OC spray. The suspect literally caught fire, and the repercussions of this

incident caused one OC spray manufacturer to go out of business.

3. Stun guns actually don't disrupt the nervous system. Rather, stun guns cause pain and shock, comparable to a kick to the groin. A stun gun shock of several seconds will put a subject down like an electronic rabbit punch. However, field tests have shown that a person can still pull a trigger while being zapped in the forearm. The net result is that stun guns are not always reliable.

4. The current can come back to the person using the stun gun. This happens when there's physical contact and the skin is wet, through sweat or rain.

These reasons are why a stun gun is a poor choice for executive protection. If the attacker is close enough for the executive protection agent to counter-attack with a stun gun, it would be quicker to use bare handed methods to neutralize him.

A better choice would be a baton, which is utterly reliable, or an OC spray, which we'll discuss next.

Aerosol Sprays

Aerosol defense sprays have come into wide use in recent years, mainly because of the recognition that Oleoresin Capsicum (OC) has a very quick and powerful effect upon an attacker. OC sprays have been on the market since the 1960s, but were not taken seriously by official agencies until recently.

One reason for the belated recognition is the decline of various tear-gas sprays, some of which are weak, and none of which work with some subjects who are high on drugs. Tear gas sprays, using CN or CS, cause the eyes to tear. The onset of symptoms is slow, often taking five or ten seconds. One reason for slow onset is that the recommended use is to spray at the subject's chest to allow the vapor to rise to his face. CN or CS sprayed directly into the eyes may cause permanent damage. Another problem is decontamination. CN or CS sprayed inside a structure can linger for hours or days.

When tear gas sprays first appeared during the late 1960s, they received enthusiastic receptions as the answer to the problem of non-lethal incapacitation. After several years' use, it became clear that these aerosols had been oversold. On the

street, tear gas aerosols incapacitated only about 70 percent of the time.

The Reli-A-Pen (left) is a true shirt-pocket model aerosol, designed to resemble a marking pen. It emits a light cone of spray that is effective only within five to seven feet. The Devastator (right) is larger, but both contain 5 percent OC.

OC works differently. Oleoresin Capsicum is red pepper extract in aerosol form, and is a powerful irritant and inflammatory agent. OC spray, as repeated tests both on volunteers and on the street have shown, acts within a second, because the method of use is to spray the agent directly at the face. The subject experiences a choking feeling as his breathing passages close. The eyes also close from eyelid swelling and irritation, blinding the subject. The subject then usually collapses, even if high on drugs or highly adrenalized.

It's worth noting that OC, like all other weapon systems, doesn't always work the way it's supposed to. According to one law enforcement trainer and specialist in the use of OC spray, "goal orientation" is a critical factor. A determined and well-motivated attacker is less likely to be stopped by OC than someone less motivated.[1]

An array of OC aerosols, from large cans carried in scabbards to smaller pocket-size models. The Bodyguard sprays emit a heavy fog, useful for crowd control as well as saturating an attacker. The smallest model at the right is the only one that's refillable, serves as a key holder, and shoots a light cone of spray.

OC spray is very good for executive protection because of the way it's used. The agent gets between his principal and the threat, spraying a cloud of OC which the attacker must penetrate to reach him. Used this way, OC spray allows retreat behind a chemical barrier.

In some situations, a small can of OC can stop a crowd. If the agent pushes his principal through a doorway, and sprays the doorway, any pursuers will have to negotiate the doorway, thereby exposing themselves to the OC to reach the protectee.

CAS-OC is a pocket-size aerosol that contains 1.7 oz. of 5.5 percent OC in a non-flammable mixture. The white can contains an inert liquid for use as a trainer. Both emit heavy cone shaped fogs.

Two models designed for low-profile carry. The one in a scabbard doubles as a key holder, and the Reli-A-Pen remains in the shirt pocket, looking very much like a marking pen.

Pepper Mace, a new formulation from Mace Security International, is a "ballistic spray," a narrow stream that selectively doses a single person in a crowd. It has an orange-flavor masking agent that covers the sharp pepper odor to prevent the spray from affecting anyone who is not the intended target. This allows precise use in a crowd. The can on the left is the active ingredient container, and the one to the right contains an inert liquid for training.

Another advantage of OC is that it's overtly non-lethal. This obviates a lawsuit relating to use of a deadly weapon. However, it's important to note that there have been a few deaths associated with the use of OC. Most of these have also involved drug overdoses combined with stress.[2]

However, there has been at least one successful lawsuit resulting from the failure of OC to incapacitate an attacker when used by a police officer. Oregon Police Officer Frank Ward sustained a fatal beating after a futile attempt to subdue the suspect with OC. His widow received an out-of-court settlement from Luckey Police Products, which produced the brand Ward had used.[3]

In 1990, there was an unusual incident in which New York City police officers subdued a violent 14-year-old boy with OC, then a shock from a Taser dart. The boy had been soaked with OC spray, which at the time was made in an alcohol solvent version under the name of "Cap-Stun." The sparks ignited the liquid, and the boy sustained burns. Most OC sprays today are non-flammable. All cited in this chapter are safe to use around sparks or flame.

Criminal law is another consideration. Few states restrict the possession or carrying of OC by civilians, while many states and cities have strict concealed firearms laws. The criminal code does not treat using OC as assault with a deadly weapon.

Sources for OC sprays:

CASCO International, Inc.
P.O. Box 166
Gap Mountain Road
Fitzwilliam, NH 03447
Phone: (800) 232-2726
(603) 585-9422

Guardian Security Products
8350 North 7th Street
Phoenix, AZ 85020
Phone: (602) 371-1023
Attn: Sam Smit

MACE Security International
160 Benmont Avenue
Bennington, VT 05201
Phone: (800) 828-8626
Fax: (802) 442-3823
Attn: Tom Archambault

Carrying weapons of any sort aboard aircraft can cause problems. Airport security is quite variable, and ranges from very tight to ridiculous. Typically, airport "security" officers are minimum wage, affirmative action employees, and some adopt airs of importance as a result of wearing uniforms. Giving little people a little power sometimes has an unintended effect.

One security expert stated that some low paid security officers exaggerate the danger when they ask the owner of a lap-top computer to turn it on and flash two different images on the screen to prove that it's not a disguised bomb.[4]

Special purpose weapons have their place, especially when protecting a client who often travels to locales where strict prohibitions against firearms are in effect. They're also useful for low-profile control of subjects who do not pose deadly threats but are merely nuisances, such as overly aggressive autograph hunters. These special implements allow controlling a situation with as little disturbance as possible.

Notes:

1. Reynolds, Joseph, and Burke, Tod W., "Cheers or Tears? A Re-evaluation of Pepper Spray," *Law and Order*, August, 1994, p. 90.
2. *Ibid.*, pp. 87-90.
3. Merrick, Jeff, "OC Spray: No Magic Bullet or 'Cop in A Can,'" *Law Enforcement News*, July 20, 1994, p. 8.
4. Keller, Stephen R., Letter to the Editor, *Security Management*, February, 1993, pp. 6-8.

14
Body Armor

The appearance of Dupont's Kevlar 29 in 1972 soon resulted in its use in soft body armor. Previously, there had been some so-called "bullet-proof" vests using steel plates. These were heavy and bulky, and were so uncomfortable that they were impractical for everyday use. Light, flexible soft fabric armor permitted police and other users to wear the vests for their entire shifts, instead of on the few occasions when they expected a shoot-out. We soon saw federal standards for body armor designed to defeat various "threat levels" and many manufacturers entered the field.

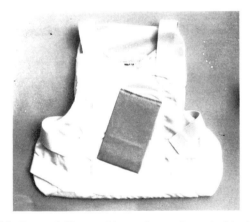

This Second Chance Monarch vest is probably the most advanced body armor at the time (late 1994) of writing. You can crumple the soft armor panels in your fist, yet they will stop magnums. A steel armor panel drops into a central pocket in front of the vest to provide extra protection from shoulder weapons.

More recently, other materials have appeared. Dupont has produced Kevlar 129, a lighter version of its fabric. Allied Signal introduced Spectra-Shield, which is stiffer than Kevlar, and less comfortable. All of these offer some improvement over the original Kevlar. The 4th generation fiber, Araflex™ is the lightest yet, and is the material Second Chance uses in its "Monarch" vest. With its Gore-Tex™ carrier, it allows evaporation of moisture and is significantly more comfortable than most other vests of the same protective level.

Soft body armor's been used mostly by police officers. There's also a significant need for body armor among those in high-risk occupations or who are exposed to other risk factors. Anyone in a high-risk occupation, such as executive protection, or who is a client, should consider body armor.

Why Body Armor?

Body armor can save a life. The protectee should wear body armor for obvious reasons. Some protectees aren't very cooperative, and convincing them that the threat is real and close enough to justify precautions sometimes is impossible. One protectee who had a fatalistic attitude and disdained wearing body armor was Indira Ghandi, India's prime minister. Ghandi was shot to death at close range outside her home by two of her bodyguards. One fired three .38 revolver rounds into her. The other used his Sten 9mm submachine gun and fired seven bullets into her abdomen, one into her heart, and three into her chest.

Still, if the protectee hires a bodyguard, he must feel threatened, and the bodyguard can build on this to persuade him to wear body armor.

Bodyguards should absolutely wear armor. There are several strong reasons for this. First, it's their job. The protectee can ultimately do what he wishes because he's paying the bills, but bodyguards are employees and must follow orders.

Bodyguards will be more effective with protection. The bodyguard is the one who takes risks in shielding his employer from danger. Anything which in turn helps to shield the bodyguard enhances his power to do his job. It's difficult enough to train a bodyguard to place himself between the source of danger and his client. Equipping him with armor that gives him a better chance of survival helps a lot. U.S. Secret Service agent Tim McCarthy sustained a serious injury from Hinckley's .22 caliber bullet because he wasn't wearing body armor when he stepped between the gunman and the president.

The VIP also should wear armor. The ricochet that went into President Reagan's chest would have been stopped by the lightest body armor made at the time, a good argument for having the principal wear body armor.

Types of Body Armor

Body armor comes in all forms and types. Most models are concealed or disguised models that mesh with the low profile often desired by bodyguards and their clients.

There are roughly two approaches. One is a package (ballistic panels and carrier) to wear underneath clothing. The other is actually clothing, with pockets for the panels built-in. Some manufacturers make clothing with Kevlar panels for special protectees. Anyone who has seen tapes of President Reagan in his raincoat after Hinckley's attempt may note how stiff the material appears to be.

The Silent Partner Tropical Vest

One of the lightest and most comfortable packages is the Silent Partner Tropical Vest, a mesh T-shirt with pockets in the front and back for armor panels. The pockets will hold more than one panel each, or panels of different weights and thicknesses. This is what Silent Partner calls their "modular system" which enables the wearer to select the amount of armor to carry, as foot-square panels of different thicknesses fit into the pockets. The lightest combination weighs 1.3 lbs., with 9 layers of Kevlar, enough to stop a .38 Special bullet. The inside panel is level I, and the one in front is level IIA. Together they make up a level II combination.

Silent Partner makes other models, all modular. There's a regular T-shirt model, and a "Diplomat" model that resembles a suit vest. The wearer can use whatever panels he needs, and doubling up on panels gives more protection.

The "Diplomat" model can hold the same panels as the T-shirt models, and is made to look like a suit vest. The buttons in the front do not open, however, and the wearer must put this vest on through the side.

Close fit is important, and although the T-shirt model may need alteration to fit snugly, the "Diplomat" model has adjustable Velcro closures at the sides and top. There are also "wraparound" models protecting the sides, with additional pockets for higher-level protection in front.

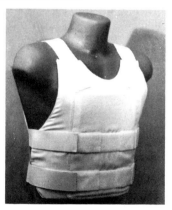

Second Chance Body Armor produces a vest with modular features, the Six-Point Adjustable, which holds Y2 panels and has a pocket for a "K30" metal plate, for additional protection. The 6"x12" plate protects the central torso.

The panels come in both male and female models, the latter having slits and Velcro tabs at the sides in order to fit the female breast. Being very light-weight, they are all comfortable to wear. A field test in the climate of the Arizona desert, one of the hottest places in the world, showed that they are practical.

This Second Chance Quilted Outer Shell contains body armor panels inside, providing protection for outdoorsmen. A VIP who plays golf, goes camping and enjoys other outdoor activities is perfect for this model, as are his bodyguards.

Point Blank Body Armor produces this Ballistic Raincoat with built-in panels that provide front, side and back armoring. This is available in several levels of protection.

Another Second Chance model is the "Investigator" jacket, a nylon windbreaker with a zip-in liner holding the wrap-around Kevlar panels. This jacket weighs 6 lbs., has Y2 panels and is for cool

weather. It's comfortable to wear, but its styling is uninspiring. This points up the fact that these vests are basically off-the-rack articles and the fit is likely to be imprecise. It's impossible to manufacture models that fit everyone perfectly, and alterations may be necessary. A ballistic garment should be a snug fit for best comfort and protection, as a loose one allows the panels to flop to the side, uncovering protected areas.

Civilians can easily sew pockets for ballistic panels into existing clothing. This gives a better fit and eliminates the cost of the carrier.

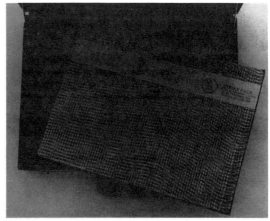

Attaché cases with ballistic panels in several threat levels are available from several manufacturers. Another choice is to buy the panel alone, and put it into your own casing.

Choosing the right one for you can be difficult. As different manufacturers make models that aren't exactly comparable in ballistic protection or comfort, it's necessary to choose very carefully. In many ways, buying armor is like buying shoes, as a try on will not necessarily be a reliable indication of all day comfort. Heavier and larger panels will provide more protection, but also more heat insulation, and the larger the panels the greater the tendency to bind and restrict movement. The unfortunate fact is that any choice will be a compromise. Nevertheless, any vest is better than none, as even a bullet which penetrates will have its velocity degraded by the armor, thus lessening the injury.

Body Armor: Technical Aspects

The basic fact is that there is no such thing as a "bullet-proof" vest. Any armor can only resist penetration by projectiles in proportion to the weight and thickness of the armor. Defining "threat levels" specifies the level of protection needed. The National

Bureau of Standards and the National Institute of Law Enforcement and Criminal Justice (NILECJ), devised a standard for body armor manufacturers to follow, but the NIJ revised it several times and caused much confusion. The current version is NIJ Standard 0101.03, and calls for unrealistic testing methods. The U.S. Office of Technology Assessment studied the standard and called for its revision.[1]

The previous standard, which made more sense, lists six threat levels:

I Projectiles up to .38 Special lead round-nose cartridge, at 850 fps.

II-A Low-velocity .357s (1250 fps), low-velocity 9mms (1090 fps).

II High-velocity .357s (1395 fps) and medium (1175 fps) 9mms.

III-A .44 Magnum, lead bullet at 1400 fps, and high velocity 9mm FMJ, (1400 fps).

III .308 Winchester FMJ at 2750 fps.

IV .30-06 armor-piercing ammunition at 2850 fps.

Not all armor exactly matches these standards. There are intermediate levels, because manufacturers tend to provide margins above the published standards. The standards themselves are limited, because they don't include all of the cartridge loads available. This isn't as important as it seems, because it's practically impossible to predict what firearm and load an assailant will use against you.

This sample of Second Chance Y-2 armor stopped a variety of bullets. Striking velocity pressed the fabric's weave into the lead.

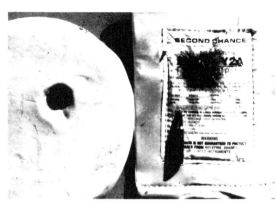

Body armor is not "bullet proof." It won't stop all bullets, only those for which it's rated. This panel of Second Chance Y2A failed to stop a .223 rifle bullet, which was far beyond its threat level rating. The bullet went through to make a clean hole in the clay slab behind the armor panel.

The wearer may know what's been used in the laboratory; he doesn't know what he'll face on the street. In America, the .38 Special is a commonly-available caliber. In Europe, the 9mm Parabellum is popular, and is becoming more widely accepted among Americans. The 9mm penetrates more than the .38 Special, even without the use of special "armor-piercing" bullets.

There's more bad news: several bullets hitting in the same spot, or close together, can still penetrate armor rated to protect against them. Protection against multiple hits is a touchy subject for body armor manufacturers, but a few, such as Second Chance, are addressing this problem with innovative construction methods.

The consensus is that a vest must be comfortable enough to wear regularly. It's better to be partly protected all of the time than fully protected none of the time. Armor left in a drawer or car is useless, no protection at all.

Body armor tends to be expensive, although usually not as costly as a top-quality suit. Price is important, but asking "What's your life worth?" doesn't help much in the everyday world of tight budgets. The body armor must be affordable.

Coverage

There's no absolute protection, and more protection means more weight and bulk. Aside from this, some vests cover only the central torso. "Wraparounds" cover the sides. Wraparounds also restrict movement slightly, are heavier and retain more body heat.

There's no absolute answer to the degree of coverage needed. The most important reason is that no vest covers the entire body, and many vulnerable areas are left open. Although in principle we aim at the center of mass, in a shoot-out shots go wild. A bullet that strikes a peripheral area, such as the brain or a major neck or leg artery, can be lethal.

The gunman who killed Luis Colosio, one of Mexico's presidential candidates, on March 23, 1994, placed a .38 Special bullet in the victim's right temple, and one in his stomach. No information is available regarding whether the murdered candidate was wearing body armor, but obviously no vest could have protected him against the head shot. The stomach shot might have been low enough to pass under the lower edge of a vest.[2]

Some attackers appear to be sophisticated enough to know how to defeat body armor. On September 28, 1994, a gunman shot Mexican politician Jose Francisco Ruiz Massieu in the neck as he was leaving a political meeting. The bullet first penetrated the window of Massieu's four-door Buick.[3]

Armor isn't the answer to all problems, although some let themselves be misled into false confidence by wearing armor. The most realistic way to think of body armor is as a small piece of portable cover.

Some models have the armor panels coming right up to the throat, but many wearers find this uncomfortable, because moving the head forward presses the throat against the edge of the armor, squeezing the windpipe and blood vessels in the neck. One officer fainted from this pressure.[4] A "V-neck" design is an improvement in comfort.

Blunt Trauma

Soft armor will "give" when hit by a bullet. The bullet makes an indentation that goes through the back of the armor. This is called "backface deformation." This allows some of the energy of the bullet to punch through and strike the body, even though the armor stops the projectile. The kinetic energy reaching the body results in "blunt trauma." This is a very frightening sounding term that can intimidate those unfamiliar with its meaning. In plain language, it's like being struck with a ball-peen hammer. This can cause a bruise, or break a bone. Still, a blunt, non-penetrating injury is less threatening than a bullet wound.

There are several ways of reducing blunt trauma. One is to wear a thick shirt under the armor. Another is to build body armor with a resistant backing. One British company has a patented process incorporating an impact reducing pad in the armor. An American firm, Silent Partner Body Armor, uses a "Poly Trauma Reduction System," a thin, stiff plastic film that reduces backface deformation.

The best and most obvious answer, of course, is to use heavier armor. If you're going to have extra weight and thickness to reduce blunt trauma, it may as well be material that resists bullets.

Waterproofing

Some ballistic panels are wrapped in plastic, which increases discomfort by blocking evaporation of sweat. Laboratory tests have shown that soaking Kevlar armor in water will lessen its resistance to penetration about 25%, but the slight amount of moisture from perspiration has no effect. Any waterproofing treatment is unnecessary, adding only to the cost of the armor.

Wear Your Body Armor!

While many protectees go through life without being shot, or even threatened by gunfire, if any prospect of violence exists there's no excuse for the bodyguard not to wear body armor. Body armor won't stop all bullets, but it will stop or slow a knife thrust, and a bodyguard expected to place himself between his client and a threat must wear it for his own safety, at least.

Climate is no excuse. There exist light-weight models that are better than ever. Moderate discomfort is no excuse. As one savvy officer put it: "Armor's hot, but a bullet's hotter."

Partial List Of American Body Armor Manufacturers

Armor Technology Corp.
2260 Rutherford Road, #107
Carlsbad, CA 92008
Phone: (619) 438-5578
1-800-932-9167
Fax: (619) 438-5574

Guardian Technologies
45472 Holiday Drive
Sterling, VA 20166
Phone: (800) 462-7880
(703) 709-7788
Fax: (703) 709-0190

Point Blank Body Armor
185 Dixon Avenue
Amityville, NY 11701
Phone: (800) 645-4443
Fax: (516) 842-5905

Safariland Ltd., Inc.
3120 East Mission Blvd.
P.O. Box 51478
Ontario, CA 91761
Attn: Donald E. Jeckell, Marketing Mgr.
Attn: Norma Osborne
Phone: (909) 923-7300
Phone: (800) 347-1200
Fax: (909) 923-7400

Second Chance Body Armor
P.O. Box 578
Central Lake, MI 49622-9989
Phone: (800) 253-7090
Fax: (616) 544-9824
Attn: Richard Davis

Silent Partner Body Armor, Inc.
612 Third Street
Gretna, LA 70053
Phone: (800) 321-5741
Phone: (504) 366-4851
Fax: (504) 364-8906
Attn: Diane Zufle

U.S. Armor Corp.
11843 Smith Avenue
Santa Fe Springs, CA 90670-3226
Phone: (800) 443-9798
Phone: (310) 949-1733
Fax: (310) 949-1501
Attn: Steve Armellino

Notes:

1. Fackler, Martin, M.D., "OTA Report Strongly Condemns NIJ Soft Body Armor Test," *Law and Order*, October, 1992, pp. 106-108.
2. White, Michael, "Suspect Confesses to Assassination," Associated Press, March 25, 1994.
3. Eaton, Tracy, "Key PRI Official Shot Dead in Car," *Dallas Morning News*, September 29, 1994.
4. Witnessed by the author during a training exercise.

15

Administration

Executive protection carries with it the same nuts-and-bolts administrative requirements as running a business or government office. The pressure is more intense, because there are lives at stake. Therefore, having to make do with a limited budget takes on a more serious aspect, and the compromises required have a greater effect.

While the U.S. Secret Service White House Detail numbers at least 40 agents to cover various posts around the clock and seven days a week, the Secret Service has reserves which it can tap to cover special situations. It can also obtain help from other government agencies, as well as state and local police forces. Private bodyguards don't have these massive resources, and have to make do with less.

There are several basic questions to settle at the start. With 8-hour shifts, and a 40-hour week, it takes 5 agents to fill one "post;" that is, keep one agent on duty in one slot around the clock. This may be surprising to anyone who hasn't ever handled administration, but let's look at the reasons why, and see how there exist possibilities for stretching manpower.

First, three agents are necessary to man each post for three eight-hour shifts around the clock. On weekends, someone has to relieve them, and there is also time required for vacations, sick leave and training days. While it's possible to ask an agent to work overtime to take up the slack, in the long run it takes five agents to man one post completely.

Some cope with the manpower problem by having 12-hour shifts. This certainly saves on the raw number of agents needed, but it has two serious drawbacks: safety and fatigue. There is much less of a margin of safety with 12-hour shifts, and asking the agents to work impossible hours leads to fatigue. It's possible to ask an agent who is winding up an eight-hour shift to work an additional eight hours to cover an absentee,

but to expect one who is on a 12-hour shift to work a straight 24 hours is unreasonable.

Fatigue degrades alertness. It's difficult enough to stay properly alert in normal circumstances, but with a burden of fatigue it's much easier to lose the sharp edge needed to cope with a suddenly appearing threat.

How Many Bodyguards Are Necessary?

This depends on the nature of the threat and whether the principal maintains a high or low profile. There are also other factors which can have a temporary effect on the degree of protection needed. If the protectee takes a trip, he'll need more close protection than if he stays in one place. The level of violence in the area may also escalate, and the client may decide that he needs more security.

The absolute minimum for around-the-clock protection is four guards.[1] This is truly a rock-bottom number, and allows very little slack. It permits only one guard to be present at a given moment, unless there is a doubling-up for a short period or unless they work 12-hour shifts.

As a practical matter, two guards per shift are the minimum for good security. This means ten agents assigned to the detail, at a cost of $5,000 a week.[2]

Why two guards? This is a critical point, one which deserves discussion in detail. Apart from the problem of alertness, there's the matter of coverage. Good general practice demands that a guard stay with the protectee constantly. If a bodyguard has to leave his post at any time, for any reason, without being relieved, he exposes the protectee. Taking meals, going to the toilet and other breaks can take a guard away from his post. Most of the time, there's no cause for alarm.

If, on the other hand, a solitary guard hears an unexplained noise at the other end of the premises, he's faced with a dilemma. If he goes to investigate, he leaves his client exposed. If he stays with the client, he has the nagging anxiety that something sinister may be developing nearby and out of sight. It may not be possible to send a member of the household to investigate. It may be dangerous, if the client is in great danger of attack.

There are other problems with having fewer than two bodyguards. Tactically, in many instances it's necessary to cover two functions, with one guard responsible for evacuating the client from the danger zone and the other assigned to hold off pursuit. In normal coverage, two bodyguards are far more effective in observing the surrounding area for danger than one, because they can divide the area into sectors. Each scans his sector more closely than would be possible if he were responsible for the entire 360 degrees. Despite all this, budgetary limitations dictate that many protectees have to make do with less.

The Team Leader

There is a need for a team or shift leader to supervise closely the moment-to-moment operations of the detail. This is not because bodyguards are less competent than other types of people, but because there are details that require immediate decisions, and there's little margin for error.

One important decision is evaluating a situation in which an agent simply doesn't show up for work. The agent may have been unavoidably delayed, or he may have been intercepted by hostile forces as a precursor to an impending attack. Providing each team member with a means of 24-hour communication, such as a cellular phone, is an important step in dealing with such contingencies.

Once the basic protective plan is laid out, the shift leader must arrange schedules. How long does a guard remain on static post? Alertness diminishes rapidly, especially when nothing's happening. The U.S. Secret Service relieves its posts every half-hour.[3] Another schedule, if there are fewer agents available, is 2 hours on duty and 1 hour off. The agents off-post are not actually off-duty, but assembled in a room set aside for this purpose. This serves as a guard room and command post.

The off-post agents form a reserve, or "alert force," ready to respond to an unusual occurrence. An agent on post may report hearing or seeing something that requires investigation. Because he cannot leave his post, the reserve agents go to investigate. In case of emergency, the reserve agents serve as a back-up force to cope with tactical needs.

Although an off-post agent may sit in an easy chair and take a nap, he cannot take off his shoes or his weapon, if he's armed. He must be ready to respond on a moment's notice. However, if he's the only one in reserve, he cannot allow himself the luxury of sleep, no matter what the hour.

Although it's desirable that the team leader stay apart from the donkey work of manning posts, in order to retain an overview of the situation and be ready to respond to any unusual happening, this often isn't possible. There simply may not be enough manpower, and the team leader must become a "working boss." The politics of employee morale also enters into it. The team leader will earn more respect from his men if he's able to show that he can carry a share of the burden as well. This shows up the difference between the two leadership styles: "You go first," and "Follow me."

In executive protection the workload has to be more evenly divided than in many other occupations. It's poor practice to assign the newer agents to "graveyard" shift and leave the more comfortable daylight assignments to those with seniority. There has to be a sprinkling of seasoned bodyguards on each shift.[4]

Many assignments will be for minimal security, with only one bodyguard assigned part-time. Many protectees either don't need or can't afford around-the-clock protection, and look after their own security when at home or at the office. Some require a bodyguard only while commuting or while on trips. Others feel comfortable with a bodyguard on duty during working hours, but can dispense with protection in the evenings and on weekends.

This is a fallacy, because if anyone with a serious intention to harm the client is stalking him, he'll soon learn when the bodyguard goes off-duty and plan his attack for the unprotected hours. It's worth mentioning this to the client, but usually it doesn't cause any changes, because the client feels that he can't afford the extra protection.

Special Tasks

The team leader should maintain security files, or delegate this duty to someone else. He should have limited access to his employer's files for various purposes. For example, a company's personnel files can be valuable in the case of a terminated employee who threatens the client. Personnel files often contain personal and medical information, and sometimes fingerprints and photographs of the employee. Any forms completed by the employee can serve as handwriting exemplars. This is why personnel files should be retained for at least 20 years after termination.

Other security files include threat assessment worksheets, building security checklists, advance survey checklists, airport security checklists, protectee personal files and bomb threat checklists.

Some of these forms must be available for completion in the absence of the team leader. He may not be able to perform advance duties at the same time as directing the protective team. As a matter of course, bomb threats are often taken by telephone operators or receptionists, not the security director. Therefore, enough of these forms should be in the hands of responsible parties.

Administration of a bodyguard detail is routine work, far less glamorous than shoot-outs and car chases. It's essential to operating an effective protective detail, and a mistake in administration may result in a gap in the defenses. This is why administration requires someone competent and experienced.

Notes:

1. *Terrorism and Personal Protection*, Brian Jenkins, editor, NY, Butterworth Publishers, 1985, p. 186.
2. *Ibid.*, p. 151.
3. "The Witnesses, Hearings Before the Warren Commission," *New York Times* edition, p. 535. This is the testimony of James Rowley, who was chief of the Secret Service at the time. The scheduling probably hasn't changed much since then, although the number of agents assigned to the president has certainly increased.
4. *Protecting the President*, Dennis V. N. McCarthy, NY, William Morrow & Company, 1985, p. 38.

16

Bodyguarding:
The Nuts And Bolts

This chapter deals with the techniques of protection under the assumption that a team will be available on a round-the-clock assignment. This is overly optimistic because many clients simply can't afford it. Having too few people increases the workload on the individual bodyguard, although the techniques are similar. We'll also cover instances of one- and two-agent operations, for the sake of completeness.

Planning

One of the lesser-known, but very successful, protection operations is the U.S. Marshal's Service Federal Witness Protection Program. In 1992 alone, there were 1,306 witnesses under actively funded protection, as well as members of their families, for a total of 3,234 persons under federal protection. The cumulative total, over the two decades or so that the program's been active, is 6,014 principal witnesses, and their families, for a grand total of 13,535 persons.[1]

The point behind these statistics is that federal marshals were able to attain a remarkable success rate because they took over their protectee's lives, uprooted them from familiar surroundings, and relocated them far from home with new identities. Most bodyguards can't do this. They can't take the president into hiding or persuade the CEO of General Motors to leave his job and change his name. Instead, they must work within the protectee's setting, and overcome the handicaps imposed by the protectee's lifestyle.

Planning will occupy most of a bodyguard's time for the first few days. It's necessary to know the principal's daily routine, and to work protective measures into it. In some instances, it will be necessary for the client to make some changes. It requires tact and persuasiveness for the executive protection agent to persuade the client to make the necessary adaptations in his daily life.

The bodyguard must also survey the client's residence and workplace. Static security is as important as security while on the move. In one sense, it's more important, because the home and workplace are fixed sites, usually known to the attacker. On the plus side, it's usually easier to defend the client in a fixed location, where there are barriers and other security systems, than it is out in the open. In some instances, the residence may be so insecure that it's advisable to relocate.

The client's home is not necessarily his castle. When a crew from the Front de Liberation de Quebec kidnapped British diplomat James Cross in Montreal on October 5, 1970, they snatched him right from his home. Posing as delivery men, they pushed their way past the maid who answered the door, found Cross in pajamas in his bedroom, and ordered him to dress. They then handcuffed him and drove him away in a taxi, changing to a private car later.[2]

On December 17, 1981, Brigadier General James Dozier was kidnapped from his apartment in Italy by four gunmen disguised as plumbers. They gained access into his sixth floor apartment without difficulty, hit the general on the head, and put him into a trunk which they carried downstairs and drove away in a van.[3]

At home, alarm systems can help increase security and reduce the need for manpower. Careful planning to integrate human and electronic security systems is necessary. For the outer perimeter, it may be possible to use a uniformed security force, but the inner perimeter should always have high-grade protective agents.

The workplace is usually safe, as many companies have their own security forces to safeguard the grounds and buildings. Indeed, the executive's bodyguard may be a member of the corporation's security force.

Commuting can be very dangerous. Ideally, it's wise to vary the times and the routes. Security specialists, lecturing upon this subject, can get quite smug in stating that unpredictability is the key to survival. In practice, it's usually impossible. The client lives in a certain place and works in a certain place. He can take whichever route he chooses at whatever time he wishes, but he begins and ends up in the same places each day. A typical city block has only two exits. A cul-de-sac is even worse, limiting the defender to only one exit. This eases planning for an attacker. However, a cul-de-sac makes it harder for an attacker to put surveillance on his target.

The client's front door is a critical danger spot. As we've seen, several notables were attacked near their front doors. John Lennon, not under protection at that moment, was shot to death by an attacker outside the main entrance to his residence in the Dakota Apartments in New York City. Emiliano Revilla, a Spanish businessman, was accosted by several gunmen outside his home in Madrid on February 24, 1988. They took him away into captivity and held him for ransom.[4]

This is why it helps greatly to have a residence with several exits. Leaving by a different one each time complicates an attacker's planning.

Best of all is an enclosed courtyard or basement garage where the protectee can enter and leave an armored vehicle out of sight of bystanders. Second best is an arrangement like the one at the White House, with its protected grounds, where the president can enter and leave his armored limousine far from the street.

For total security, the residence and the workplace need to be kept secret. This is impossible for most protectees. The Federal Witness Protection Program works this way, though. The protectees receive new identities, residences and employment. This elusiveness gives total security, except for those who "blow their cover." One such was Joseph Bombacino, and the consequences were fatal for him, as we'll see in the chapter on bombs.

For commuting, the choice of vehicle depends on the client, his lifestyle and what he can afford. If he's a high-profile person, and can afford the extra protection requirements this brings, he can have a limousine. A more modest business executive is better off with a plain car, with no distinguishing features. This tends

to confuse an attacker, as does using different vehicles drawn from a company motor pool.

The driver should have a defensive driving course under his belt. His ability to handle the car skillfully in a crisis can save lives. Competent instruction in defensive and offensive driving is available, as noted in the chapter on "training." There won't be much space devoted to driving techniques here, because these are truly "hands-on" skills, and it's impossible to learn them from a book alone.

The question of whether or not the driver should be an armed bodyguard is controversial. Some feel that each member of the protective team should be trained to the highest level, to enable doubling up and "covering" for each other. The other viewpoint is that executive protection is a special skill, as is driving, and the two do not mix. On the balance, the view that driver and bodyguard should be cross-trained seems to have more merit. This is true from the viewpoint of versatility, as well as administratively. A driver cross-trained as a bodyguard can "cover" when the bodyguard is absent. The reverse is also true.

This is not only because of budget constraints which dictate making the most of the fewest people. A driver who has a solid grounding in bodyguarding techniques will better understand his place in the scheme of things. He'll hold up his end of the team's effort because he'll understand better what they expect from him and why. A bodyguard who understands the emergency maneuvers possible with a car will also be in a better position to understand and anticipate tactics in an emergency, and to plan accordingly.

How many vehicles and protection agents are available? The chapter on ambushes lays out the advantages of using more than one vehicle. Having more than one permits boosting security by deception. The client can ride in the follow-up car, leaving the high-profile limousine with only the driver.

Keeping A Low Profile

The most basic concept of executive protection is to keep a low profile. There are several components to this.

The first objective is to avoid standing out as a likely target. Keeping a low profile helps minimize the client's apparent importance. Keeping a high profile can advertise both importance and vulnerabilities. Let's consider one possibility:

The client decides to hold a huge reception for his daughter's sixteenth birthday. This involves news releases, invitations, caterers, crowds and a lot of confusion. The disadvantages for the client are that this lets anyone who is interested know that he has the money to afford such an extravaganza, and therefore must be an important man. There will be people coming and going, which will create a security nightmare for the protective staff. They probably won't have the manpower to check out all of the tradespeople with legitimate business, although they may be able to improvise ways of ensuring that those who present themselves at the door really are who they claim to be. Keep in mind, though, that passes can be forged or stolen. The guest list may include some undesirables. There may also be gate-crashers. Even innocent gate-crashers pose dangers, because they may divert security people away from more serious problems.

Routine precautions are to avoid such conspicuous gatherings and to keep a low profile. Keeping a low profile includes many steps.[5] Among them are not having custom license plates on the automobile, using a common type of car, and not dressing in a flamboyant manner. Other steps to lower the profile are:

- Don't have custom or obviously expensive luggage. Also, don't put the client's home address on the luggage tag.
- Don't have an assigned parking space marked with the client's name at the office.
- Don't live in an especially opulent part of town.
- Don't have a telephone listed in the client's name. It's futile to have an unlisted number, because these aren't really secret, and a little effort can reveal it. Instead, have the telephone listed in the name of an administrative assistant or bodyguard.
- Don't be too much of a socializer, or hold large parties that may be newsworthy. Remember, the larger the guest list, the better the odds are for a gate-crasher.
- Avoid personal publicity. This includes public meetings with public figures. Take care not to have the client photographed at public affairs. The best way of doing this is not to try to snatch the photographer's camera, which will only attract attention, but to stay inconspicuous if it's absolutely necessary to attend.
- It's also wise to avoid social functions that publish guest lists.

- These precautions also take in the client's family. The wife may compromise her husband's precautions by shopping at the most expensive stores in her chauffeur driven Rolls-Royce.
- The bodyguard should also keep a low profile. Apart from avoiding childish behavior such as displaying guns and handcuffs to all who ask, he should make a serious effort to blend in and pass as an ordinary member of the protectee's "crowd." It's safer to let a casual observer think that the bodyguard is a friend or an "administrative assistant" than to announce that he's the "goon." An increasingly important point is that the bodyguard can be a female, perhaps posing as a secretary, and this is a good argument for recruiting females for executive protection.

Information Control

As we've already seen, gathering information about a target is the necessary preliminary to a "hit." Information control is critically important, and covers restricting any information that might help an attacker.

The basic principle of information security is "need to know." Nobody without a need to know should have access to any information about the protectee. This includes employees.[6]

Attackers try to find out about a target's habits and routines. In many instances, especially in foreign countries, their efforts may include making the acquaintance of and "pumping" servants and employees. This is one reason why the client should never discuss plans, especially travel plans, in front of employees with no "need to know." One serious mistake some make is to discuss sensitive matters in front of servants whom they believe don't understand English.

There should also be a program of active indoctrination of all family members and household servants not to give out information to strangers. A special caution is appropriate with telephone inquiries. One method of answering the telephone without giving anything away is to say the last four digits of the telephone number. Another is simply to say, "Hello."

Another important routine should be never to tell any caller when the protectee will be arriving. The staff and protectee should also be aware that many "wrong number" or "hang up" calls may be a method of finding out if the premises are occupied.

An important precaution is a "duress code." This is a code word, normally used in daily speech, that indicates that all is well. Omitting this word in conversation alerts the listener that the speaker is talking with a gun at his head. It's a precaution to cope with the possibility that attackers have seized the office or captured the home. A procedure of regular telephone "check-ins" helps monitor vital events throughout the day. This is a duty that the bodyguard can carry out while at the office, without compromising his vigilance.

One technique that enhances the value of telephone check-ins is establishing traveling times between places the client and his family frequent. This is to gain the earliest possible warning when they become "overdue." In this, as in many other aspects of protection, detail work is important. Driving times between home and office will vary, depending on the hour. The bodyguard, driver, or other staff member should record driving times at various hours during the day, to prevent both false alarms and complacency.

The telephone can easily be an information leak. It's impossible to ever be sure that the telephone isn't tapped. The "bug detectors" that some enterprising electronic companies sell at inflated prices can only detect bugs placed nearby. They can't alert the user to taps placed in the central office or on the other end of the wire. Therefore, it's vital never to discuss sensitive information on the telephone.

Counter-surveillance is necessary, although it's possible to exaggerate. Watching for people or cars that pass repeatedly is one technique. This is difficult if the client lives on a busy street, as the volume of traffic will mask surveillants. As previously noted, a dead end street helps detect attempts at surveillance because of the dearth of traffic. Another advantage of a dead end is that it makes drive-by shootings much more difficult.

Electronic Privacy

Industrial espionage and information gathering are facts of modern life.[7] Part of the bodyguard's duties may also be to ensure the client's security from electronic eavesdropping. If this is the case, the bodyguard should have a working knowledge of electronic surveillance and of de-bugging methods.

One source for bugging and anti-bugging devices is:

Shomer-Tec
Box 28070
Bellingham, WA 98228
Phone: (360) 733-6214
Fax: (360) 676-5248

There are two essential steps to assuring freedom from bugging. The first is never to discuss sensitive information casually, in public places or on other premises where unauthorized people might overhear it. The second step is to provide secured offices for confidential discussions. The reason these two points are so critical is that verbal discussions often precede writing down new plans and products, and the eavesdropper can obtain confidential information very early, often before dissemination to authorized persons.[8]

The technical side of eavesdropping protection involves locating an interior room which is protected from casual entry, ascertaining that its construction is solid enough to prevent casual eavesdropping, and using sound insulation and sound masking (background noise) to prevent directed eavesdropping. Sound masking isn't merely turning up the radio when having a confidential discussion, but using a special sound generator to emit vibrations that make picking up a conversation more difficult.[9] Finally, protection means sweeping the room electronically, to ensure that no "bugs" have been planted.

Note that in the corporate environment, anti-eavesdropping and electronic sweeping counter-measures are the responsibility of the security department, which probably has specialists to relieve the bodyguard from this duty. This is all to the good, because it avoids overloading the bodyguard with supernumerary duties.

It may not be possible to be completely free from electronic eavesdropping, which is why the bodyguard should have an array of methods which can be employed to take advantage of the situation. One way is to make fake reservations by telephone, to mislead an attacker. Another is for the protectee to mention fake plans or travel arrangements during casual telephone conversations, knowing they'll be picked up by a potential assailant.[10]

Computer Databases

Direct surveillance, by shadowing the client, bugging his phone and office and suborning his employees, is becoming less necessary because today it's possible to form a good picture of a target's lifestyle and habits by electronic means. This goes beyond bugging and other forms of direct electronic eavesdropping. Automobile registrations, utility bills, credit card use records and other databases allow a potential attacker to learn almost everything worth knowing in order to plan an attack without directly approaching his target. There are private data services that ferret out such information about almost everyone in the country.[11]

This has already happened. Rebecca Schaeffer, TV actress, was located by Robert John Bardo, who stalked her electronically and discovered her address, telephone number, vehicle, and where she shopped and dined. With this information, Bardo was able to track her down and shoot her to death.[12]

The way to make an attacker's life more difficult is to avoid leaving an electronic trail. Some precautions are:

- Have the client's vehicles registered in another name. His corporation may be the owner of record. Lacking that, registering the vehicles in the name of a relative with a different surname will cover that point. Other choices are registering the vehicles in the names of bodyguards and friends. In any case, changing the registrations and obtaining new license plates help defeat both electronic tracing and direct observation.

- Make all purchases and travel arrangements in another name. Hotel and rental car reservations can be in the name of the client's bodyguard, secretary, administrative assistant or others. Corporate credit cards help in this regard, as long as the protectee is not the only person in the company authorized to use them.

- Pay cash if possible, both as a regular method of evasion and in an emergency. The limit is that payments of ten thousand dollars or more are required to be reported to the Internal Revenue Service, but this is a generous limit, and most purchases and travel costs are so far under the limit that they will not attract attention.

- Unless the client's residence is so well known that it's public knowledge, utilities, including cable TV, should be billed to his company, landlord or other party, to avoid having his name on record.

- The client's mailing address should not be his home address. This is the easiest point to cover because of the easy choices available. The client's mail, even

personal mail, should come to his business address, a post office box or a mail drop. If the choice is a P.O. box or mail drop, the client should never pick up his own mail, to avoid being ambushed at a fixed point. Someone else, not necessarily the bodyguard, should pick up the mail. A practical point about private mail drops is that the post office will not accept a change of address order if the client decides to move. He'll have to notify each correspondent and publication individually.

- Magazine subscriptions, especially those to publications that suggest lifestyle (yachting, flying, illegal drugs, sexual perversion, etc.), should always be in an alias, in conjunction with a mail drop. Mail drops accept corporate listings, and allow several other names to receive mail at the corporate address. It's not illegal to subscribe to publications using a fictitious name.

- Medical care, including hospital stays, should always be under an alias. Entertainers employ this technique of evasion frequently, and are able to secure cooperation from doctors and hospitals by paying their bills promptly. Doctors and hospitals are mainly interested in the money anyway, and a corporate guarantee of prompt payment will elicit cooperation.

Other Precautions

One important precaution is to examine all packages, including mail, as they may be threatening. Letter bombs come in thick envelopes. Refer to the chapter on bombs.

When planning a trip, one choice is making reservations under another name. Never giving a home address when making reservations or registering at a hotel is also wise. Using several names during a trip can make the protectee especially hard to trace. All of this will be nullified if the bodyguards use their own names. They'll have to if they are required to show ID, but if this is the case, they can still avoid revealing the client's name, by renting rooms and making travel reservations under their own names.

The consensus is that the best location for the protectee's room is several floors up, for protection against easy assault from the street. The secure zone is above the second floor and below that tenth, to ensure that the room is not beyond the reach of a fire ladder.[13] This covers the possibility of the protectee's becoming trapped in case of fire, and is one of the small details the bodyguard must note constantly. Choosing a room at the end of a hallway lets the bodyguard take the next room, giving partial protection against eavesdropping. It also minimizes traffic in front of the protectee's door, which makes screening those who approach easier. A room next to a staircase or elevator is undesirable because of the constant traffic.

Bodyguards should occupy adjoining rooms so that they are close by if needed. This enables them to mount a watch on the client's door, and conveniently stand guard in front of it, if necessary. It's usually unnecessary to book the entire floor, and it will always attract attention. A good compromise solution is to book four or five rooms in a row. This then leaves open to doubt exactly which room the protectee will occupy, in case anyone's planning to plant a bomb or a bug.

Whatever the case, the bodyguards should always examine the room before the client enters. The room should be under guard even when the protectee's away, but manpower limitations may make this impossible.

The client's luggage is also important. It should always be in a secured area, or under surveillance, especially while in transit. Planting harmful objects in luggage is a well-known maneuver. Another precaution is to make sure that all of the luggage is actually that of the protectee and the bodyguard team. An extra, unexplained piece of luggage may be an innocent one, or it may be more sinister. Another hazard is the client's luggage being used to smuggle illegal drugs. It's important not to leave luggage unattended at an airport or hotel, and not to carry packages aboard aircraft for acquaintances.[14]

Avoidance

It's important to avoid certain clear dangers:

Isolated places sometimes are dangerous. If far from help, the danger is greatly increased. By contrast, if the isolated place is "home ground," with lots of help nearby, there are certain definite advantages.

Certain situations are inherently dangerous, and the bodyguard should avoid them. A client can get mugged as easily as any other citizen. The bodyguard should not assume that just because he's armed, or skilled in martial arts, he's invulnerable to a common mugger. Even if the bodyguard has a successful encounter and defeats the mugger, the incident can be annoying to the client. There will be statements to

make to the police, and possibly unwanted publicity, especially if the protectee's a public figure or entertainer. The best policy is to avoid any confrontation, especially an unnecessary one.

Crowds pose potential danger and impair mobility. The problem with a crowd, if trouble strikes, is getting the protectee out. Always try to leave yourself an "out," for quick evacuation.

Crowds in shopping malls offer excellent cover for attackers. It's important to remember that the president of the United States can have a shopping mall's security staff serving as part of the protective force around him, but this is practically impossible for a protectee of less than national importance. In any case, shopping mall security officers are often not geared to executive protection needs.

Mall security officers are often unarmed, and oriented towards preventing shoplifting and motor vehicle theft, as well as keeping out panhandlers and other undesirables. Security procedures are very lax, compared to those at airports, where electronic gates are commonplace. Security officers are often low-grade, low-paid and poorly trained hired help.[15]

If the protectee must make public appearances, it may be wise to hire uniformed guards and take additional security measures. Plainclothes reinforcements are especially worthwhile because they can mingle with the crowd. There are two great advantages to this. One is that it's smart to have "back-ups" nearby. Both police and criminals use back-ups, and keeping a force in reserve can help a bodyguard team through a difficult situation. The other reason is that if a threat develops within the crowd, the agents within it are the ones most likely to reach it in time.

In this regard, it's important to remember that assassins and kidnappers can have back-ups too. Never assume a crisis is over because the attacker has been apprehended or otherwise neutralized. Leaving the scene quickly is the best defense against secondary attacks launched by back-ups.

Another protective technique is to photograph the crowd at each appearance. Saving the photographs for later comparison can be valuable, because scanning successive photographs and finding the same face in different locales can alert you that someone's "stalking" your client.

Liaison with local security is worthwhile, because this provides a source of reinforcements. Even rent-a-cops can be useful for perimeter guard.

Close Static Protection

Control access to the protectee. Use walls, fences and other barriers to limit free access. This economizes on manpower and enhances security. Whenever there's a hiatus in the action, try to get the protectee into a closed space.

In certain public places, there are tactics to minimize the client's exposure. In a restaurant, for example, the client should always be away from a window. If there are alcoves, seating the client in one will minimize exposure. The bodyguard should sit so that he can see the entrance as well as the area around his client. Having his back to a wall reduces the perimeter he must scan. Having other team members at another table is helpful because they can serve as back-ups if needed. A member of the team should immediately scout for a rear exit, in case emergency departure becomes necessary. The bodyguards should plan to finish their meals first, so that they can be ready to go when the protectee leaves. This requires that they order meals which are quick to fix. Asking the waiter often helps. In a pinch, a sandwich is quicker than a "hot plate." It's also important to pay for the meal when it's served, to avoid delays upon departure.

There have been "hits" in restaurants, but most have been Mafia killings. The target has usually been a well-known "man of respect" who did not take precautions because he thought his exalted status was protection enough. "Crazy Joe" Gallo was shot to death in Umberto's Clam House in Manhattan. By contrast, Albert Anastasia died in a barber's chair.

On The Move

The bodyguard should always be the first to enter a room, moving ahead of his protectee to ensure that there's no threat. The "away from windows" rule applies, and a further precaution is to draw the drapes or lower the blinds. In a public restroom, the bodyguard should enter first, as with any other room, and stay with the protectee. It's not possible to take a stance outside the door and prevent others from entering a public place. If the bodyguard and protectee are of opposite sexes, restrooms may become a problem. The bodyguard can sometimes simply knock on the door and ask if anyone's inside before allowing the client to enter.

Elevators pose a similar problem, but worse. Again, the bodyguard should "check out" the elevator before his client enters, and then stay very close to him inside. Upon leaving, a quick look up and down the corridor is essential before the client leaves. The tactics of using elevators give both bodyguard and protectee practice at closely coordinating their movements without appearing conspicuous, and the client soon can learn to respond to his guard's "body language" and move appropriately without verbal commands.

Escalators are troublesome, but not necessarily threatening. A heavily protected client will justify having an agent on the opposite escalator for side protection, but in reality the threat is minimal. An attacker would have to have perfect timing to launch an attack from the opposite escalator.

Stairs can also be a problem if they're of the open center type. This permits a vertical attack, and the bodyguard should urge his client to stay close to the wall. In a tight-security situation, extra guards can be detailed to ascend a few flights, and others can take up stations below the protectee.

Streets are potentially very dangerous, especially for pedestrians. The Swedish prime minister, Olaf Palme, was shot to death by a pistol wielding assailant while walking from the theater. A passing car can be the launching platform for a killing or a kidnapping, demonstrating that the client is even more exposed on the pavement than when riding in a car. The only reason why there are far more protectees attacked while traveling in cars is that most ride, not walk.

A client who walks or jogs each morning is taking a chance. President Truman was able to go for his morning walks, and Clinton goes out jogging, but both had enough U.S. Secret Service agents along to insure their safety. The best solution is to avoid going outdoors unnecessarily. Jogging in place is about as good as full scale jogging, and doesn't expose the client. If he insists on going outside, it's best to avoid a regular time and route.

If a protective team is available, stationing an agent on the opposite sidewalk gives better coverage of windows and roofs on the client's side. Otherwise, agents on his side of the street would have to crane their necks to peer up, and would observe at a very narrow angle.

If there are enough resources, an escort vehicle trailing the client is a wise precaution. This was one of the ways the U.S. Secret Service protected President Truman when he took his morning walks.

At The Office

At the office, take a positive role in screening visitors. Don't depend on a secretary or a maid to do this. They're not professional protection officers, and can be fooled. In some instances, they can be "bought." Establish a visiting list of people known to your client. Each day, scan the appointments book. Be especially watchful of strange names and faces. Always check with your client before admitting anyone not already "cleared" in to see him.

It's also important to brief oncoming shifts to prevent embarrassing errors. Explain to the client that errors, when they happen, are for his protection, and indicate that the guards are acting alertly.

One possible technique is electronic "frisking." An electronic gate, such as those used at airports, costs thousands of dollars. It also may be unnecessary. One extremely cost-effective device is the small, handheld electronic frisker. This permits a surreptitious frisk, which can be very important in certain situations.

The surreptitious frisk is necessary when there's a risk of the person taking offense. One such example would be the important guest about whom the bodyguard has some nagging doubts. Pushing such a person up against a wall, police style, could easily lose the bodyguard his job. Another is the suspicious person in a public place. It isn't always possible, especially at airports, to prevent the approach of strangers. Any attempt to frisk a suspicious person can lead to an assault charge, especially if the bodyguard is not a police officer. A small, handheld metal detector that gives a silent alarm is valuable in this case. A third case is searching a female.

Close Protection on Foot

Ideally, the close protection agents form a screen around the protectee, scan the surroundings for threats, and act to shield and remove the client if an attack develops. Let's begin the discussion with the supposition that only one agent is available:

One agent should always stay behind his client. This protects the principal's most vulnerable area, his rear. The protectee can look out for himself in front, to a certain degree.

The proper distance is one pace or closer. The client should always be within arm's reach. The bodyguard will have to be able to reach out to his client to get him down out of the line of fire, if neces-

sary, or jump in front or to his side to shield him. The bodyguard should not be too rigid in his positioning, and he should try to place himself between his client and the most likely risk.

Two agents should be on opposite sides of the client, one slightly to the front and the other slightly to the rear. With three agents, two should be in front and one at the rear. With more agents available, the effort should not be to make one tight ring around the client, but to arrange a defense in depth. It may be tempting, if the manpower is available, to form a "human wall" around the principal. This can be a cumbersome formation, and may be hard to maintain if rapid movement is necessary. If the intent is to keep an attacker from having a clear shot at the protectee, quick movement will be even more effective. None of these formations are absolute. They should change to meet changing situations.

Another reason for keeping a loose formation is to avoid bunching up, in which case an assailant can take everyone out in the first short attack. One burst of automatic fire can injure or kill everyone in a tight group. One grenade can accomplish the same thing. Dispersal is safer. Dispersal provides defense in depth and is much harder to breach. This is true while on foot or in vehicles.

Observation

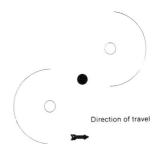

With two bodyguards, one walks slightly in front and to the side of the client, and the other on the opposite side from him. Each scans his area of responsibility. The forward agent scans the front and sides, and the rear one scans the rear and sides. Note that with two agents, each has to cover at least 180 degrees, and even overlap slightly, to be certain of not missing anything.

While on the move or when static, agents should scan the area around themselves and their protectee. The areas of responsibility are preassigned, but logical. The surrounding area is divided into sectors. Each scans his own sector.

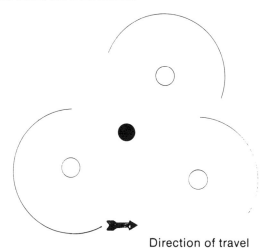

Direction of travel

With three bodyguards, each is responsible for a sector of about 120 degrees. As before, the sectors will overlap to assure complete coverage.

In scanning, it's important to keep the eyes moving. Threats can develop very quickly, and are easy to miss if the agent slows down or fixates on one object of interest.

Some bodyguards feel that an attacker will keep watching the protective agent's eyes, and make his move when he's looking elsewhere. This is why bodyguards used to wear reflective sunglasses. This became obsolete because it became too well-known. It's better to train to use peripheral vision.

There are various theories regarding how to scan. One is to divide the area into layers, and scan the closest layer first, then move on to the next, etc. This is the technique taught at the U.S. Army's sniper school, and it doesn't necessarily apply here. There isn't time to conduct a leisurely scan of people and objects at various ranges.

It's best to follow natural instincts. Movement is what attracts the eye, and it's also movement that can be threatening to the client. Assassins may lurk, surveying the scene, but they do not begin attacks by remaining still. An assassin will wait quietly, blending with the crowd, until the moment he judges is best. That's when he moves, and the movement will probably be very sudden. There may be the sudden display of a weapon. Sometimes the attacker will assume a firing stance, even before the weapon

becomes visible. The guard must also be alert for thrown objects. They may be harmless, but maybe not.

Various "profiles" of dangerous people have been developed. There is an American assassin profile, which describes the typical assassin as young, male, a "loner," and not part of a conspiracy. This description is too loose to be useful. Moore and Fromme, the two women who attacked President Gerald Ford, did not fit this profile because they were female. Another woman was arrested in Colorado in September, 1992, after stalking President Bush.[16]

There are also some psychologists, psychiatrists and other charlatans who claim that they can instruct bodyguards on how to spot threats by facial expressions or behavioral cues. The widely shown videotapes of the Wallace and Reagan shootings show the attackers' faces clearly, and this makes it obvious that they'd be hard to pick out from the crowd. Arthur Bremer, who shot Wallace, was wearing a wide smile and looked very much like an enthusiastic supporter until he started firing.

The police officer/bodyguard will already know the lesson that police officers learn very early: "Watch the hands." This is the basic principle of observation regarding anyone who approaches the protectee. In some instances, the bodyguard won't let anyone approach unless he can see their hands. While it may not be possible to restrain someone physically, the bodyguard can place himself between the approaching person and his client, refusing to move aside until he can see their hands.

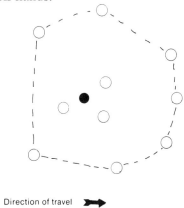

Direction of travel

A loose formation with ten bodyguards. There are two concentric screens of agents. It's best not to use tight formations, with everyone walking in step, because this makes it too conspicuous. The outer screen can blend into the crowd, ever watchful for the early signs of an attack, and ready to intervene. The team leader is in the close group of three.

Apart from searching for suddenly moving people, it's wise to seek out objects and situations that may be threatening. A partly open door is a feature that requires further checking out. A bodyguard who sees this should place himself between it and his client. A team member should move to check it out.

An occupied car parked with the engine running is a cliché, but it sometimes happens. This is another reason for an alert, and again team members should place themselves between the car and the client. In such a case, the priority should be to get the client out of range as soon as possible.

One important point is not to react to a diversion. Some assassins will stage a fight or use other diversions to distract the protectee's bodyguards and draw them away from their client. This is what happened when Malcolm X was killed in 1965. He was making a public appearance when a fight broke out at one side of the stage. The bodyguards, drawn to the disturbance, left their client uncovered for a few crucial seconds, long enough for the killers to rise from their seats, draw weapons and gun Malcolm X down with a shotgun round, 9mm- and .22-caliber bullets. The killers escaped, too.[17]

The agents must shout warnings of attacks. It's important to alert the entire crew as quickly as possible. Have them use the clock system. Describe the weapon and person, as for example:

"Two o'clock! Man with a gun, ten feet!"

Immediate Action Drills

There should be well rehearsed and established procedures for countering a threat. Once the first to see the threat sounds the alert, an automatic plan should go into motion. This requires a clear division of roles, and everyone must perform within his role unless ordered otherwise. With fast breaking events, it's not likely that many orders will come during the first few critical seconds.

Without a well rehearsed immediate action drill, the results can be catastrophic for the client, or even comical. Indian Prime Minister Rajiv Ghandi was addressing a crowd at an open-air rally when an attacker concealed in bushes opened fire on him. Ghandi stopped his speech and told the head of his protective detail that someone appeared to be shooting at him. The chief and his detail all rushed to the bushes, leaving Ghandi exposed on the podium, instead of evacuating him. Fortunately, the assassin was acting alone, and Ghandi survived the experience.[18]

The inner ring shields the client, and attempts to evacuate him. The exact sequence of events will depend on how close the threat is. In some instances, it will be worthwhile to get the client down, or at least below the level of the crowd. One way of doing this without pushing him forcefully to the ground is to reduce his height:

Taking a client down out of the line of fire. The bodyguard strikes the backs of the client's knees with his own, while shoving down hard on his shoulders.

The client's height has now been reduced so that the bodyguard shields him. This may be enough for momentary protection while other agents deal with the attacker. If necessary, the bodyguard can drive his client all the way to the ground, supporting him to avoid injury.

Another way to get the client away from danger is to pivot him. This is possible when there are two or more guards. In a crowd, reception line, or when the protectee is walking along a line of people, one bodyguard stays very close behind him. He keeps one hand on the client's belt. If he sees danger, he encircles the client's chest with his other arm, pivots the client around him and marches him to the rear. The pivoting motion is forceful and quick.

The bodyguard grabs his client in two places: by the belt and around the chest. The hand holding the belt must be thrust through, with the fingers under the belt for a firm grip. The bodyguard throws his weight into pivoting the protectee. It's surprising how small the bodyguard can be and yet pivot the client quickly, taking advantage of body mechanics.

The simplest and most effective disarm is to grab the weapon and turn it towards the attacker. This points it away from the client, and puts the attacker in danger if he should pull the trigger. A simple two-handed grip, as shown, is effective and workable.

The outer ring tries to blunt or stop the attack. The moment of contact with an attacker requires some very clear thought. Many will think first of reaching for their weapons, but in fact it's usually quicker to "swarm" over the attacker. Swarming requires several agents to smother the attacker with their weight. It's the method of choice when he's in reach, because jumping him will be quicker than drawing a weapon and firing.

With only one or two bodyguards, swarming is out of the question. A disarm is a more useful tactic:

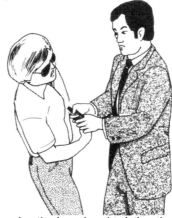

Grasping the barrel and twisting the weapon out of the attacker's hand completes the disarm. A knee to the crotch will disable him and prevent further aggression.

Another reason for avoiding gunfire is the danger to innocent people. Firing in a crowd can also start a panic, putting the client in even more danger.

Finally, gunfire usually isn't quick enough. Some segments of opinion see the solution as having a weapon with enough "stopping power."[19] This doesn't take into account the lag between firing a shot into a human body and seeing the effect. The desired effect is instant incapacitation, but it usually doesn't happen that way. There are many documented instances of people sustaining fatal wounds from large weapons, even shotguns, and living long enough to return fire or turn and flee. Every bodyguard should understand the concept of the "dead man's five seconds."

This point is so crucial that it's worth a more detailed discussion. The only way of getting an assured "stop" is to fire a shot into the brain or spine. To be sure of a hit while the people involved are moving, it's necessary to place the weapon up against the attacker's skin. If the bodyguard is that close, he can deflect the attacker's weapon. He'll also get there faster if he doesn't stop to draw his own weapon.

It may be necessary to conduct an exercise to convince all members of the team that drawing weapons can be slower than swarming. One way to do this is to set up a tackling dummy, and measure the time needed by each member of the team to tackle the dummy from various ranges. Then measure the time needed for each to draw, fire his weapon and score a hit. It will be immediately apparent that for each person there's a range at which it's equally quick to open fire or to rush the target. Beyond this, gunfire is faster. Closer, the choice is swarming.

A good example from recent events is the attack by John Hinckley on the Reagan presidential party in 1981, and the response from the Secret Service agents on the scene. The agent closest to Hinckley had his vision blocked by the crowd, but started for him when he heard the shots. He dived at Hinckley and drove him to the ground.[20] Other officers immediately piled on top. Hinckley was subdued and captured by weight of bodies, not martial arts skill.

Secret Service agents assigned to George Wallace also did not open fire when Arthur Bremer fired. Instead, they swarmed at him, overpowering him by weight. It's critical to note that in both the Reagan and Wallace shootings the attackers had emptied their revolvers before the first agent reached them, although one agent was able to deflect Bremer's aim as he fired his last shots.

Some close-in problems are less dramatic, but require skill in handling. A common one is the hand-shaker who doesn't want to let go. The bodyguard must intervene, but not start a fight by punching the hand-shaker out. One low-profile way of handling this is the thumb peel-away:

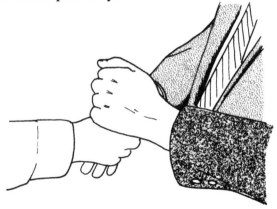

This is how the thumb peel-away looks to the crowd.

From the other side, we see how the bodyguard grasps the subject's thumb and starts to bend it back towards the wrist.

Grasping the thumb more securely, the bodyguard continues to peel it back and away from the protectee's hand. The thumb peel-away is a good way to force a person to let go without inflicting shattering pain or striking a blow. It can become painful if he resists, but hardly anyone does. This is another example of body mechanics.

Getting the client to safety is paramount. The team leader should see to this even as others neutralize the threat. He should not assume that a lone attacker is truly alone. There might be "back-up" attackers. Another possibility is that there might be more than one attacker, but one jumped the gun and attacked prematurely. Yet another possibility is that a second attacker has been delayed because of the crowd's blocking his view, or because of a difficulty with his weapon.

All of these possibilities make it essential to evacuate the client as soon as possible. If the client is within a few feet of a vehicle, the team leader gets him into it and takes off.

This type of vehicle looks ungainly, but it makes an excellent back-up and headquarters vehicle for a bodyguard team. It can be parked outside a home or office. It can follow in a procession. It can creep along close to the curb to follow a party on foot. It can contain an array of weapons and special equipment that might be needed by the team. It serves as a mobile rest area, and even contains a toilet, which is very important when bodyguards must spend long hours on duty. The cooking facilities can provide meals, and the vehicle can carry armor for extra security in case it becomes necessary to bring the client inside for his safety. Finally, such a vehicle makes an excellent roadblock in case it becomes necessary to stop pursuers.

If the protective team is large enough, a stay-behind party impedes pursuit. The minimal size for a protective team to make this tactic effective is hard to judge. At the barest minimum, it takes only one guard to try to impede an attacker while his client flees as best he can. With two guards, one goes with the client and one stays behind. With a larger team, the deputy team leader takes charge of the stay-behind party, which might be only one guard. Often, simply using gunfire can stop a pursuit cold for long enough to allow the principal to escape. In other instances, a vehicle can block the road. On foot, locking a door can create a significant barrier.

Special Problems and Techniques

From the foregoing discussion, it's obvious that unarmed combat skills are very low on the list of priorities. This is true despite the views of "experts" who teach such skills. We must take into account the pecuniary interest of those who teach, and what they stand to gain from acceptance of their viewpoint.

Physical combat with an assailant is possible, and its most likely form is a struggle for control of a weapon. Unlike the lessons in "disarming" taught in karate schools, this won't go according to plan because the attacker will never be standing directly in front or behind the bodyguard. The method will be to grab the weapon or the hand, whichever the bodyguard can grab, and redirect the weapon. As we've seen, only the simplest methods will work under stress. With all that, developing a martial art skill is useful for general physical conditioning. A bodyguard may find it interesting to work on a job-related skill for enjoyment.

Airline travel can be a special problem. Terrorist attacks on airlines and their facilities have been sensationalized, but they represent a real problem. Let's lay out a few obvious facts about airlines and security in air travel:

- The majority of the world's airlines are safer than the downtown streets of many major American cities.
- Only a few airlines are victims of terrorist attacks. The most obvious one is the Israeli airline, El Al, for reasons that have to do with the Israeli government's difficulties with its neighbors. As a coping measure during the Gulf War, several airlines suspended service to Israel. These included Alitalia, Pan Am, Polish LOT, SAS, South African Airways and Cyprus Airways.[21]
- American flag carriers are safer than most. Between 1983 and 1992, 3 U.S. flag airliners had bombs explode aboard them, and one was the Boeing that went down over Lockerbie, Scotland. 14 bombs exploded aboard other countries' airliners during the same period. Of 185 airliners skyjacked between 1984 and 1992, only 23 were American. 162 were foreign airliners.[22]
- It's impossible to prevent terrorist attacks absolutely. While a system of pre-flight screening of passengers and baggage can prevent attacks in

flight, the response of the terrorists has been to attack ground facilities. We still read of an El Al ticket office being blown up, or a shooting of passengers at the boarding area.

• There have been many millions of dollars spent around the world on "security." Airlines have offered reward money, as has the U.S. Government, for information regarding terrorists.[23] This has not prevented terrorist attacks.

From this, we can draw certain clear conclusions. The most obvious one is to avoid the problem areas. Even buying a ticket in a downtown office can be dangerous if someone is intent upon attacking a certain airline by parking a car bomb outside.

It's a mistake to think that you or your client will remain uninvolved. Terrorists don't ask for passports before opening fire or setting off a bomb. Bullets don't have anybody's name on them. They're marked: *To whom it may concern.*

The safest bet is to use the airlines of countries that are not attracting terrorist attention at the moment. It's easy to see, by reading newspaper headlines, which countries are involved in controversies with parties that attack airliners and airline facilities.

It's also safer not to linger around an airport. Attacks can and do occur at boarding gates and ticket lines, and staying away from them until the last possible moment is a sensible precaution. Some relatively safe areas in airports are the restaurants, as they haven't usually been attacked. "VIP" lounges are also relatively safe.

There are also certain airports which are notoriously insecure. This may be because officials don't screen passengers diligently enough, leading to the smuggling of weapons on board aircraft. It can also be because these airports are convenient targets for terrorists. A few of the airports that have been involved in recent incidents are the ones in Rome, Athens and Vienna. Whatever the reasons, incidents happen at those airports.

A special problem that can occur if you and your client are traveling incognito, is encountering the special "risk analysis system" now in force at certain airports and with certain airlines. American carriers operating from high-risk countries are mandated to use this system, according to FAA regulations. This is a high-security system, adapted from that used by El Al, of keeping a close watch over all luggage, catering, cargo and passengers.[24]

While normally passengers do not have to show proof of identity to buy an airline ticket or board an airliner, the high-risk system can be a hindrance to anyone traveling under an assumed name, and you and your client should be aware of this. The system involves individual interviews with each passenger, and checking of tickets, passports, baggage tags and other documents. Carry-on luggage gets special attention, including physical search and x-raying while empty.

The close questioning involves details police officers normally pursue when checking identities, such as asking the passenger his address, name of employer, date of birth and other personal details that the officer can check with I.D. documents. The interviewer may also ask the passenger his ultimate destination, names of people or companies he plans to visit, hotel reservations, details of railway tickets or rental car reservations and names of others in his party.

Questioning is also designed to put psychological pressure on someone already under tension because of the risk involved in a skyjacking. Passengers who appear to become more nervous or anxious during questioning will find themselves subject to even closer examination.

This type of questioning makes it essential to either make arrangements in advance with the airline, or to be able to answer all questions without hesitation or any appearance of uncertainty. Bodyguards should also be aware that the system involves physical search, including a pat down inside a booth, and even partial or total disrobing. This precludes carrying weapons of any sort through the checkpoint, because even a fingernail file or scissors will receive scrutiny.

As a practical matter, such passenger checks are directed mainly towards those who fit a certain profile developed through experience. The passenger who arouses the most suspicion and attention is the young and physically fit male traveling alone, on a one-way ticket, and who appears to be a member of an ethnic group noted for terrorism. This doesn't totally exclude women, as Leila Khaled made a name for herself during a noted skyjacking incident during the 1970s, and Kim Hyon Hui planted a bomb on Korean Flight 858. However, it serves to concentrate attention on those passengers who appear most likely to be threats. By contrast, the middle-aged fat lady will receive only cursory inspection.

Enhanced security precautions in force at some airports are often useless. The reason is that airports are divided into "secure" and "insecure" areas, and the secure area is the section containing the gates. Once a passenger passes through security checks dividing the two areas, and embarks upon a flight, when he arrives at his destination he'll disembark into the "secure" airside. When he changes planes to continue to his destination, there will be no more security checks to hurdle. Terrorists know this, which is why they book flights originating at airports where security is lax, and change to the target flight at the airport with tight security, which they have already bypassed.

Another type of public conveyance vulnerable to terrorism is the cruise ship. The Achille Lauro was attacked in October, 1985, and in July, 1988, three terrorists opened fire on board the City of Poros, killing nine passengers.[25]

Both of these incidents took place in the Mediterranean, noted for the politically unstable countries that dot its coastline. If your client likes cruises, at least avoid those originating in, or passing through the Mediterranean.

The threats are many, and the array of techniques for protecting your client are equally varied. Keep your eyes, ears, and mind open, and you will keep ahead of the situation.

Notes:

1. *Sourcebook of Criminal Justice Statistics*, Washington, DC, U.S. Department of Justice, 1992, p. 71.
2. *You're The Target*, Shackley, Theodore G., Oatman, Robert L., and Finney, Richard A., New World Publishing, Ltd., 1989, pp. 49-50.
3. *Ibid.*, p. 56.
4. *Ibid.*, p. 54.
5. *Executive Protection Manual*, Reber, Jan, and Shaw, Paul, Schiller Park, IL, MTI Teleprograms, 1976, pp. 137-177.
6. *Ibid.*, pp. 148-149.
7. Butler, Charles W., and Schultz, Norman O., "Devising an Intelligence Collection Plan," *Security Management*, March, 1993, pp. 66-68.
8. Chanaud, Robert C., "Keeping Conversations Confidential," *Security Management*, March, 1993, p. 43.
9. *Ibid.*, pp. 43-48.
10. *Providing Protective Services, A Practical Guide For Police*, James A. King, San Diego, CA, EPS International, 1990, p. 151.
11. *Privacy For Sale*, Jeffrey Rothfeder, NY, Simon & Schuster, 1992, pp. 63-88.
12. *Ibid.*, pp. 13-15.
13. Flores, Thomas V., and Nudell, Mayer, "Executive, Protect Thyself," *Security Management*, January, 1993, p. 40.
14. *The Executive Protection Bible*, Martha J. Braunig, Basalt, CO, Executive Protection International, 1992, p. 238.
15. Wilson, Carolyn, "Securing America's New Town Centers," *Security Management*, June, 1992, pp. 41-43.
16. Associated Press, Sept. 23, 1992.
17. *Providing Protective Services, A Practical Guide For Police*, James A. King, San Diego, CA, EPS International, 1990. p. 16.
18. *You're The Target*, Shackley, Theodore G., Oatman, Robert L., and Finney, Richard A., New World Publishing, Ltd., 1989, p. 79.
19. *On Assassination*, Cooper, H.H.A., Boulder, CO, Paladin Press, 1984, p. 121, note 8.
20. *Protecting the President*, McCarthy, Dennis V.N., NY, William Morrow & Company, 1985, pp. 56-57.
21. Richardson, Alan, 6th. "Airline Cuts Flights to Israel," *USA Today*, January 8, 1991, News p. 4.
22. Hubbard, Don L., "Who's Really At Risk?," *Security Management*, vol. 38, no. 3, March, 1994, p. 40.
23. Sharn, Lori, "Airlines Set to Offer $1M For Terrorists," *USA Today*, April 2, 1990, News p. 3A.
24. Boynton, Homer A., "An Eye on Airline Security Technology," *Security Management*, June 1992, p. 22A.
25. Robbins, Clyde E., "Making Security a Port of Call," *Security Management*, June, 1992, p. 14A.

17

The Automobile

Automobile travel is inherently dangerous, and especially so if someone's trying to kill you. It's also dangerous if nobody's trying to kill you, but we'll deal only with the extraordinary dangers here. You're vulnerable to various methods of assassination. President Kennedy was killed by rifle fire while traveling in a car. Another recent example is the killing of Admiral Carerro Blanco in Spain, by assassins who used a "stand-off bomb," an explosive charge buried in the road, which was set off by remote control. Dictator Rafael Trujillo was killed in his car by assassins using submachine gun fire. There are other dangers: Aldo Moro and Hans-Martin Schleyer were kidnapped out of their cars.

We're going to deal with this problem by dividing it up into two aspects: the hardware and the tactics. First, we'll look at the hardware, which consists of the vehicle itself and the modifications possible to enhance its protection. The next chapter will deal with the ambush, both theory and practice. The ambush is the basic tactic in vehicular attacks, and there are ways to counter it, even without a specially protected vehicle.

High-profile vs. Low-profile

There are basically two ways to travel by road: high-profile and low-profile. The motorcade is high-profile and used mainly by politicians. With the publicity usually accompanying a motorcade, protective agents have their hands full. They have to employ massive protective measures to counter possible threats. Typically, they deploy hundreds or thousands of local police, and borrow agents from other offices to make up the numbers required. The motorcade is usually a clumsy procession of vehicles, all in close touch by radio, and the protectee is surrounded by agents on foot, on the running boards, as well as by

motorcycle officers. Anyone who has seen a presidential parade knows what's involved.

This stretched limo is a typical high-profile vehicle, and stands out prominently on any street in the country.

The low-profile vehicle is much more desirable because it avoids the danger of presenting a conspicuous target. A low-profile car blends in with other cars. Typically, it's a common model of a common make in the area. In the United States, a Ford or Chevrolet sedan is a good choice. In some areas, Chevy vans and "four-wheelers" are common. Certain imports are also common enough to pass with little notice, especially on the East and West Coasts. A Toyota or Nissan is common enough. Either way, there are some precautions to take, even without fitting special equipment.

One precaution is to be sure that the car is always in good shape. Keeping it well maintained, and the gas tank always at least half full, are wise precautions.

Another precaution is a "stash car," a totally different vehicle to serve as a spare if the protectee's vehicle becomes disabled, or if it appears desirable to change vehicles. The stash car is kept out of sight, but close enough to be available quickly as a getaway vehicle.[1]

On a higher level, with a suitable budget, a few modifications are advisable. Note that vehicle armor isn't the most cost effective precaution. Historically, armor did not protect many of the high-profile protectees from being killed. President Kennedy was shot to death despite his car's armored body. In other attacks, the aggressors used guns or explosives powerful enough to penetrate the armor.

The main problem with modifications is that they all add weight. A full bore modification job, following the recommendations of those who modify automobiles for executive protection, can add several thousand pounds to the car and cost tens of thousands of dollars or more. We'll cover some of the options available.

Resistance to Projectiles

Armoring the car provides some protection against bullets from hand weapons. Traditionally, automobile armor was steel plate. Steel plate is still the best way to provide protection against very heavy gunfire, but there are lighter materials that give good protection without the extreme weight penalty.

Steel armor is sometimes used in cars. Ballistic plate known as "T-1," for example, will give protection against any handgun in its ¼" thickness. A panel of ½" T-1 will stop .30-caliber rifle bullets. Jessop Steel Co. manufactures "Dual-hard" plate, which will, in its ¼" thickness, stop .30-caliber military ball ammo, but not "armor-piercing."

Fiberglass is another choice. Because its structure is fibrous, and not crystalline, as with steel, Fiberglass does not "spall" when hit by a projectile. "Spalling" is when a piece of the armor's backface is thrown off by the force of impact, creating a secondary missile that can cause injuries.

Another material for synthetic armor is Lumagard™ Fiberglass Structural Armor, made by American Acrylic Corp. This glass fiber reinforced structural polyester is made in various thicknesses according to the amount of ballistic protection needed. Type I armor, providing Level I protection, is $^3/_{16}$" thick, and other thicknesses range up to 1¼", which provides Level IV protection against .30-06 rifle fire. This material comes in 4' x 8' sheets, and can be cut and drilled for application inside vehicles and fixed structures.

Soft armor is useful for protecting most of the area of a car. This can be ballistic nylon or relatively lightweight Kevlar armor, which is the same material used in soft body armor. It's relatively easy to remove

body panels to install Kevlar armor. It's also simple to line the floorboard with it, under the carpet. Armoring the windows is another matter. This requires special glass, some of which is up to three inches thick. Even the thinnest armor glass requires reworking the window lift mechanisms and widening the window slots to accommodate the extra thickness if the windows are designed to be still operable. If the car is air-conditioned, the windows will be permanently shut, which is simpler and less costly. As a practical matter, armored windows aren't any use if left open.

The choice of material's worth discussing. The best material is a laminate of glass and polycarbonate (Lexan). The glass outer shell breaks up the bullet, or at least flattens its nose, and the inner layer of polycarbonate has the elasticity to stop the projectile from penetrating totally. Outside layers should be glass, to avoid scratching.

ARMORED UTILITY VEHICLE

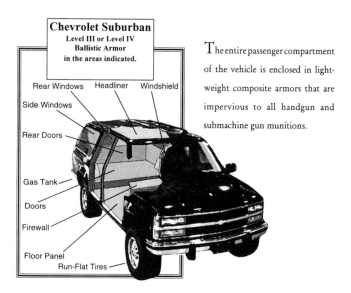

Chevrolet Suburban
Level III or Level IV
Ballistic Armor
in the areas indicated.

Rear Windows Headliner Windshield
Side Windows
Rear Doors
Gas Tank
Doors
Firewall
Floor Panel
Run-Flat Tires

The entire passenger compartment of the vehicle is enclosed in lightweight composite armors that are impervious to all handgun and submachine gun munitions.

This Chevrolet Suburban, by Safe Car, Inc., incorporates many armored panels and safety features. Contoured armor panels maintain the low profile of the vehicle. This attention to detail keeps it from looking like a tank.

Safe Car, Inc. makes a glass-polycarbonate laminate, bonded under heat and pressure, to avoid the problem of the inner surface spalling. Thus we see that bullet-resistant window glass consists of a sandwich of hardened glass and Lexan layers. The glass breaks up the bullet, and the Lexan plastic is resilient enough to "give" and hold the sandwich together. This is the plan. It doesn't always work out.

One possible problem is that installing the window armor is too expensive, or is impractical for another reason. The doors may be too thin. This then dictates tactics, making it necessary to duck below window level when under attack. Another problem is that bullet-resistant windows may still fail for other reasons. The bullet that killed Leaman Hunt in February, 1984, slipped through a rubber window grommet.[2]

Even with the windows armored, the resistance of the glass may be less than the protection afforded by the opaque armor installed in the body panels and the floorboards. Augusto Pinochet's armored car had its windows shot out during an ambush, and only the protection offered by the door and body armor saved him from death. If the attackers use weapons that will penetrate the windows, ducking is still the best choice for protection. In any event, the bodyguard should always urge his client to get down on the floor when an attack develops, while taking the necessary chances of exposure to defend the car.

An easy to overlook point is a radiator shield. While the occupants may be safe from gunfire, a puncture in the radiator can stop a car quickly. Another possible weakness is the gas line, which often runs unprotected under the chassis where rocks and bullet fragments can pierce it. This will bring your car to a quick halt and ruin your day.[3]

Protection is relative. No matter how thick the armor, there's a weapon that can defeat it. A car armored to resist handgun bullets can still be penetrated by rifle fire. Armor designed to defeat rifle bullets will almost melt when hit by a rocket launcher. It's safe to assume that a well organized and competent terrorist group will have estimated the protection level and planned to use weapons that can overcome it.

What use, then, is an armored car? There are two uses. One is protection against the casual or poorly-equipped assassin who doesn't have a weapon that defeats the armor. The other is to buy valuable seconds by offering temporary protection while the driver gets his client out of the danger zone.

Let's review the most important point to understand about armor: It's not bullet-proof, only bullet-resistant. Thicker armor will protect against more powerful weapons, but it's heavier and more expensive. Every armoring job done on a vehicle is a compromise between degree of protection, weight and cost.

On-board Electronics

The security specialist may see a need for a radio on a commercial frequency to communicate with corporate headquarters or a command post. A transmitter on the police band may be legal in some areas, and if the VIP has official status, it's certainly acceptable for his vehicle to be so equipped. For less affluent protectees, a cellular phone is adequate in the United States, because of the universality of the "911" number.

For extra security, a vehicle locator system manufactured by Auto-Trac uses the Global Positioning System (GPS). It monitors vehicle location, and controls alarms and panic buttons. A computerized map display in the central security monitoring office provides constant up-to-date vehicle location for the security officer.

A Smooth Belly-pan

This helps slightly with aerodynamic efficiency, but the main value is to reduce the chances of tampering. Covering all of the cavities under a car body with a smooth panel riveted in place eliminates the opportunity to do a quick job of placing an explosive device. It also makes it easier to spot evidence of tampering.

Window Curtains

These add very little weight, but make it much harder for a gunman to detect and aim at a particular individual inside the car. They're worth having even if the window glass is bullet-resistant, because they provide an edge over the attacker. Remember, the attacker may have a weapon that will penetrate even bullet-resistant glass.

Tinted windows are another choice, but are less advisable because, unlike curtains, the tint cannot be drawn back or removed if not needed. A tinted windshield, even where legal, can be a driving hazard at night.

Reinforced Bumpers for Ramming

Sometimes ramming a roadblock is the best way to escape from an ambush. Having a rigid bumper that won't crumple allows the driver to ram without fear of damaging his radiator or buckling his fenders into the tires. It doesn't do much good to ram if the vehicle becomes disabled while so doing.

A point to note about ramming is that vehicle weight is very important. The momentum (mass times velocity) must be enough to knock the blocking vehicle out of the way for this tactic to succeed. This is a strong argument for using a large and heavy car.

"Run-flat" Tires

There's no such thing as a "bullet-proof" tire, any more than there is a "bullet-proof" vest, despite the efforts of some fiction writers. But, there are tires designed to be partly usable after being punctured by gunfire. These vary in construction. Some have inner cells that retain some air if the outer casing is pierced. Others have a heavy rubber lip that prevents the tire from collapsing completely if the air pressure drops. Yet others have a heavy goo inside that immediately seals a hole, if all works well. The theory is to enable the car to continue with its tires shot out.

Another approach is the wheel tire well insert, which fills the central wheel well and prevents the tire bead from dropping into the well when pressure drops. Without the insert, the tire bead can drop into the well, and the tire can come off the rim. The insert does not, however, maintain any pressure in the tire, and driving on the flat tire will destroy it. That's the least of the problems, though. Loss of control is more serious, because it's no longer possible to execute maneuvers such as the J-turn quickly with a flat tire.

One variety, the "run-flat" system made by Rodguard Corporation, takes this a step further. A solid skeleton wheel (the "runner") rides inside the tire on a runner, and prevents total collapse of the tire if pierced or shredded. The skeleton wheel keeps some rigidity in the tire for emergency maneuvering.

That's the theory. In practice, there have been several instances of cars driven long distances with ordinary tires shot out. It's more a matter of driving skill and willingness to accept great discomfort and loss of maneuverability from riding on the rims.

Special tires are much more expensive than ordinary ones, about $2,000 per set.[4]

Tear Gas Dispenser Nozzles

These are for dispersing a rioting crowd or more determined attackers who are not protected against gas. The prospect of this happening is small, but if it does, tear gas can be a life saver. When Vice-President Nixon's limousine was trapped in Caracas, Venezuela, by a hostile mob, such devices would have been useful.[5]

Allied with this is a sealed car body and an air conditioning system to prevent the occupants from being affected by the gas. Part of the system would have to be a tank of oxygen to replenish that consumed by the occupants. Such a system would also protect against an attack with lethal gas. It hasn't yet happened that a car's been ambushed with a gas attack, but there's always a first time.

Oil Dispenser

This consists of a tank and nozzle for depositing an oil slick on the road behind the car to make the surface slippery. The oil slick, an old moonshiner's trick, is for impeding pursuit. This is one of the few defensive systems that can be jury rigged.

An alternative to this is a container of caltrops that spills its devices out onto the road at the touch of a switch. The main problem here is carrying enough of them to create a dense pattern sure to catch a pursuer's tires.

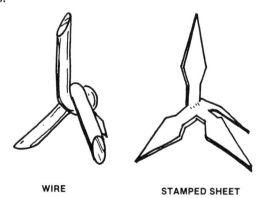

WIRE   **STAMPED SHEET**

Caltrops can be fabricated from wire or stamped, hardened steel. Either will puncture a tire and release the air, although the tire doesn't go flat instantly.

Gun Ports

These are gaps in the armor, just large enough to permit firing at attackers. These are utterly invisible from the outside because the sheet metal covers them. However, using them can be a problem. Firing guns inside the vehicle can be noisy, and attaining accuracy without aiming is difficult.

Heavy-duty Suspension

Executive vehicle modifications can add a couple of thousand pounds to the vehicle's weight, and a beefed-up suspension becomes essential.

A More Powerful Engine

More power is necessary to compensate for the sluggishness induced by the extra weight. If performance is at all important, this is mandatory. If the vehicle will always travel as part of a procession, and never need speed and acceleration to evade attackers, this is less important.

A point worth noting is that modern cars are getting smaller, and therefore it's more difficult to add the weight of armor and other accessories. Family sedans don't take well to full-bore armoring. If the perceived need is for less than Level IV armor, it's possible to cope without adding too much to the vehicle's weight.

Another possibility is to use a different style of vehicle. A four-wheeler, such as a Blazer, Bronco or Silverado has a truck chassis, and the beef to handle the extra weight. Some choose mini-bus style vehicles, as these are also built on heavy-duty chassis types.

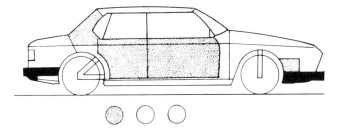

Armor panels cover most vital areas of an automobile, although weight limits coverage. A thoroughly armored vehicle may be too heavy for the performance desired.

Other modifications and equipment to consider are an armored blanket to throw over the protectee for additional shielding, a bomb blanket, a first-aid or paramedic kit, oversize rear view mirrors, Lexan shields for the headlights, a siren, fire extinguisher, and an extra spare tire.[6]

The cost of such modifications depends on the type and the company doing them, and they can be as high as $20,000 to $125,000, plus the cost of the car. With various luxury cars and accessories that some protectees demand, the total cost can exceed $200,000.[7] An economical job is available for less than $4,000, but this consists of only armoring to Level II.

Costs can vary greatly, as we've seen. Much depends on the quality of the work. At the end of this chapter is a short list of carefully selected suppliers known for quality work.

For the skilled mechanic, it's possible to install a do-it-yourself armoring job at a fairly low cost. Using commercially available Fiberglas armor giving Level III protection, it's possible to armor a family sedan for between $1,000 and $2,000. The same treatment for a van will cost between $2,000 and $4,000. This does not include windows, and when under attack it would be necessary to duck below window level for protection.

Vehicle Security

It's basic to keep the car secure to avoid tampering. Tampering can be simple or more complex. It can range from pulling out the ignition wires to immobilize the car, to planting a bug or a bomb on board.

Governments have the resources to keep their official vehicles under 24-hour guard. Private agents often don't, and have to use other means.

One is to keep the car locked up in a secure garage when not in use. The garage should have adequate intruder detection alarms. This isn't always possible, especially when traveling, and the security agent must take other precautions.

Car alarm systems set off a siren or bell in the car, or send a signal to a remote pager that the bodyguard carries with him. The simplest systems, available at neighborhood electronic outlet shops, consist of a trembler switch, often advertised as a "motion detector." This switch closes if the car is moved or rocked. This is practical only if the car will be parked in a remote area, but not if it has to be left on the street, because passers-by will bump against the car and set off the alarm.

Conventional sensors on the doors and windows are much better, but also much more costly. These can also be attached to a radio to send a signal to a pager.

Another security accessory for use if the car's been left unguarded is the remote starter. This device is akin to radio remote controls for model aircraft, and it starts the engine by radio signal. This is a precaution against a bomb wired to the ignition. Although highly touted, this device is hopelessly inadequate against real world threats. The reason is that nobody but the crassest amateur wires bombs to the ignition anymore.

A simpler and better method is to wire the detonator to the brake light. This increases the odds that the target will be in the car when the bomb detonates. Yet another method is to have the detonator wired to a tilt switch precariously balanced on a frame member. When the car moves, the switch tips over or falls off, closing the circuit. Yet another way is a more sophisticated arrangement, wiring it to the odometer. This will have the bomb going off after a certain distance, and is useful for sabotaging a car that is stored at a remote location. With this system, the chauffeur comes to pick the car up, but the bomb doesn't go off until the car's covered mileage enough to take it to where he's picking up the protectee.

A radio-controlled bomb enables the assassin to verify that the target's actually in the car before detonation. It only requires that the person with the push button be within sight of the car at some point along the route.

Because of the sophisticated ways of wiring a bomb, the only fairly-safe method is to search any car left unattended. There's a professional short cut to reduce the time required, or even to eliminate some searches. The bodyguard should carry a can of talc or powdered chalk in the car. After everyone's out of the car, and it's parked where he'll leave it for some time, he sprinkles a light deposit of powder on the door handles and around the car. The key is a light sprinkling, unnoticed by an attacker who leaves his footprints in the powder. This won't work on all surfaces, and it's useless if there's a lot of foot traffic around the car, as on a busy street. Otherwise, it'll disclose if anyone's approached the car. More importantly, it'll show where the approach was, and cut drastically the time needed for a search.

A thorough car search takes many hours, but developing some skill will cut the time somewhat. More important is familiarity with the car. The bodyguard or chauffeur must know the car thoroughly, so that he can tell at a glance when opening the hood if anything's out of place or whether there are wires that shouldn't be there. Familiarity with the car will also tell him whether the car's had a new ignition coil installed recently, as the bright new one may be a disguised bomb. What better way of concealing a bomb than disguising it as an engine component normally wired to the ignition?

A bomb could be placed almost anywhere within the engine compartment. One key to searching is to look for wires that don't belong.

In searching a car for explosives, a good precaution is to lock it before leaving it. This not only makes it more difficult for an enemy to gain access, but he may leave signs of forced entry if he's hurried or unskilled. Scanning the surface of the car for fingerprints and grease spots may reveal evidence that someone's been at it recently. Using a dog, or electronic sniffer may help to detect explosives, but private bodyguards normally don't take specially-trained dogs with them wherever they go. An obvious and unfortunate fact is that assassins are becoming ever more sophisticated, and some of them are aware that wrapping explosives in plastic can make detection much harder by sealing in the characteristic odors. There's also the definite prospect that a dog may not have been trained to detect a particular explosive.[8]

After the preliminary examination, it will be necessary to risk getting dirty by going under the car. A quick look with a flashlight and inspection mirror will do for the first stage, but there are places under the car that can't be seen or reached from anywhere but underneath, and this requires crawling under the car.

An inspection mirror and a small flashlight are very helpful for inspecting hard-to-reach spots. An excellent flashlight for this is the Streamlight Junior, because it's rugged and reliable, and the price includes a couple of Mallory Duracell batteries. Available from Streamlight, Inc. 1030 West Germantown Pike, Norristown, PA 19403. Phone: (800) 532-7488.

You sometimes have to get down there and get dirty. Only getting underneath and eyeballing it yourself will assure you that there isn't a bomb under the car, or that someone hasn't cut a brake line.

Some of the signs of tampering are dirt or grease, clean spots in normally dirty areas, scuff marks, bright metal, fresh paint or undercoat or the odor of either one, and extra wires or objects. Total familiarity with the normal appearance of every part of the car is very helpful when seeking out unusual objects.

The underside of a car is more complicated than it appears at first sight, and it's important to look very

carefully. The clever bomber knows all of the professional "tricks," such as smearing road dirt on his handiwork to blend it in. He also knows the barely-accessible locations that challenge a searcher's patience. The days of a bundle of dynamite sticks held together with tape are over. Bombers can fashion plastic explosives into unusual shapes to fit in small nooks and crannies. One favorite place is on top of the gasoline tank, between it and the car body.[9] There's barely room to slide the fingers into this space, and it's up and out of sight. Only a flashlight and inspection mirror will do to make sure this space is clear.

The detonators can be wired to a variety of fuses. Some are heat-sensitive, and are placed next to, or inside the exhaust pipe. Others are mechanical, and have a wire attached to a wheel or an axle. Some respond to pressure. All must lead to the explosive charge, and this usually means wires.

Inspecting the interior is also essential, because the bodyguard has to consider the possibility of an electronic listening device, or "bug." Checking the glove compartment and door pockets is only the first step. He must also check out all the seats because of the possibility of a pressure switch. Checking all of the controls is another step, and he should pay special attention to all radios and other electronic equipment because these are perfect places to conceal a bug.

Check out the inside as carefully as you checked under the hood and the body. What are those papers on the floor? Were they there when you left the car? What's in that thick envelope? If you have any reason to think someone's been at the car, it's better to get another vehicle, because checking this one out thoroughly will take a long time.

An absolutely thorough search, covering all possibilities, can take hours. A quick but good search takes about 15 minutes.[10] This is because it's necessary to take some risks when searching. There's always a very slight possibility that a door has been gimmicked to set the bomb off when opened. Checking for this thoroughly, taking no chances, is often impractical, and the bodyguard simply has to trust to luck. This seems terribly unprofessional but it's true most of the time.

Sources Of Supply for Material Discussed in this Chapter:

American Acrylic
400 Sheffield Avenue
West Babylon, NY 11704
Phone: (516) 422-2200
Fax: (516) 422-2811
Attn: Bill Schnell

American Acrylic provides light-weight synthetic armor plating for automobiles, as well as for fixed structures, in varying thicknesses, according to protection level desired.

American Body Armor
85 Nassau Place
Fernandina Beach, FL 32234
Phone: (904) 261-4035

Auto Trac
(vehicle locator system)
9330 LBJ Freeway, Suite 380
Dallas, TX 75243
Phone: (214) 480-8145
Fax: (214) 907-2292

Custom Armoring Corp.
20 Keeler Street
Pittsfield, MA 01201
Phone: (800) 499-3104
Fax: (413) 443-1572

International Logistics Sys.
234 MacLean Blvd.
Paterson, NJ 07504
Phone: (201) 881-0001
Fax: (201) 357-0077

Lenco Industries (armored vehicles)
442 Merrill Road
Box 668
Pittsfield, MA 01201
Phone: (413) 443-7359
Lennie Light, President

Protection Development International
Corporation (vehicle armor)
P.O. Box 2048
Corona, CA 91718-2048
Phone: (909) 734-7531 or 734-5920
Fax: (909) 734-7570
Attn: Norman E. Smith, President

This company provides vehicle armor for a variety of applications, including limousines, sedans, vans and trucks. Light-weight armor is applicable to helicopters as well. This company also can provide extra features, such as gunports, air/life support systems, siren, run-flat tires, gun racks, ram bumpers, armored radiator, remote start, reserve fuel tank, and oil slick and gas dispensers.

Rodguard Corp.
1355 Clinton Street
Buffalo, NY 14206
Phone: (716) 823-1411
Fax: (716) 823-1607
Attn: Richard Hauck, Vice-Pres.

Safe Car, Inc.
3015 N. Bryant Blvd.
San Angelo, TX 76903
Phone: (915) 657-8182
Fax: (915) 658-4380
Attn: Matthew Cardon, Marketing

Silent Partner Body Armor
612 Third Street
Gretna, LA 70053
Attn: Tim Zufle
Phone: (800) 321-5741
Fax: (504) 364-8906

Tetradyne Corp. (armored vehicles, incl. vans)
1681 South Broadway
Carrolton, TX 75006
Reg Anderson, President
Billy Brown, General Manager

Notes:

1. *The Executive Protection Bible*, Martha J. Braunig, Basalt, CO, Executive Protection International, 1992, p. 82.

2. *You're The Target*, Shackley, Theodore G., Oatman, Robert L., and Finney, Richard A., New World Publishing, Ltd., 1989, p. 107.
3. *The Executive Protection Bible*, Martha J. Braunig, Basalt, CO, Executive Protection International, 1992, p. 166.
4. *Terrorism and Personal Protection*, Brian Jenkins, editor, NY, Butterworth Publishers, 1985, p. 151.
5. *Secret Service Chief*, U.E. Baughman and Leonard Wallace Robinson, NY, Popular Library, 1963, pp. 178-180.
6. *Executive Protection Manual*, Jan Reber and Paul Shaw, Schiller Park Illinois, MTI Teleprograms, 1976, pp. 108-109.
7. *Terrorism and Personal Protection*, Brian Jenkins, editor, NY, Butterworth Publishers, 1985, p. 151.
8. *Dead Clients Don't Pay*, Leroy Thompson, Boulder, CO, Paladin Press, 1984, p. 61.
9. *The Specialist*, Gayle Rivers, NY, Charter Books, 1986, pp. 171-173. Other accounts of car bombings are in earlier pages, from p. 143 on.
10. Several years ago, the author watched U.S. Secret Service agents check out a car slated to carry a former president. It took two agents, working in tandem, only 15 minutes to go over the car thoroughly.

18
Countering Ambushes

The ambush is the basic tactic of attack when your protectee is on the move. What makes it difficult is the great variety of techniques and tactics open to the ambusher. To prepare to defend yourself and your client against an ambush, you must first understand the basics of the ambush. Let's take you through what an ambush really is, to understand how the ambush plan often breaks down. Getting through the gaps in the ambush is the key to coming out alive, as we shall see.

Ambush Theory

The prerequisite to an ambush is information about the intended victim. The ambusher must know who is coming down the road, approximately when, and what protection there will be. This provides the basic framework upon which to plan an ambush. There are three basic elements to the ambush:

The Stopper

This is a way to stop the victim to make him a still target and prevent him from escaping. It can be a log in the road, a vehicle or a ruse. If the purpose is kidnapping, a person dressed as a street worker can wave the car down. In a narrow street, a car in front can stop, preventing further progress. Tire slashing devices such as spikes or caltrops will damage the target vehicle's tires. From this we see that there's a great variety of ways to make the victim stop.

For best results, the victim should be taken by surprise. The stopper can be a roadblock located around a bend in the road. Another way is to have a vehicle parked at the curb or in an alley suddenly pull out into the street to block it.

The stopper can take several forms, some using deception. A pedestrian, apparently drunk, stumbling into the middle of the street forces the driver to stop. A

woman wheeling a baby carriage, as happened in the Schleyer kidnapping reviewed below, is another trick. Attackers can dress up as soldiers or policemen and set up a "roadblock" to stop the target car. This has happened in several instances, allowing a kidnapping without the use of weapons.

The importance of the stopper is hard to overstate. As we'll see, there have been successful actions without using one, but they depend heavily on marksmanship, firepower and luck. An attack by gunfire alone is most successful when the target is moving slowly. A protectee's vehicle will often travel at high speed when possible, because this gives an additional degree of protection.

Motorcycle attacks, with a gunman on the rear seat, often take place in crowded traffic where the target can't maneuver and evade the gunman. During one attack, a red light served as the stopper. After a broadcast in Bogotá, Colombia, producer Jorge Pulido and announcer Ximena Godoy left the government owned Inravision Studio. Two blocks from the studio, Pulido stopped his unarmored Renault sedan at a stoplight. A waiting gunman got off a red Suzuki motorcycle and blasted the car with a 9mm Ingram submachine gun. Pulido took bullets in the throat and shoulder, while Ms. Godoy was wounded in the leg. The gunman mounted the motorcycle, and made his escape with an accomplice.[1]

The Killing Zone

This is where the main action takes place. The ambushers presumably have heavy enough weapons to accomplish their task. An important feature of the killing zone is that there be no cover available for the victim, and enough cover for the ambushers. Another is that the victim's vehicle must be traveling slowly enough to make a good target.

When Charles de Gaulle was president of France, his bodyguards often drove him at high speed with minimal escort. This saved him in the Petit-Clamart incident, where the plan was to hose his car down with gunfire as he passed by. The problem for the ambushers arose when de Gaulle's car arrived somewhat later than originally foreseen, which had two effects. The daylight was fading fast, and the traffic was lighter than during the rush hour, permitting higher speed through the killing zone. In another incident, the attackers used a lay off bomb planted alongside the road leading to his country home. The speed of de Gaulle's car, and the partial failure of the bomb to ignite, aborted the effort.

If their purpose is kidnapping, not killing, they have means of extracting their victim from the car and overpowering his bodyguards. This can be tricky, because disposing of the bodyguards without producing a dead victim is hard to manage when armed bodyguards are in the same car as the victim. Still, kidnappers of both Aldo Moro and Hans-Martin Schleyer succeeded despite a retinue of bodyguards.

The Plug

This is a block behind the victim, to prevent his escaping by turning around. Again, this can be a vehicle or another physical obstruction. A vehicle is usually the best way to create a plug, because the way has to be clear for the victim to pass moments before the plug comes into place.

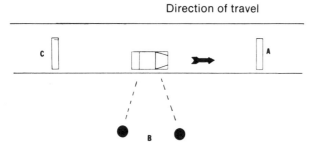

Direction of travel

The Stopper, "A," prevents the car from going any farther. The ambushers, from behind cover at "B," pour gunfire into the vehicle in the killing zone. The Plug, "C," prevents the driver of the ambushed car from escaping by a "bootlegger's turn" or other evasive maneuver.

A practical point is that the ambush is not restricted to use against motor vehicles. Pedestrians can fall victim to ambush, as can people on horseback or bicycles. An ambush doesn't necessarily take place out of doors. It can also happen inside a building.

Engineer and armaments expert Gerald Bull had just returned from abroad, and was unlocking his front door in Brussels, Belgium, when a professional assassin put two bullets in his neck with a suppressed pistol. He'd been designing a long-range super cannon for Iraq, and had previously worked for both Iran and Israel, enemies of Iraq. That, and the $25,000 left untouched in Bull's wallet, led to the suspicion that professional hit-men from one of these countries had "terminated" Bull.[2]

It's also important to note that ambushes aren't all run "by the book." Because of time, space and personnel limitations, many ambush leaders take short cuts and the ambush does not have all three elements. If there's a lot of firepower available, the plan may be an ambush by fire, with members of the ambush team depending on gunfire both to stop their target and prevent his escape.

Egypt's head anti-terrorist officer died in a gunfire ambush outside his home in April, 1994. Major General Raouf Khayrat was shot to death by Muslim extremists as he drove away from his house. He did not have bodyguards with him, making him more vulnerable to assassins who already knew where to find him.[3]

Ambush by gunfire alone doesn't always work, as we've seen. In other instances, the plan may be to deploy a stopper, and then use gunfire to prevent escape. A recent innovation is the traveling motorcycle ambush. A motorcycle with a driver and a passenger pulls up alongside the target car. The rear rider opens fire. This is the tactic used in the Buback assassination, which we'll consider later. In Bogotá, Columbia, six senators were wiped out in five days by these motorcycle attacks. In Sicily, Mafia attackers killed several law officials using motorcycles. The motorcycle attack has become the second-most popular method for attacking targets in vehicles.[4]

Terrain is very important. Locating the ambush site around a bend in the road or over the crest of a hill aids in gaining surprise. In urban locales, cover is so widely available that an ambush party can easily hide. Sometimes the terrain doesn't permit the ambush to be well executed. Surprise may not be perfect, because the ambushers are partly exposed.

Countering Ambushes

There are basically two ways to counter ambushes. The preferable one is to avoid the ambush altogether. The second is to run or fight your way out.

Avoiding an ambush requires a certain amount of vigilance. Basic to counter-ambush planning is avoiding a pattern in travel, since such a pattern can help an ambush planner immensely. As we'll see in studying specific ambushes, the targets displayed habits which helped the ambushers predict their locations at specific times. In selecting the route to travel, it's helpful to try to avoid locales that are "set-ups." The bodyguard should have scouted various routes in advance and decided upon their relative safety.

Making a personal reconnaissance is very important. One of the best-trained and best-coordinated bodyguard teams, the protective agents of the U.S. Secret Service, employs an "advance man" reporting back on the routes, so that the escorting agents can plan adequately.

The advance agent should establish driving times for the various routes necessary. This is especially important in a strange city. If it's necessary to get the client to the airport, and the driver doesn't know how long it takes to get there, the schedule will be disrupted. Another point to watch is to establish driving times at the same time of day as slated in the plan. A trip that takes a half-hour in light traffic can easily take twice as long during the rush hour. The bodyguard needs firm information to lay out his time-table.

A thorough knowledge of the geography is not enough. The guard should also know the locations of police stations and hospitals along the route, and the shortest routes to them in case of need. The bodyguard should note any overpasses and underpasses, which are potential ambush sites.

There are other features favoring ambushes which will usually exist along the route. Windows are potential sniping points. Manhole covers may hide "lay-off" bombs. Trash cans and mailboxes along the route may also conceal bombs. Unfortunately, the bodyguard can't do anything about most of these, as it's impractical to stop and search each one. Only government protective agents, by mobilizing local police, have the manpower to provide this level of security.

Commuting to and from work at the same times every day greatly increases vulnerability. Following the same route is likewise dangerous. A planner of ambushes will be stymied if the intended victim is unpredictable. An example of what can happen to someone who neglects this principle is the Aldo Moro kidnapping.[5]

The Moro Kidnapping

Aldo Moro, a former premier of Italy, was well guarded. He had five armed bodyguards who accompanied him on his rounds each day. His major error was to attend mass each morning at the same church and at the same time. This gave the ambushers an invaluable edge: they knew where he'd be at a certain time each day. Moro's car was a Fiat 130, and the back-up car was a Fiat 128. Moro's car was not armored, although this may not have been a critical factor.

Preparation was extensive. Conspirators sabotaged the telephone network in the area and lured police away from the site with fake bomb reports. They also slashed the tires of a flower vendor who normally took up station at that intersection and might have been in the way.

The kidnap group was comprised of eight men and one woman. One morning they intercepted Moro by staging an "accident." Using a stolen car, they cut off his car near an intersection, causing Moro's car to collide with it. This was the stopper. The plug was Moro's escort car right behind him, which was quickly immobilized with gunfire. Two attackers emerged from the ambush car and several more came out from behind nearby concealment. The gunfight was short and sharp. The attackers left 90 empty cartridge casings behind them on the street. Two more casings were the result of action by one of the police in the back-up car, who was able to draw his pistol and fire two shots before being gunned down. This guard wounded one attacker slightly.

In Moro's car, the driver and chief bodyguard were sitting in the front seat. This made it relatively easy to take them out without hitting Moro. Once the attackers had eliminated the bodyguards, they bundled Moro into a nearby getaway car and hustled him off to captivity.

The Buback Assassination

An abbreviated ambush occurred in the killing of West German Chief Prosecutor Siegfried Buback.[6]

This time a red traffic light served as the stopper. Two assailants on a motorbike drew up alongside Buback's car, and the passenger sprayed Buback's car with gunfire. Buback's bodyguard sat in the back of the car with him. The gunfire killed both Buback and his guard, and gave the driver a wound which was eventually mortal. In this case, varying the route would not have done much good, as the tactic used was a "traveling ambush."

The Schleyer Kidnapping

A classic ambush occurred in the kidnapping of Hans-Martin Schleyer.[7] Schleyer, a German businessman, traveled in a limousine with a driver. Three police guards followed in an unmarked car. The way the incident came down suggested very strongly that the assailants had good information about Schleyer and his entourage.

Shortly after Schleyer left his office in Cologne, a yellow Mercedes in the opposite lane swung towards his limo. A baby carriage was rolled into the street, and the driver of Schleyer's car braked sharply. The follow-up car, too close behind, rammed into the rear of Schleyer's limo. Five assailants fired on the follow-up car from the left side of the street. They were very well prepared, with two .223-caliber assault rifles, a submachine gun, and two shotguns firing slugs. They were also armed with handguns. They killed the police escort before they were able to organize any effective resistance, although one police officer got off a short burst from his submachine gun and another fired a couple of rounds from his pistol. The police bullets had no effect.

Another ambusher shot Schleyer's driver at close range, being careful not to endanger Schleyer himself, whom the attackers wanted alive. With the field cleared, the party extracted Schleyer from his car and took him away, leaving no trace for the police to follow.

The lessons to learn from all three ambushes described are that an ambush is possible almost anywhere, at any time, and often in unexpected circumstances. Protective measures have their limitations. Varying the routes and times are helpful, but limited because the protectee must start from home and end up at work. Whatever the routes may be, he starts and ends at the same two points. This gives potential attackers a "handle" on him.

The target's home is a fixed point which he leaves and to which he must return. Action Direct shot French General Rene Auban when he returned home after work, as we've seen. This group used the same plan against Georges Besse, chairman of Renault. His chauffeur had let him off about 100 yards from his front door at 8:30 P. M., and he was walking the rest of the way when two waiting ambushers shot him to death.[8]

Another important lesson relates to alertness. It's important for all members of the team to keep alert to possible dangers. Observation of the road should be divided between them.

Ideally, there should be at least two bodyguards in the car with the protectee. The driver should not be among this number, although it helps if he's had some bodyguard training. An important point is that the driver takes his orders from the bodyguard, not the protectee. The chief of the detail sits in front next to the driver and keeps an eye on the road for security. This division of functions is critical, and explains why the driver should not be the only one in the front seat. The driver's job is to drive and to watch for road hazards. The bodyguard's job is to watch for security hazards. Each looks at the road and the surroundings from a different viewpoint. It's imperative that the team be well coordinated, with plans worked out in advance so that they can cope with an emergency with little confusion or loss of time.

Another bodyguard should be in back with the protectee as the last line of defense in case of an incident. His job is to scan the sides and rear of the road to detect possible threats. He should also keep a watch for surveillance. There might be two or more vehicles involved in either surveillance or attack. Some of them may be driven by women. A vehicle driven by a woman doesn't usually attract suspicion.[9] The bodyguards should use the same system of voice signals as they would to warn of perceived threats while on foot. Radio contact with the follow-up car will also help.

If there's only one bodyguard and a driver, the bodyguard's place is up front next to the driver. This gives him maximum visibility to scan the road for hazards. If an attack develops, he'll surely draw fire, especially if he fires at an attacker. Having him up front draws fire away from the principal. The principal is more on his own in the back seat, and the bodyguard should have carefully briefed him to get down on the floor if an attack should come. There may be another problem. The protectee may cherish his privacy and not wish a bodyguard in the back seat with him. He may also have other people sharing the space, leaving no room for a bodyguard.

If the budget permits, there should be a second vehicle with at least two guards inside. This car can carry heavy weapons that might be awkward in the client's car. The client may have additional passengers, and a submachine gun on the seat, shotgun on the floorboards or rifle in a case might seem out of place.

The second car has two functions. One is support, in case the client's car is stopped and comes under attack. Because experience shows that most attacks come from the front, the second car should lead the convoy.

The second function is to impede pursuit so that the client's car can flee. The second car has to keep close to the lead car to prevent another vehicle from wedging itself between them and separating them. This is likely to happen as much by accident as by design, but it can lead to a fatal lack of support if they become separated for very long. This means that the driver of the second car has to be on his toes, in order to avoid the twin evils of rear ending the lead car and losing it. Losing the lead car can happen very quickly and easily in a city. A red light can separate them, and if the driver of the lead car is unaware, he can lose his follow-up totally.

This is where teamwork is important. The driver of the lead car must both watch the lights and keep an eye on the car behind. If there's a delay, or if a car pulls in between the two, he must slow down to give the other driver the opportunity to catch up. He must also "time" the lights, so that both cars arrive while the light is green or red.

In some high-budget protective operations, there will be a point car staffed with bodyguards. This car should travel at least half a block in front of the client's car to give ample warning of any problems along the way. In certain instances, the client's car should drop back even farther. When coming to a hill's crest or a blind corner, the client's driver should slow down enough to give the lead car time to negotiate the bend or hilltop and evaluate the road beyond. This space and time cushion should be enough to allow the driver to stop and turn around if the lead car reports danger ahead.

A follow-up car is also extra security. Having a three-car convoy is a guard against a "box-car" attack, in which one attacking car cuts off the protectee's vehicle in front while another blocks it from the rear. The lead and follow-up vehicles can forestall such an attack by aggressive ramming before the pattern is complete.

Riding with weapons exposed is sometimes permissible, because of the potential danger. Usually, public relations will dictate that weapons be kept out of sight. The protectee doesn't want to appear surrounded by thugs or "heavies." A good compromise is to keep weapons on the seat or floor of the car. This is easily permissible in cars in which only bodyguards ride.

If it's necessary to carry a carbine at the ready, be sure it's a help and not an obstruction. Carrying it between the legs like this means that you'll be obstructed leaving the car.

This scene seems fairly safe. There's little cover close to the road on the right side, and no cars parked along the curb. With no pedestrians in sight, there's little chance of a staged pedestrian "accident."

This is better. Carrying it inboard means that you can swing your legs out quickly.

In leaving the car, swing your legs out fast, then dive for the ground. You pull your carbine after you.

Observing the route ahead can be fatiguing, because it demands constant alertness. The driver and the bodyguard must scan the road for warning signs, although the responsibility for security is mainly the bodyguard's.

Familiarity with the route helps. The bodyguard can determine the normal level of activity, and be especially alert if it's "too quiet" or if there's an unusual level of activity. Watching the pedestrians for unusual or furtive movements can alert the bodyguard

to danger ahead. Pedestrians carrying large packages that may conceal weapons are worth a second look. So are pedestrians dressed too warmly for the season, because long coats can conceal weapons. Both the driver and the bodyguard must scan the road at least a block ahead for signs of a stopper. Having over a block's warning allows the driver to turn down a cross street if he sees a potential problem.

The perspectives of the driver and bodyguard on a protective assignment are different from when they're leading their normal lives. Road work that may be run-of-the-mill in normal times is always cause for caution when conveying a protectee. Even if legitimate, the slowdown makes for an easier target.

At a stop light, the driver and both bodyguards should scan the cars behind and on either side. This is a precaution against the traveling ambush.

This is potentially alarming because it's a narrow street. The person opening his car ahead may be legitimate but what will the driver do if he suddenly springs out into the center of the road?

It is also important to watch the cars parked along the side of the road. Note if they're truly parked or if there's someone inside. This could be a tip-off to an unhealthy situation. A gathering of pedestrians can be a sign of something unusual. Cover near the road can hide attackers. Sometimes they're not totally hidden and an alert bodyguard can take warning. Watching the alleys and side streets is also important.

The stop sign is cause for concern. More important is the driver's door of the car ahead.

This is a good situation. The clear road ahead allows high speed, reducing the time in any danger zone. Also, if one of the oncoming vehicles turns in to block you, it's possible to evade by steering into the oncoming lane or the broad shoulder.

It's also important to watch the front tires of cars which are parked along the road. If a tire is turned out towards the street, note if there's anyone behind the wheel, waiting to pull out. This could be a stopper or a plug, pulling out behind your car when you brake. It could also be a "crash car," to force you to stop.

As noted before, speed is protection. This is because high speed dictates more "lead" when using gunfire and also allows less time to fire. In this regard, too much attention has been given to sniper attacks against moving cars. The successful attack by Oswald against President Kennedy has two atypical features. The motorcade was traveling at about 11 miles per hour, and the president rode in an open car. Most protectees don't present such exposed and slow-moving targets. French President Charles de Gaulle survived an ambush at Petit-Clamart partly because his Citroen sedan was moving at about 70 mph. Although his attackers used automatic weapons and hit his car many times, not one shot hit the four people inside de Gaulle's car.

Observing the simple precautions can be critically important. It's vital, when escorting a client, not to stop for reasons that normally might call for a stop, such as filling the gas tank. The tank should be filled beforehand. Of course, you don't stop to help a distressed motorist and you don't pick up hitch-hikers. This is also an important procedure for the driver to follow when off-duty or when driving to pick up a protectee. Stopping can give an attacker the opportunity to damage the car, or to plant a bomb. It can also help an assassin to disable the driver and disguise an impostor as the chauffeur. This can give a dedicated aggressor the wedge he needs for an attack. Keeping the car doors locked will prevent an attacker from slipping into the car when stopped at a light.

The beginning and end of a trip are the critical points because an attacker will usually know the locations of the two points. 84% of attacks against vehicles happened within ¼ mile of home. Picking up and dropping off a client are usually the moments of maximum concern, especially in an urban area. With many people around, an assassin or kidnap team can easily blend in with the crowd and approach to a dangerously close distance. This is why it's preferable to have the client enter and leave the car in a controlled space such as a courtyard, instead of on the street. The limited access is a safety factor which makes the bodyguard's task easier. Neglecting it can have serious consequences.

On the street, there's need for extra care. The bodyguard must be on the pavement first, to scan the area. Only when he considers the street safe will he signal the client to come out of the building. Another bodyguard may accompany the client to the car. Upon arriving, the bodyguards leave the car first to scan for danger. When they judge it safe, the client leaves the car and moves quickly towards the building's entrance. The bodyguards make an effort to shield him if they're numerous enough, but at least one of them must move ahead to check out the building before the client enters.

Ambush Reactive Tactics

There are two main points to make regarding counter-ambush tactics:

1. Whatever happens, do something! It's extremely dangerous to hesitate while trying to calculate the appropriate move.
2. A competent bodyguard team will have tactics rehearsed well ahead of time, and will have established several "immediate action drills," with each member knowing his role beyond doubt and without hesitation.

By far, the most desirable reaction to an ambush is to leave the area immediately. The bodyguard seeks an opening in the ambusher's plan, and exploits it to make an escape. The stopper may be inadequate. If it's a car, there may be a gap, or the car used may be too light. In such a case, ramming forcefully can move the roadblock out of the way enough for the protectee's car to get away. In ramming, the best bet is to ram the lighter end of the blocking car. The blocking car's engine has enough mass to impede a getaway if the driver makes the mistake of ramming the car in the engine compartment. Ramming the other end causes the car to pivot around the heavy end, and helps to clear the block quickly.

It's hard to exaggerate the importance of keeping in motion, because velocity makes for an elusive target. It also keeps up momentum in case it becomes necessary to ram.

Moving straight ahead, if feasible, is the fastest way out because there's no wasted motion. This is what President de Gaulle's driver did during the Petit-Clamart ambush when the attackers were firing at the car with full-auto weapons. De Gaulle's car and its police follow-up car were doing over 70 miles per hour when the attack began, and the driver put his foot on the gas and took off. This is also what Secret Service agent William R. Greer, driver of Kennedy's car, did when Oswald opened fire. He accelerated sharply and pulled out of the procession to get the car away from the target area and to safety.[10]

The alternative is to reverse and retreat. Sometimes the ambusher forgets or neglects the plug, assuming that surprise and gunfire will immobilize the victim. An alert driver can take advantage of this to reverse direction. There are maneuvers taught for this at various driving schools, but a practical point to watch is that many city streets are too narrow to permit fancy maneuvering. Heavy traffic also makes it difficult.

When ambushers attacked Chilean President Augusto Pinochet's convoy on a rural road on September 7, 1986, they blocked the road at a curve with a car and trailer. The attackers devastated the lead car, killing five bodyguards, but the driver of the follow-up car cleared the road to allow Pinochet's driver to turn around and flee. The heavy armor in Pinochet's vehicle saved him and his grandson from serious injury, although Pinochet suffered a slight wound from flying glass.[11]

A "box-car" attack can block retreat, and is especially effective against a single car. A driver who sees such an attack developing can disable the following car by stopping suddenly and damaging the other car's engine. A sharp collision can also drive the following car's fenders into its tires, stopping it cold. This is where heavy duty "ramming" bumpers are very helpful.

A problem comes when an attack is developing. The warning signs are not always clear, and can easily be ambiguous. Gunfire or aggressive ramming can injure innocent people and lead to civil and criminal liability if actually unjustified. The moment when the bodyguard or driver decides to counter-attack can be critical. This is why one valuable tactic is overtly evasive driving to forestall or evade an attack. If the driver sees signs of an impending "box-car" for example, he can make a sudden turn at an intersection. This will throw off at least the lead element of the "box-car" team. Having radio communication between the protectee's and the follow-up car helps because the follow-up car can receive a warning of the impending sudden maneuver and be in a position to support it.

If the driver of the follow-up car sees another car attempting to follow the principal's car into the sudden turn, he can ram and disable it. If he suspects that a car behind him might be running surveillance, he can take the turn and stop suddenly, blocking the progress of the following car. If there's a lead car in the protective convoy, this car can proceed to the intersection beyond the one where the principal's car turned off, then follow on a parallel street.

The vehicle itself can be a formidable weapon. It's most effective against relatively unprotected attackers. A gunman on a motorbike is very vulnerable to a sideswipe. Ramming an attacker who is firing at the vehicle can also be effective, depending on the range and speed of the vehicle. A car moving at 30 miles per hour covers 44 feet per second. At 60, it covers 88 feet per second. It may be quicker for the driver to run an attacker down than for a bodyguard to try to unholster his weapon and take aim from a moving car.[12]

The attack can be a mobile attack, with an assailant's car trying to run the protectee's vehicle off the road. This is a situation in which vehicle weight is important. A lot of mass is hard to displace, and if the principal's vehicle is a massive limousine or van, an attacking car will have a hard time trying to run it off the road or otherwise cause a crash. The vital rule for the chauffeur is not to give in to first impulse and steer away from a vehicle sideswiping him. Turning into it will lessen the force of the impact because the other vehicle will have a shorter "run" at him.

A defense against such an attack consists of alternate braking and accelerating to prevent the attacker from either cutting in front to block or ramming the rear end to force a change of direction. The counter-attack, of course, is gunfire. This is practical because, whatever the speed of the vehicles over the road, their relative speed will be low. Firing from one vehicle to another then has a high probability of hitting.

A mobile attack can also mean that the attacker's vehicle pulls alongside while the attacking team opens fire. Response to this can be either ramming or gunfire. A narrow street, normally considered a liability, can be an asset here, because it prevents an attacker's car from pulling alongside. A tip-off to such an attack is a car with the windows open when the weather's either too hot or cold.

Standard operating procedure dictates that, at the first sign of trouble, the bodyguard sitting with the protectee pushes him down onto the floor.[13] This will be the safest place, especially if the windows aren't armored. If there's a ballistic blanket in back, the guard will throw it over the principal. The conventional tactic is for the bodyguard to shield the client with his own body, but this has its disadvantages.

A ballistic blanket is a much better alternative than having the guard shield the protectee. Lying on top of the principal takes the bodyguard out of action at a time when his firepower is most needed.

The bodyguards must face the possibility that the client's car will be either boxed in or disabled. This is the moment for "Plan B." If there's a follow-up car, it can move in to take transfer of the protectee. This may be advisable if the gunfire has subsided or if the second car is armored. In any event, someone should be on the radio to summon help.

The most dangerous outcome of an ambush is having to fight it out in the killing zone. The only redeeming feature is that there's often cover available because the ambushers can't find an ideal ambush site. Cover can be vehicles parked along the curb or nearby buildings. In some instances, the driver can create his own cover by turning into an alley if he sees no chance of getting by the stopper. This often causes a pause in the gunfire because the attackers have temporarily "lost" their target.

An important point is whether or not the protectee's vehicle is armored. An armored vehicle can serve as cover, but there are better ways to use this cover. If the gunfire is from both sides of the road, it's wisest to stay in the car if it's plain that the armor is stopping the bullets.

If the attackers have planned well, they'll have weapons more powerful than those the armor will defeat, and in such a case it may be best to scramble out to get under other cover. However, if the gunfire's coming from only one side, getting out of the car on the side away from the source of gunfire will mean that the bullets have to penetrate both protective layers to reach their targets. This may be enough to stop them. In making such a decision, it's vital to be sure that there are no attackers on the other side.

Unless the ambush has occurred in a very isolated place, a radio call for help should bring reinforcements within a few minutes. With help on the way, a holding action by the bodyguards may be enough to defeat the attack. An ambush is, in principle, a short attack. Usually, if it's to succeed, it does so within a minute or two. One attack that failed was the attempt on Augusto Pinochet's life, which may have taken as long as ten minutes, according to one report. Ambushers aren't prepared to fight a protracted battle in most instances, and if the attack fails they'll retreat and try again another day. In any event, they're under great pressure to leave the scene quickly because of the imminent arrival of the police.

Guarding the protectee while traveling by motor vehicle is a demanding task. It requires constant alertness. Like protection in other settings, the undramatic precautions are usually more important than sudden and improvised actions in the face of danger.

Notes:

1. "The Deadliest Beat," *Time*, November 13, 1989, p. 76.
2. Bierman, John, "A Doomsday Gun Mystery: The Murder of A Canadian-born Arms Expert May be Linked to Iraqi Plans to Build A Super-cannon," *MacLean's*, April 23, 1990, v103, n17, pp. 22-23.
3. "Top Anti-Terrorist Officer Slain in Egypt," Associated Press, April 9, 1994.
4. *You're The Target*, Shackley, Theodore G., Oatman, Robert L., and Finney, Richard A., New World Publishing, Ltd., 1989, p. 81.
5. *Terrorism and Personal Protection*, Brian Jenkins, editor, NY, Butterworth Publishers, 1985, pp. 73-75.
6. *Ibid.,* p. 50.
7. *Ibid.,* pp. 51-52.
8. *You're The Target*, Shackley, Theodore G., Oatman, Robert L., and Finney, Richard A., New World Publishing, Ltd., 1989, p. 47.
9. *Executive Protection Manual*, Reber, Jan, and Shaw, Paul, Schiller Park, IL, MTI Teleprograms, 1976, p. 165.
10. Testimony of William Greer and Roy Kellerman before the Warren Commission, pp. 47-53.
11. *You're The Target*, Shackley, Theodore G., Oatman, Robert L., and Finney, Richard A., New World Publishing, Ltd., 1989, pp. 77-78.
12. *Executive Protection Manual*, Reber, Jan, and Shaw, Paul, Schiller Park, IL, MTI Teleprograms, 1976, p. 167.
13. Testimony of Lyndon Johnson before the Warren Commission, pp. 6 and 7. Johnson stated that, although his car was never under attack, at the sound of the first shot Secret Service agent Rufus Youngblood turned from the front seat, hit him in the shoulder, and told him to get down. Youngblood kept pushing Johnson down, then vaulted over the seat back and shielded Johnson with his body.

19
Coping With Bombs

Bombs are almost ideal assassination weapons because they allow the perpetrator to be far from the scene. In effect, a bomb permits remote-control killing. Bombs are amazingly easy to make, using smokeless powder, fertilizer, fuel oil, flour, and other commonly available materials. One bomber used nails for shrapnel. The World Trade Center bomb used fuel oil and fertilizer.

Both overseas and in the United States, bombs have proven to be an effective means of assassination, with the bonus of minimal exposure and risk to the bomber. Letter bombs especially offer anonymity to the bomber.

In Britain, the Irish Republican Army has effectively used bombs to kill its enemies. Behind the fog of propaganda regarding bombs killing only innocent persons, have been some very real and very effective strikes. In 1979, an IRA bomb killed Airey Neave, Member of Parliament, as he drove his car out of the House of Commons car park. Neave was only one of four British MPs to fall victim to the IRA.

The latest MP killed was Ian Gow, murdered in July, 1990, with a car bomb. This incident followed closely the bombing of the Carlton Club on June 25, and another explosion at the stock exchange on July 20. In a public statement, the IRA took credit for placing a 2-kilogram bomb under Gow's gold Austin Montego as it was parked outside Gow's home in Hankham, Sussex. Although Gow's name had been on a captured IRA hit list, discovered in 1988, Gow had been slack about his safety. He had a published address and phone number, and had left the keys in his car when he'd parked it the night before he was killed.[1]

South America has more than its share of bombers, some of whom direct their efforts at American diplomats. Peru serves as an example. The U. S. Embassy in Lima was bombed by the Sendero Luminoso (Shining Path revolutionary group) in 1981 and in 1982. Private businesses were also targets. The Sendero Luminoso also bombed the Bank of America office, the Coca Cola Company, and a dairy farm working with the Carnation Company.[2]

Disruption

Bombs are not necessarily used for selective assassinations, but often to disrupt and destroy facilities. In some areas, bombs appear to be emerging threats. Hospitals and other health care facilities have seen a decline in armed robberies from 1986 to 1991, but the incidence of bombs and bomb threats has risen from about 20 to well over 40 during the same time.[3]

Bombs are not necessarily terrorist weapons, although that assessment depends heavily upon how we define "terrorist." One survey of over 10,000 bombs planted in this country during the last decade found that 90 percent of bombs were planted by criminal bombers.[4]

Bomb Threats

The first subject with which to deal is the "bomb threat." If telephoned, it is often a hoax, but it impales the security specialist upon the horns of a dilemma. If the threat concerns a building, is it wise to evacuate? The bodyguard is often the only security trained person on the scene, and often will be asked his opinion.

Bomb threat forms (Photocopy Appendix VI as much as you need to) should be in the hands of every person with a telephone extension. Anyone receiving a threat should begin filling out one of these forms, and try to keep the caller on the line while signaling for someone else to pick up an extension. Bomb and other threats are good reasons to have telephones equipped with "Caller ID."

Another security measure is to observe nearby pay phones while the caller is on the line, because experience shows that most bomb threats are made from pay phones close to the plant.[5] Caller ID can even pinpoint the phone used, if the security manager has prepared a list of numbers and locations.

Although in principle the safest course is to evacuate everyone from the area immediately, this is often the desired result of the bomb threat. If the bomber were intent upon killing anyone, he wouldn't give warning. Threats have been phoned in by employees seeking an afternoon off, pranksters, and even school children who wanted a break from the everyday.

If the bodyguard or security manager is reasonably certain that the premises are secure, he may decide that evacuation is unnecessary. With proper security precautions, a bomber should not be able to gain access to plant his bomb. This has to be the basis of a decision not to evacuate. Otherwise, it would appear to be a callous risking of human life.

Some established groups, such as the IRA, provide telephone warnings in advance of the explosion, so that they may later claim to have allowed enough time for evacuation, thereby showing they care about innocent lives. However, such warnings have invariably been vague regarding the bomb's location or too late to permit complete evacuation, according to an authoritative source.[6]

A crucial dictate is never to take anything for granted. The security officer or bodyguard should not relax after finding a bomb. Some bombers use secondary devices. The first bomb, while not exactly an inert decoy, is left in an obvious spot to fool security officers. It may even detonate, and if there's no thorough search after the explosion, the secondary bomb remains undetected while the building's occupants return. Sometime later, the second bomb detonates.[7]

An insidious type of bomb threat by a sophisticated bomber is designed to force evacuation of a well secured building, thereby placing the occupants near an area within reach of the bomber. Having placed his bomb where he estimates the evacuees will gather, he detonates it when the evacuation is complete.[8] A security agent ordering the evacuation of a building after a bomb threat should first inspect the area where evacuees will congregate, searching nearby trash cans, dumpsters, etc.

Types of Bombs

The bomb may be open or disguised. Automobile bombs are often open, the bomber trusting the victim's lack of awareness. Other types of bombs may be carefully and cleverly disguised or hidden. One example is the suitcase bomb that used to be the plague of the airlines. One device, placed in a flight bag, had a 30-minute timer and an anti-tampering device to cause detonation if anyone tried to dismantle it.[9]

More recently, bombers have disguised their bombs by packing the explosive, detonator and timer in electronic appliances such as radios, cassette players, etc. The bomb that destroyed the Pan American airliner over Lockerbie, Scotland, was one of these.

The bodyguard has to take bombs seriously for several significant reasons:

- Their use is common. This is partly because a bomb offers safety for the assassin. He can place his bomb long before detonation and get away unnoticed.
- Bombs can be very cheap and simple to make. Propellant salvaged from cartridges will serve to make an acceptable bomb. The fuse can be very simple, and inexpensive to construct.
- Bombs can be quite small. This permits placing the bomb almost anywhere, in almost anything. A letter bomb containing only an ounce of high explosive can be lethal. A bomb in a telephone mouthpiece can be small yet lethal because of its closeness to the target's head. Israeli hit men used one of these to eliminate an Arab enemy in Paris.

Letter Bombs

Attempts on an individual may take the form of letter bombs. These have been used extensively by Middle East factions, such as Israelis who used them against German scientists working on Egyptian rocket projects. We've had domestic letter bombs as well. Sometimes, exploding letters and packages kill innocent persons, such as Patricia Wilkerson, a secretary who opened a package addressed to her employer in 1980.

A 75-year-old woman who opened a letter bomb addressed to her brother was injured in April, 1994. Alice Caswell, living in Brooklyn, New York, was in critical condition after a thick letter bomb containing, among other items, two .22-caliber cartridges, exploded. The letter was addressed to her brother, Richard McGarrell, a retired U. S. Customs Service inspector.[10] McGarrell, however, had not lived at that address for 15 years, suggesting that the letter bomb was an effort to settle a very old grudge.

The fuse mechanism may be of several types.

The Time Bomb

This has a timer or clock set to detonate the bomb after an interval. This is what inspired the many jokes about ticking packages, but a mechanical timer is obsolete. The many quartz timers available today are silent, and much more reliable. The extreme reliability of the quartz timer allows a bomber to emplace his bomb months before the moment of detonation. If the bomber knows that his target will be at a certain place at a certain time, he has a chance to place his bomb and remain entirely unsuspected at the time. Any witnesses will have forgotten him by the time the detonation occurs. This is what happened to the bomb placed in the hotel at the Brighton Conference, which missed catching Mrs. Thatcher by a narrow margin. A bomb built into a structure during the course of construction or repairs can easily pass unnoticed because the installation takes place long before the protective staff arrives.

A time bomb is useful in a building, but it can also serve as a car bomb, if the bomber knows that his target will be in the car at a certain time. If split-second accuracy isn't necessary, a chemical delay fuse is useful. In this, acid eats through a wire which holds the firing pin back. When the wire's eroded enough to give way, the striker fires and the bomb detonates. Chemical delay fuses have short duration, usually not more than a couple of hours.

The Mechanical Fuse

This depends on some sort of mechanical action to detonate. A trip-wire attached to the fuse can set the bomb off. This can be either a pull or release type. One of the simplest hybrid types to construct is so simple that it can be homemade. This is the spring clothespin with two electrical contacts separated by a piece of cardboard. The cardboard has a string attached, and anyone tripping the string pulls the

cardboard from between the two contacts, closing the circuit.

The mechanical fuse can serve as a car bomb. A wire or string is attached to a fixed object, and this triggers the bomb when the car moves. It can also be wrapped around the drive shaft, eliminating telltale wires coming out from the car. When the car moves, the drive shaft turns, winding the wire around it and pulling the trip.

In another type of mechanical fuse, a striker shaped somewhat like a mousetrap delivers a sharp blow to the primer when tripped. This is the sort of fuse used in grenades, and it's also useful in a letter or package bomb. Opening the package lid releases the pressure and allows the striker to fly over and hit the primer.

Yet another type of mechanical fuse is the barometric fuse. This responds to a decrease in air pressure, and is very limited in use. Its only application is to detonate bombs placed aboard aircraft. The fuse has an air chamber and a diaphragm, and a decrease in the outside pressure forces the diaphragm outwards. This provides the mechanical action to release a striker.

The barometric fuse may be combined with a timer for a special purpose. If the intent is to destroy an aircraft, the timer may be set to arm the bomb only after the aircraft is out of the country, so that the barometric fuse detonates the bomb upon take-off from a foreign airport. Another use for a combination fuse is to destroy the aircraft when it's high over the ocean, so that the evidence vanishes into the depths.

The Electrical Fuse

The electrical fuse is extremely versatile, allowing use in many situations. The fuse for an automobile bomb, for example, may be a simple connection from the ignition wires to a blasting cap. Another method is to place one fuse wire on the battery's positive terminal, with the other wire attached to a simple clamp on the fan belt. When the engine turns, the fan belt moves the clamp into contact with the fan pulley, closing the ground circuit. Yet another is the simple spring clothespin attached to the hood.[11]

An old method, still effective, is to attach the fuse wires to the brake light. In April, 1974, federal witness Joseph Bombacino, living under an alias in Tempe, Arizona, stepped on the brake pedal while backing out of his apartment's parking space. The resulting explosion sent pieces of his Lincoln Continental over the three-story roof and onto a nearby freeway. The person who placed the bomb was never caught, and was probably many miles away at the time of the blast.

Another type of fusing is to attach the wires to an electric light switch in a building. Flipping the switch sets off the bomb. Some bombs are attached directly to lamps and light sockets, and turning on the light brings the detonation.

Remote Control Bombs

Remote control bombs are perhaps the most versatile. They have been used in several spectacular assassinations. There were a couple of attempts on De Gaulle with remote-control bombs, and in Spain, Admiral Luis Carrero Blanco was killed in his car with this method, which employed electric wires to activate the bomb. This has also been called the "lay-off bomb." The attackers rented a basement apartment on the admiral's route from church to his office, dug a tunnel under the street, and laid 200 pounds of dynamite in the tunnel. The explosion blew the car up over a five-story building.[12]

West German attackers used a lay-off bomb on a bridge in an attempt against General Alexander Haig on June 25, 1979. When the NATO commander's Mercedes was on the bridge, they fired the bomb, but had not allowed for the speed of the convoy. Haig escaped unhurt, but the explosion damaged his follow-up car, injuring three bodyguards.[13]

Don Bolles, an investigative reporter for the *Arizona Republic*, was killed by a radio-operated bomb placed in his car in 1976. The recent killing of Spanish policemen by a lay-off bomb placed in a van shows that this type of explosive device is still popular today.[14]

In Beirut, President Rene Moawad fell victim to a lay-off bomb in late November, 1989. The President left a mansion in West Beirut, heading home in his armored Mercedes limousine. He was escorted by several other vehicles, which were carrying heavily armed bodyguards. Less than a minute after departure, a remotely controlled bomb containing about 400 lbs. of explosive, placed in an abandoned shop along the route, detonated. Moawad, several of his bodyguards and several soldiers lining the route, were blown to bits, and it took 2½ hours to find his body.[15]

Alfred Herrhausen, CEO of the Deutsche Bank and advisor to German Chancellor Helmut Kohl, was killed by a lay-off bomb near his Bad Homburg home one December morning in 1989. Herrhausen normally traveled in a convoy with two other automobiles and four bodyguards. Leaving for work at about 8:30 A.M., his chauffeured and armored Mercedes 500SE passed a bicycle bomb, which then exploded and sent Herrhausen's car flying into the air. The limousine's armor was not enough to protect Herrhausen, who died on the spot. Police found a wooden box with an arming switch attached to a wire leading to the bicycle laden with the explosives. As reconstructed, the explosion was caused by a photoelectric cell which triggered the bomb when Herrhausen's car was next to it. The arming switch was necessary to prevent premature explosion caused by other passing cars.[16]

The Mafia got credit for a remotely controlled bomb that exploded in Palermo, Sicily, killing Prosecutor Paolo Borsellino and six bodyguards. The explosion took place as they approached Borsellino's armored automobile, injuring 15 other people as well. Two months before, a lay-off bomb had killed his predecessor, Prosecutor Giovanni Falcone.[17]

Attempts Against Airliners

Some bombers try to get their devices delivered by a surrogate. One ruthless bomber was Nezar Hindawi, who induced his pregnant Irish girlfriend to take a package containing a bomb aboard an El Al airliner at London Airport. She didn't know the package's contents, and would have perished in the explosion.[18]

In this attempt, Hindawi hid over 3 lbs. of high explosive in a flat package in his girlfriend's suitcase, knowing it would not appear on the x-ray. The fusing mechanism, with its timer and batteries, was hidden inside a pocket calculator, which, with its battery and chip, provided a perfect disguise for the circuit. An El Al security agent discovered the large explosive charge during a physical search when he thought it felt too heavy for an empty case.[19]

Defense Against Bombs

The first line of defense is good security. Bombs have to be delivered, or in rare instances, the victim goes to or passes by the bomb. Basic security precautions can negate the bomber's efforts. Even casual security is better than nothing. 80 percent of bombs used against businesses were planted outside. 18 percent were discovered in building lobbies and other common areas. Only 2 percent were inside a particular person's office.[20]

One point to watch is the bomb left on a car seat. This may not be the main bomb, but merely part of it, or one designed to fool the security officer into thinking he's found the bomb and solved the problem. A much larger bomb may be hidden in the trunk or under the back seat.[21]

Access control goes a long way towards limiting the bomber's opportunities. If the bomber can't hand-carry his bomb, he'll have to find another way or abandon the attempt. Defense against bombs in vehicles requires keeping the vehicle secured and searching any vehicle that has been left unattended, as discussed in the chapter on automobiles. Having the vehicle "hardened" against bomb blast can be effective, but it's unwise to depend on armor too much. Armor is no defense against a bomb placed inside the vehicle, and a lay-off bomb can be of almost any size needed to defeat the armor.

The suddenness with which a bomb attack can develop on the road is breathtaking. When an armored Jeep Cherokee containing Salvadoran Attorney General Roberto Garcia Alvarado stopped for a red light in downtown San Salvador, a pedestrian stepped forward and placed a limpet bomb on its roof. The driver and bodyguard were slightly injured in the explosion that took the life of Alvarado, who had been sitting in the back seat.[22]

Anyone handling incoming mail should pay special attention to suspicious appearing letters and packages. These include oversize and excessively thick envelopes, those with foreign postmarks, any with strong odors, those without known return addresses, and any which seem greasy or "funny" to the touch.[23]

Some senders of letter bombs use Express Mail to ensure rapid delivery, and they may mark the envelope "Personal" or "Confidential" to ensure that only the addressee opens the envelope.[24] A simple precaution upon receipt of such a suspicious envelope is to telephone the alleged sender to verify that it's genuine.

Another danger sign is a thick letter with too much postage, a hallmark of the inept bomber. To prevent recognition, inept bombers avoid having their letter bombs weighed at a post office window, and put excessive postage on them to ensure that the post office will deliver them. Postal scales are so cheap, and so commonly available, that a bomber who makes his letter bombs conspicuous with excessive postage is almost brain dead.

The adept sender of letter bombs won't make these stupid mistakes. He'll weigh his letters and put on the right postage; no more, no less. With a little cleverness and professionalism, he'll procure another firm's envelopes, printed with their return address. He may also secure a few of the target company's business reply envelopes, which arouse less suspicion. The really clever letter-bomber will obtain, or have printed, envelopes with the return address of the target company. He'll make sure the post office returns the envelope to the "sender" by putting on an undeliverable address, insufficient postage, or both. If he's after a specific individual, he may even type his target's name under the printed company logo.

The return address may not offer a clue, and may even be familiar. Obviously, a person mailing a package can write any return address on the wrapping. The bomb that killed federal judge Robert Vance bore the address of one of his friends, judge Lewis P. Morgan. When he opened it, the explosion killed him and seriously injured his wife.[25]

This is why it's wise never to take anything for granted when examining mail. Any letter thick enough to contain a bomb, or which looks or feels funny, should receive special examination.

There are ways to check these out. One traditional way is to x-ray any suspicious package or letter. This will usually reveal if it contains what it's supposed to hold. Electronic sniffers are also useful, and more reliable than dogs.

Dogs are a special case. Although explosives-detecting dogs are available, they're expensive, and must be retrained regularly. To train a dog to sniff explosives, it's necessary to keep some on hand, which means keeping it for the dog's useful life because he needs refresher training at regular intervals.

Dogs also will not respond to explosives they haven't been trained to sniff out. This can lead to a dog's missing a bomb. Some types of explosive, such as the Czech-made "Semtex," do not emit an odor dogs can detect.[26] A determined and clever bomb-maker knows that he can fool a dog by masking the odor of the explosive with another odor to which the dog hasn't been conditioned to react. A strong perfume can overpower the dog's sense of smell.

Very few security specialists have explosives sniffing dogs. Their application is so limited that it's often not worth the expense of keeping one. Most explosive dogs are in the hands of police agencies and government security departments. Most are trained at the U.S. Air Force facility at Lackland Air Force Base, in Texas. The bodyguard who suspects a bomb should call the police, who have the dogs and the trained specialists to find the bomb and render it harmless.

For the specialist who needs an explosives dog, one source is:

Rudy Drexler's School for Dogs
50947 CR-7N
Elkhart, IN 46514
Phone: (219) 264-7514

Because the lay-off bomb is usually planted along a route the target is known to take, defense consists of not following a known route. This isn't always possible. This type of bomb is excellent for use against a motorcade. The bomber is part of the crowd, and is far enough away to remain safe from the blast. He stays close enough to keep the site of the bomb in sight. When the target vehicle passes over or near it, he presses the button on a radio control in his pocket.

The U.S. Secret Service has the authority to obtain local cooperation in having manhole covers sealed, and likely hiding places for lay-off bombs searched, before a motorcade. The private protective agent has no such authority, and must depend on avoidance and secrecy to keep his client from falling victim to a lay-off bomb.

The methods that protect against ambush (not following a regular route and varying the schedule) also tend to protect against lay-off bombs. If the protectee is a government official in a motorcade, he's probably got enough security policemen checking the route inch-by-inch before he drives over it. As we've seen, even this sometimes isn't enough.

Disarming Bombs

Defense against suspected bombs of other types is to keep a respectful distance. It's unwise for an untrained person to attempt to defuse them both in principle and because some are designed to explode when opened or even touched. A mercury switch will close the circuit if the package is tilted or moved.[27]

Another type of anti-tampering device is the collapsing circuit. This design uses electrical power to keep the contacts of a relay open, and cutting one of the wires causes the circuit to collapse and the contacts to close, thereby completing the firing circuit. The explosives disposal officer must be very sure of the wire he's cutting.[28]

One widely disseminated piece of advice is to shut down all radio transmitters upon discovery of a bomb, on the theory that radio transmissions may set off the detonator. The main effect of this advice is to disrupt communications during an emergency. The practical point about bombs and radio transmissions is that if the detonator were vulnerable to radio waves, it would have gone off while the bomber was carrying and planting it.[29]

Disarming bombs should not be part of the bodyguard's job, because his responsibility is to stay with his client and get him away from dangerous situations, not cope with them on the spot. If the bodyguard tries to render a bomb harmless, instead of leaving this task to a specialist, he leaves his client exposed while his attention is on the bomb.

Notes:

1. Phillips, Andrew, "Hitting A Soft Target," *MacLean's*, August 13, 1990, v103, n33, pp. 32-33.
2. *Sendero Luminoso: Peruvian Terrorist Group*, U.S. Government Printing Office, Department of State Bulletin, December, 1989, v89, n2123, pp. 49-53.
3. "Hospital Crime Survey," *Security Management*, November, 1993, p. 15.
4. "Big News On Bombs," *Security Management*, September, 1993, pp. 20-21.
5. *Ibid.,* p.21
6. *Braver Men Walk Away*, Peter Gurney, London, Harper Collins Publishers, 1993, pp. 149-150.
7. *Ibid.,* p. 119.
8. *The Executive Protection Bible*, Martha J. Braunig, Basalt, CO, Executive Protection International, 1992, pp. 207 and 211.
9. *Federal Bomb Intelligence, U. S. Government Guide to Terrorist Explosives*, Boulder, CO, Paladin Press, 1991, Commercial Reprint, pp. 9-13.
10. "Reward Offered For Letter Bomber" Associated Press, April 6, 1994.
11. *Federal Bomb Intelligence, U. S. Government Guide to Terrorist Explosives*, Boulder, CO, Paladin Press, 1991, Commercial Reprint, pp. 8-9.

12. *You're The Target*, Shackley, Theodore G., Oatman, Robert L., and Finney, Richard A., New World Publishing, Ltd., 1989, p. 72.
13. *Ibid.*, Page 73.
14. Associated Press, July 15, 1986.
15. Marlowe, Lara, "Agony in Beirut," *Maclean's*, December 4, 1989, v102, n49, pp. 26-27.
16. "Terrorism: Target For The Red Army Faction," *Time*, December 11, 1989, World, p. 54.
17. Zuckerman, M. J., "Mafia Blamed in 2nd Killing," *USA Today*, July 20, 1992, News p. 1A.
18. *You're The Target*, Shackley, Theodore G., Oatman, Robert L., and Finney, Richard A., New World Publishing, Ltd., 1989, p. 44.
19. *Braver Men Walk Away*, Peter Gurney, London, Harper Collins Publishers, 1993, pp. 176-185.
20. "Big News On Bombs," *Security Management*, September, 1993, pp. 20-21.
21. *Braver Men Walk Away*, Peter Gurney, London, Harper Collins Publishers, 1993, p. 107.
22. *Time*, May 1, 1989, World, p. 51.
23. *Executive Protection Manual*, Reber, Jan, and Shaw, Paul, Schiller Park, IL, MTI Teleprograms, 1976, p. 171.
24. *The Executive Protection Bible*, Martha J. Braunig, Basalt, CO, Executive Protection International, 1992, p. 204.
25. Carlson, Margaret, "Murder by Mail," *Time*, January 1, 1990, p. 33.
26. *You're The Target*, Shackley, Theodore G., Oatman, Robert L., and Finney, Richard A., New World Publishing, Ltd., 1989, p. 45.
27. *Braver Men Walk Away*, Peter Gurney, London, Harper Collins Publishers, 1993, p. 117.
28. *Ibid.*, p. 92.
29. "Big News On Bombs," *Security Management*, September, 1993, p. 21.

20

Kidnapping:
A Special Case

Kidnapping places a special burden on the security manager. After other kinds of attack, the security manager knows whether he's succeeded or failed. He can pat himself on the back, set up new procedures to correct perceived deficiencies, or begin looking for another job. After a kidnapping, though, he has the responsibility of recovering his client, and this may put him right in the middle of a power struggle involving conflicting needs.

We can generalize that kidnappers don't necessarily intend to harm their victims, and in fact often try to keep them in good health. A kidnap victim who dies loses his value. In some cases, however, the kidnappers kill the victim. This may happen because the negotiations break down, or because they fear being identified by the victim.

One critical point is whether the victim can later identify his kidnappers. The kidnappers can easily keep the victim blindfolded, or wear masks in the victim's presence, to avoid this. The victim who only sees masked captors can take reassurance from this. On the other hand, if the captors don't bother to hide their faces, he can be pretty sure they plan to kill him, and should take any opportunity for escape, however risky. We'll take another look at this situation in a later chapter.

Another important point is reaction to a successful kidnapping. Some authorities, such as Carol Edler Baumann[1] and Richard Clutterbuck, claim that a hard-line policy of refusing to pay ransom is best because it deters kidnappings.[2] But, others point out that if the government makes it illegal to pay ransom, families simply will circumvent the government to get their relatives back. They'll either not notify police, or try to sneak ransom payments to the kidnappers.[3]

There are two basic kinds of kidnapping: political and for profit. The first kind involves political demands, with the release of the victim contingent on compliance. The second kind is strictly for money, and is a straight criminal enterprise. Confusing the issue is the political group that uses kidnapping as a fundraising method.

The Middle East has seen political kidnapping and hostage taking become common practice, alternating with outright killing. Malcolm Kerr, President of Beirut's American University, was shot to death near his office on January 18, 1984. The university's librarian, Peter Kilburn, was kidnapped on December 3, 1984, and killed in 1986, along with two British hostages, in reprisal for the American air raid on Libya that year. William Buckley, CIA station chief in Beirut, was kidnapped March 16, 1984, and held hostage, dying in captivity.[4]

Only five other countries, including Colombia, Italy, Lebanon, Peru and the Philippines, outrank the United States in sheer number of for profit kidnappings.[5] However, considering our population, the American kidnapping rate is pretty low. Tolerance for kidnapping is very low in the United States, and police agencies have high-tech means of tracking kidnappers when they recover the ransom.

Kidnap/Ransom Insurance

This falls into the category of precautions. One choice for both affluent individuals and corporate clients is insurance against this contingency. Several companies, such as Chubb, Staward-Smith and others offer such coverage. A major selling point for such insurance is that, in case of an incident, the insurer provides not only financial coverage, but the assistance of a private security company to help recover the victim.[6] Incidental services also provided in some contracts are negotiator's fees, travel and accommodations, rewards for information leading to the kidnappers and recovery of the victim, and loss-of-earnings coverage.

There are certain conditions of such insurance. Its existence must not be disclosed, presumably to avoid encouraging kidnappers. Clients must not be committing an illegal act, and as a corollary must cooperate with law enforcement agencies.[7] This can put the client between a rock and a hard place, because in some countries paying ransom is illegal. This is the fine print that can make a policy useless.

The negative aspect of using employees or contractors of insurance firms in negotiations is that they actually work for the insurance firm, neither the victim nor his company. Their main interest is their employer's interest.

Sources for Kidnap Insurance are:

Corporate Risk International
11250 Waples Mill Road, Suite 320
Fairfax, VA 22030
Phone: (703) 359-3901 or 359-3902
Fax: (703) 359-3903
Attn: Sean M. McWeeney, President

CRI also provides a customer handbook on crisis management planning and executive protection. This 32-page handbook lists tips for maintaining a low profile, getting through airports, overseas travel, sources of up-to-date information, and other relevant topics.

Professional Indemnity Agency, Inc.
409 Manville Road
P.O. Box 130
Pleasantville, NY 10570-0130
Phone: (914) 747-1818
Fax: (914) 747-3737

Other Kidnap Precautions

Any executive protection agent with a client that may be kidnapped should obtain a basic file of information from his client and his family. These should include a full physical description, including a dental chart and list of surgical scars. Medical information, such as blood type and a list of prescription drugs currently used, should be included. Such information can be crucial if the victim is diabetic, for example, and takes insulin or an oral drug.

A set of fingerprints is important, partly to identify the body if the kidnappers kill their victim, but also to identify amputated fingers provided by the kidnappers

as purported evidence that they truly have the victim in custody. This has happened in a couple of cases.

A recording of the victim's voice, for voice-printing, is essential if kidnappers provide an audio or video tape as proof of custody. Handwriting exemplars are important as well, to authenticate any notes or letters purportedly written by the kidnap victim.

The potential victim should have a duress code and an authentication code. The duress code is a code word he can slip into a communication to show that he's being forced to make a statement. The authentication code is a code word or phrase that he includes in a communication to indicate that it truly comes from him. This could be his mother's or father's birthdate, nickname, or other personal information not likely to be known beyond the immediate family. These trivial details also serve to prove that the kidnap victim is still alive.

Another type of precaution uses an electronic tracker to locate the kidnap victim and/or his vehicle. A small transmitter is hidden inside the vehicle, or on the protectee's person. A special receiver using dual antennas shows the transmitter's direction, and a signal strength meter provides an approximation of distance.

Sources for tracking transmitters and receivers include:

Executive Protection Products, Inc.
1325 Imola Avenue West, #504
Napa, CA 94559
Phone: (707) 253-7142
Fax: (707) 253-7149

The Privacy Connection, Inc.
23133 Ventura Boulevard
Woodland Hills, CA 91364
Phone: (818) 225-8007
Fax: (818) 225-7516

Electronic tracking provides an edge to rescuers, because by knowing the victim's location, they can mount a rescue operation that takes the kidnappers by surprise. This is why every effort should be made to provide high-risk clients with electronic trackers. Concealing a transmitter inside a shoe heel is one choice. If resources allow, a second transmitter should be provided in case a search by kidnappers reveals the first one.

A practical point is battery life. This is why it's desirable to have an on-off switch easily accessible by the victim. To save battery power, he can transmit on a pre-arranged schedule, such as ten minutes on the hour. A limited schedule such as this one can greatly extend battery life, and is crucial because it's often impossible to prepare a rescue operation before a battery becomes exhausted from continuous use.

Battery reserve is also important to confirm a victim's location. Kidnappers have been known to relocate their victims one or more times during their confinement, and being able to confirm the victim's precise location just before the attempt enhances the odds of success.

Aftermath

If an executive is kidnapped, his employer's efforts to free him may become the subject of a lawsuit. When kidnappers abducted Gustavo Curtis, manager of a Beatrice Foods subsidiary in Bogotá, Colombia, the company refused to pay the $5 million ransom because of its suspicion that he and his wife were involved with the plot. After having the wife submit to a polygraph test, the company did pay $430,000 to free Curtis. Curtis and his wife subsequently filed suit on the grounds that the company had neither done enough to protect Curtis, nor to free him after his abduction. The judge dismissed this case, but its implications made it clear that employee safety is the employer's concern.[8]

A company may buy kidnap/ransom insurance for its personnel, or it may self-insure. Either way, there's an expectation that the employer will take responsibility for correcting situations that arise from assigning an employee to a position that puts him in harm's way.

Notes:

1. *Terrorism and Personal Protection*, Brian Jenkins, editor, NY, Butterworth Publishers, 1985, p. 38.
2. *Ibid.,* p. 258.
3. *You're The Target*, Shackley, Theodore G., Oatman, Robert L., and Finney, Richard A., New World Publishing, Ltd., 1989, p. 54.
4. "The Undeclared War," *Time*, August 14, 1989, The Nation, p. 16.
5. Revzan, Henry A., "The 'Secret' Response to Kidnapping," *Business Horizons*, May-June, 1990, v33, n3, p. 79.
6. *Ibid.,* p. 79-81.
7. Leach, Norman S., "Executive Protection: An Ironclad Defense," *Security Management*, February, 1990, v34, n2, p. 84.
8. *Ibid.,* p. 84.

21
Legal Problems

Licensing

Civilian bodyguards usually operate under the umbrella of a private detective agency. The laws in many states require that a private detective be licensed, which may be a formality but can also be a serious process. In some states, all that's required is to fill out an application, pay the fee and submit to fingerprinting. The whole process takes ten minutes. In other states, there's a long delay between application and granting of the license, to allow time for an investigation regarding the suitability of the applicant.

In some instances, executive protection specialists operate as members of a corporate security department. The director of security is in charge of uniformed guards, locks, alarms and other access control systems, issuing badges to employees and providing protection to the top executives. For this last function, he hires a few specialists, preferably with sound backgrounds in the field. In certain rare instances, the company may pay for training these agents, or for "refresher" courses.

"Selling" the need for executive protection is the hardest part of the corporate security director's job, because many executives feel no need to be protected, or feel that they can look after themselves. (Personal account by the director of security of a major corporation.) In any case, executive protection specialists are usually required to be bonded.

Bonding

In some jurisdictions, the law requires a private investigator to be bonded, and in any event clients sometimes require this. Individuals seeking bodyguards often consult a private investigative agency, partly because of the impression of private detectives they get from crime fiction, Hollywood and television.

Some private investigative agencies also advertise bodyguard services.

Bonding is a cash deposit to insure honesty and proper performance of duties. In actuality, the security agents or private investigative agencies don't put up the large sums required because they simply don't have that much money. Instead, they hire a bonding company to furnish the bond, much as a prisoner hires a bail bondsman to "front" the money for his release. The bonding company, in turn, does not put up the money itself in many jurisdictions, but merely furnishes an affidavit that it can pay if required.

The bonding company takes a risk in bonding employees. This gives it the leverage to impose certain qualifications, as does an insurance company. Actually, bonding is a form of insurance. The applicant will be obliged to fill out a personal data form, which serves as the basis for the bonding company's own investigators. The applicant, in effect, winds up getting a "security clearance" from the bonding company.

Liability

The bodyguard is liable for his actions. So is his employer. The laws vary from state to state and from country to country, but the trend is clear. Civil liability is growing, and litigation for liability is a growth industry.

One law a protection agent should always keep in mind is the Federal Civil Rights Act: Title 42, 1983. While this applies mainly to police officers who use unjustified force under color of law, it can also apply to a bodyguard because of its broad wording. The statute reads:

"Every *person* who, under color of any statute, ordinance, regulation, custom, or usage, of any state or territory, subjects or causes to be subjected, any citizen of the United States or other person within the jurisdiction thereof to the deprivation of any rights, privileges or immunities secured by the Constitution and laws, shall be liable to the party injured in any action at law, suit in equity, or other proper proceeding for redress."

The bodyguard can be both criminally and civilly liable. This corresponds roughly to malpractice among doctors. Police officers can also be prosecuted under Title 42. After several Los Angeles Police Officers were acquitted of state criminal charges, former Sergeant Stacey Koon and Officer Lawrence Powell were convicted in federal court and sentenced to prison.

A wrongful death because the bodyguard shot the wrong person can land him in very hot water. So can other, less violent, actions.

Photographers are often nuisances to people in show business, and sometimes a screen actor's bodyguard will confiscate the film or camera.[1] If this happens after a photographer has trespassed on the protectee's private property, it's a stand off, unless the bodyguard has seriously injured the photographer. Normally, they both agree not to prosecute.

If it happens in public, however, the law is squarely on the photographer's side. A prominent person is normally held to have less of a right to privacy than someone who is unknown, and in any event, appearance in public is usually implied consent to be photographed, according to statute and case law in most states. A bodyguard who attacks a photographer is not only legally in the wrong, but he's acting very unprofessionally. This is because while he's dealing with the photographer, an assailant can be attacking the protectee. He can then be sued by the protectee for having failed to protect him. In practice, being photographed is an inevitable nuisance for the rich and famous. A photographer can easily use a telephoto lens to stay out of reach of the bodyguard.

Police Powers

Another set of legal problems comes from the bodyguard's civilian status. Unless the executive protection specialist is a police officer in that jurisdiction, his rights and privileges are those of a civilian, and this can cause severe problems in some situations.

In the United States and many English speaking countries, the law is still loosely based on old English "common law," which allows certain basic rights,

such as self-defense and "citizen's arrest." However, these can often be more trouble than they're worth. The concept of "citizen's arrest" may not be formalized in the law, and there is no such thing in the statutes of many nations, but the common sense practice of holding a criminal for the police is tacitly recognized. The bodyguard, however, is not very interested in making an "arrest" whether sanctioned by law or not. That's not his job, and the requirements of his job usually dictate that he leave the arresting to others.

In some countries, police officers provide "courtesy" to officers from other jurisdictions, and even to foreign officers. This can lubricate the way, but it's best not to depend too heavily on "courtesy," which varies with the individual officer extending it. Some are jealously protective of their rights and privileges, and will not tolerate anyone usurping their police powers. Others, especially police of certain foreign countries, have a financial reward at stake, as we shall see.

Firearms

The problems involved with carrying firearms for defense are often misunderstood. Part of the reason for this is the variety of laws and policies in effect, which makes it difficult to come up with hard and fast rules. Even in the United States, laws vary sharply from state to state, and from year to year.

Generally, a police officer working a bodyguard detail in his own jurisdiction can carry a concealed weapon, even if he's "moonlighting." In some jurisdictions with very restrictive firearms laws, such as New York City, retiring police officers can apply for concealed firearms permits with the certainty of having the application approved.

Traveling to another state, the police officer finds that he has no jurisdiction, and that his right to carry a firearm is exactly the same as that of citizens of that state. This is where "courtesy" from local officers comes in. The retired officer, on the other hand, has a more tenuous claim upon this "courtesy," and has good reason for concern.

The civilian executive protection specialist has a simpler, but more serious, problem. He has to follow the law exactly, and this can sometimes lead to complications and some "catch-22s." In some states, a permit is required to carry a concealed weapon. The permit may be easy or difficult to obtain. In other states, carrying a concealed weapon by any but police officers and military personnel is prohibited, and there's no permit available for civilians. In still others, there's a permit needed for mere ownership of a firearm. In some cases, the restriction applies only to handguns and other "concealable" weapons.

The following is a quick summary of state and local laws restricting possession and carrying of concealable firearms, compiled from several sources. Major problems are that some laws are badly written, are ambiguous, and have significant loopholes. New legislation and court decisions change the picture as well. This is why it's best to obtain an up-to-date reading on such laws before starting on a trip.

States prohibiting open carry of firearms are: Arkansas (with intent to employ it as a weapon against a person), Illinois, North Dakota (loaded), Oklahoma (loaded), Tennessee (with the intent to go armed), Texas, Utah (loaded), Vermont (carrying with the intent or purpose of injuring another, open or concealed) and the District of Columbia.

States requiring licenses to carry a firearm openly are: Alabama (license to carry in a vehicle openly or concealed), Connecticut, Florida, Georgia, Hawaii, Indiana, Iowa, Maryland, Massachusetts, Michigan (license to carry in a vehicle openly or concealed), Minnesota, New Jersey, New York, Pennsylvania (license to carry in a vehicle openly or concealed), Rhode Island, South Carolina and Washington (loaded).

States that issue concealed carry permits are: Alabama, Alaska, Arizona, California, Colorado, Connecticut, Delaware, Florida, Georgia, Hawaii, Idaho, Indiana, Iowa, Louisiana, Maine, Maryland, Massachusetts, Michigan, Minnesota, Mississippi, Montana, Nevada, New Hampshire, New Jersey, New York, North Dakota, Oregon, Pennsylvania, Rhode Island, South Carolina, South Dakota, Tennesse, Texas, Utah, Virginia, West Virginia and Wyoming.

There are also local laws and peculiarities in enforcing the laws. In Illinois, the cities of Evanston, Highland Park, Morton Grove, Oak Park, Winnetka, and Wilmette, prohibit handguns. New York City's firearms laws are severe, and even BB guns are banned. Theoretically, a person may apply for a concealed carry permit in New York City, but in practice, only those with political connections get them. Possession of an unlicensed weapon, or carrying concealed without a permit, is a felony in New York City, but concealed carry is only a misdemeanor in Arizona.

Enforcement practices vary. There is very strict enforcement in New York City and Washington, DC, but in Arizona persons who look neat, clean and respectable are extremely unlikely to be stopped and searched by police. A loophole in Arizona law allows concealed carry in a holster made to look like a belt pouch, purse or other innocent apparel.

The problem becomes very sticky when in transit from one state with liberal gun laws to another, if it's necessary to cross through a state with restrictive laws. There's no legal way to do it without obtaining the necessary permits, if available. Another way is to hire locals with permits to assist with protection while passing through that jurisdiction. This is, incidentally, one important reason to fly instead of driving to your destination.

The law in some states has a "kink" in it that makes carrying a firearm doubly dangerous. For example, in New York, a killing, even an accidental one, while committing a felony is automatically "Murder One." The intent of this law was to hold criminals responsible for any deaths resulting from the crime, such as a fatal traffic accident while making a getaway. The flaw is that if someone kills another, even with justification, while using an illegal firearm, he can be prosecuted for first-degree murder.

In states with restrictive gun laws, it's smart and expedient to hire off-duty police officers to assist. The principal's civilian bodyguard remains in charge, and the local officer provides the muscle and firepower in a confrontation. The officer can stay behind and deal with the threat while the bodyguard evacuates his client.

Traveling to foreign countries with firearms is almost always a problem, because few have firearms laws as liberal as American ones. Another problem is that of the "ugly American." Foreigners resent those Americans who enter their country and throw their weight around. Any action suggesting that the American is trying to play "Big Daddy" will arouse resentment and, if the act is illegal, action from the local police.

An American arrested overseas for possession of an illegal firearm can expect no effective help from his consulate or embassy. No diplomat will take the trouble to try to get "off the hook" an American citizen who violates the host country's penal code. Many countries don't have jury trials, bail, protection against self-incrimination, the right to a speedy trial and other things Americans take for granted. Many foreign prisons are rigorous, with inadequate food and sanitation. Guards and police officers often don't speak English, and some treat prisoners brutally.[2] Foreign judges can also "throw the book" at someone whom they feel merits it.

An additional hazard is that if there's a lot of anti-American sentiment in that country, the person convicted may face a prison sentence of several decades, although it may seem harsh by American standards.

Even in countries which we consider our allies, importing firearms is usually problematic. In Britain, for example, only official federal security agents, such as Secret Service agents protecting the president, can pass through British customs with their weapons. A loophole in the law comes from the possession of a diplomatic passport, which grants the holder immunity to search and prosecution. In many instances, diplomatic bodyguards have diplomatic passports because they have "cover" jobs such as "second assistant secretary" or some such.

The British police partially compensate for this drawback by providing, in certain carefully selected cases, a follow-up car with armed British police bodyguards. This protection is usually for foreign diplomats, because the police recognize that they can carry weapons under their immunity, and they don't want foreigners staging their shootouts in the middle of London. The British police will go so far as to train diplomatic chauffeurs in evasive driving at the Foreign Embassy Driving Course at Hendon.

Among the Third World nations, the picture is confused. If the bodyguard is protecting the potentate within his own kingdom, the protectee is the law, and there will be no problem. In other instances, there can be severe problems, and these touch directly upon what a client can expect from a bodyguard. It's too much to expect the protection specialist to risk a prison sentence for his principal, and legitimate clients understand this and allow for other means.

Some advise "stashing" weapons in safe deposit boxes in various parts of the world, to be available when needed for protective work.[3] This makes good reading for those who enjoy pouring over exciting accounts of clandestine activities, but it's not realistic. It's certainly possible to smuggle in weapons, despite increasingly stringent airline screening of baggage, or to buy or borrow indigenous weapons, but carrying them is something else.

There is a way to obtain armed protection for a client in a Third World country without using diplomatic passports or knowing the leader, etc. This method hinges on the corruption common in these countries. The police supplement their official incomes by receiving payments for special services rendered to those who can afford their prices.

The key to obtaining official police protection is contacts. The "contact" is usually the local representative of the corporation, who knows the important people in the locale, and can direct the security agent to the proper person to pay. In other instances, the contact can be an attorney living in the country, or an executive of a local company with which the protectee's corporation does business.

The usual pattern is for the contact to introduce the security team leader to the local or district police chief.[4] The security specialist states that his VIP needs armed protection, and asks if the local police chief can arrange it for a suitable fee. The chief asks the security agent how many officers he needs and for how long. Upon receipt of this information, he names a fee. If it's satisfactory, the security agent pays it directly to the local official, because that's the way the system works. The fee contains a suitable profit margin for himself after paying his officers.

There are some practical points to watch in this sort of arrangement. One is to be aware that the fees can vary a lot from country to country and from year to year. A rough estimate is five thousand dollars for the services of five police officers for a week. The local contact is important in this arrangement because he knows the prevailing rates.

Another practical point is to be selective about accepting police agents for this duty. The security team leader must remain aware that he's a customer, not a supplicant, and he must retain the right to interview and select prospective armed bodyguards. He needs the same sort of talent that he'd recruit in the States: agents who are healthy and fit, have a certain amount of "common sense," are not trigger happy, and who understand that the first priority is to protect the principal, not glory hunting. It's preferable to have officers who have some protection experience, not uniformed types who know only patrol duties. It's important to make this requirement known to the local contracting officer.

An additional point regarding hiring local police officers for armed protection is that in some countries suing Americans is a profitable pastime. This is important to any corporation that does business in that country. Even tourists are often aware of this, because of the requirement to take out local vehicle insurance on the threat of being jailed indefinitely in case of an uninsured accident.

A corporation whose security agent shoots someone, or incurs liability in another way, is in for a serious problem. Using local police side steps these problems, because the citizens of Third World countries usually do not sue the police. What seems to be an exorbitant fee at first sight becomes very reasonable in view of the potential hassle it saves.

Legal Advice and Staff

Corporation security officers need the services of the staff lawyers. These can be invaluable in smoothing the way, because their services in many ways parallel those of the executive protection staff. The principle of operation is to avoid problems rather than have to solve them afterwards. The lawyers can brief the security agents on the legal picture, both at home and elsewhere.

Having a legal staff is crucial because of the "deep pockets" doctrine accepted by many courts. It often happens that, when there's an injury and a consequent lawsuit, the judgment goes against the one who can afford to pay the bills, not the one who really is at fault. The thinking is that the victim must receive compensation, and that the responsibility for paying the bill lies with the party with the "deep pockets."

This places any corporation or wealthy client in danger of being sued. Even without the "deep pockets" doctrine a wealthy person or corporation is more likely to be sued than an indigent. Having a full-time legal staff is a worthwhile precaution. The small agency or operator should have a lawyer on retainer, to ensure his availability for consultation.

Notes:

1. *Dead Clients Don't Pay*, Leroy Thompson, Boulder, CO, Paladin Press, 1984, p. 55. There are descriptions of bodyguards confiscating film and cameras. This seems very macho, but can lead to serious liability in certain circumstances.
2. *The Executive Protection Bible*, Martha J. Braunig, Basalt, CO, Executive Protection International, 1992, Appendix D.
3. *Dead Clients Don't Pay*, Leroy Thompson, Boulder, CO, Paladin Press, 1984, p. 30.
4. Account by a corporate security director who has first hand knowledge of how this system works.

22

Special Problems:
Things We Don't Normally Discuss

A bodyguard can find himself involved in some strange situations, as do police officers, clergymen, and doctors. The bodyguard has to possess the mental equilibrium and flexibility to cope with unusual problems, some of which bring great danger to both him and his client.

Flaky Clients

Let's begin with a simple problem: the client who engages you, changes his mind, and feels no obligation to cover any expenses you laid out to be at his disposal. One bodyguard was contacted by a potential client and told to have a team ready to meet him at a distant resort. The client postponed his trip twice, then canceled, leaving the team financially stranded.[1] Obviously, avoid this type of client, and take steps to protect your interests when accepting assignments. One way to cope with a new and unfamiliar client is to ask for cash up front to cover immediate expenses. A flake who does not intend to honor his commitments will refuse, and you can act accordingly.

Another way to handle this type of problem is to ask for airline tickets, and an account to cover lodging.[2] This is a diagnostic test, and quickly separates the sincere client from the ruthless manipulator.

Personal Relationships

While a bodyguard's positive feelings for his client are assets because they help the relationship, these can occasionally go too far. The Kevin Costner film, *The Bodyguard*, depicts a romantic relationship between a female client and her bodyguard. In one very limited sense, this has been a reflection of real life. Princess Stephanie of Monaco became romantically involved with Daniel Ducruet, her bodyguard. Patty Hearst married her bodyguard, and President Gerald Ford's daughter, Susan, likewise

married her U.S. Secret Service agent. The rumor mill has linked Geena Davis with executive protection specialist Gavin de Becker, and both Princess Diana and Dolly Parton have allegedly been linked romantically with their bodyguards.[3]

Bodyguards to the stars may be able to afford to become romantically involved, especially if they're single and well paid for "special services." Some people are "groupies," and a well muscled body and sidearm are turn-ons for them. However, in workaday life, especially in the business world, this becomes less likely than in the make-believe atmosphere of show business and royalty. A male bodyguard who becomes involved with his employer's wife is merely seeking trouble, especially if he, too, is married. A female bodyguard involved with her male executive boss may consider it a step up, but her employer's wife may object, as may her own husband.

Another problem arises with the female protectee who "will sexually taunt and tease the bodyguard, setting him up for an infraction of security policy or sexual assault charges."[4] There are enough problems involved in protecting someone from a threat without this prospect arising. Assigning a female bodyguard can forestall this type of problem.

Romantic relationships can also bring about nasty surprises, especially if the protectee is a homosexual who develops a crush on his heterosexual bodyguard. Likewise, the heterosexual female protectee with the hots may be bitterly disappointed upon discovering that her "hunky" protection agent prefers his own sex. The complications can be so far reaching, and the results so dangerous, that a policy of firmly avoiding any sort of romantic entanglement on the job is best. This applies to other bodyguards on the team, not only the leader.

Female Bodyguards

The U.S. Secret Service has been using females for protective duties for at least two decades, and apparently they have been able to continue the practice. The Secret Service is a special case, however, because of the generous personnel allotment they're able to devote to protective duties. Among other things, this allows relieving each agent on post regularly. Private bodyguards, however, have to make do with limited resources, and some special problems arise. One is bathroom calls. A male agent can urinate into a bottle or bush behind the premises. It's not that easy for a female, and the discomfort involved is discouraging enough to drive many females from the field once they discover that the real hardships are no more glamorous than bathroom calls.

With all that, there is a place for females in this occupation. The growing number of female executives indicates a need for bodyguards who can go with them into the gym and the bathroom.[5] Protocol may dictate a female agent for the wife or daughter of the main protectee. An adaptable woman who understands that she'll be working in a male dominated field, and who can put up with more than her share of discomfort, can succeed in executive protection.

The Uncooperative Protectee

This seems like almost a contradiction in terms, because a client who hires a bodyguard should work with him to get his money's worth. This isn't very unusual, though, because people often have conflicting motives and needs. Doctors know this very well, because one of the serious problems in medicine is the patient who doesn't follow his doctor's advice. Just as a patient may ignore advice to stop smoking or get more exercise, he may also ignore the bodyguard's advice to wear an armored vest and drive a less conspicuous car.

There are two types of uncooperative protectee: the one who finds the changes to his lifestyle too onerous, and the other who feels he needs no protection. Working for either can be a huge hassle.

The protectee who objects to lifestyle changes requires very tactful handling. It's important to convince him of the need to modify his daily routine. An additional difficulty can come from his wife, who may object to protective measures for herself. If she's convinced that her husband's the only one who may be kidnapped or killed, it'll be hard to change her mind unless someone else in a similar situation comes to grief. This is often the deciding event, and we'll discuss its effects later on.

The protectee who feels that he's not in danger and doesn't need protection isn't a direct client. He may be an executive of a company which has a policy of providing protection for all executives above a certain grade. If he's young and physically fit, or simply feels that he's lucky, he may disdain protection. It's hard to convince a person of this type that executive protection is either necessary or prudent. One approach is to present protection as a sort of status symbol. It is, because only executives above a certain grade are entitled to the services of an executive protection specialist, and if the idea is "sold" to the protectee in the right way, the agent can win him over. Sometimes, however, only outside help will make a difference in attitudes.

This outside help may come in the form of an attack on a peer. Just as people tend to lock their doors and windows after a burglary, a killing or kidnapping can stimulate interest in executive protection. This type of event will often win over even a recalcitrant wife. If another executive's children have been kidnapped, the point of the program will come home to her.

Other protectees may have special requirements, and fulfilling them can bring a great deal of trouble to the bodyguard who isn't prepared. In some instances the difficulties can be serious enough to lead the bodyguard to give up his employment rather than take the risks involved.

The Ego-Tripper

This is the reverse of the uncooperative protectee. A few individuals who hire bodyguards don't really need them, but spend the money because they see having an executive protection specialist at one's side as a status symbol. It implies to friends and associates that they're important enough to be worth knocking off or kidnapping, and allows them to strut around with an enhanced sense of importance.

One danger for the executive protection specialist who concludes that his client is ego-tripping is that there may exist real danger for the client. The client may not be in danger from political terrorists, but still may encounter a street level mugger. The situation may also change, and a real threat may develop without the bodyguard's being aware of it.

Another danger can be that the client may insist that the bodyguard be armed to enhance his image. Traveling armed in locales where there are strict gun laws is a liability, as we've seen, and this kind of client unwittingly lays a sucker trap for himself and his protection specialist.

The best practice is, of course, to take on only a client who is not a "flake," but a bodyguard needing work cannot always select his clients with the care he should. An executive protection specialist who hires on with this type of client should not view his assignment as a racket in which he can relax, because nothing's going to happen anyway. Complacency can be dangerous, and a bodyguard who loses a client will be handicapped in seeking future employment.

Illegal Enterprises

Some people who seek protection against criminal attack are themselves involved in illegal enterprises.[6] One obvious example is the drug dealer who takes a bodyguard along to an illegal transaction for protection against the other party's bad faith. A worse example is the client who takes a bodyguard along for protection because he intends to rip off the other party.

Both of these situations are bad from a tactical standpoint, because the client is exposing himself to unnecessary risks. The basic philosophy of executive protection is avoidance, not confrontation, and any bodyguard who goes along on what promises to be a confrontation stands to lose.

There are two further dangers, one from the law and the other from the other party's associates. Law enforcement officers will perceive that bodyguard as a member of the criminal enterprise, and may well arrest him as part of a conspiracy. If a death results from the confrontation, it will be hard to avoid criminal liability for it because it will have occurred during a criminal transaction.

In a criminal transaction, the other party's reaction can be explosive and far reaching. To him, it won't matter that the executive protection specialist isn't sharing in the profits of the criminal transaction. The other party will see him as part of the gang, and if a deal goes badly, he may take reprisals. At times, drug gang reprisals become rigorous and bloody, because the offended party seeks revenge by gunning down the dealer and his associates, not sparing their families.

These are all good reasons for carefully avoiding illegal enterprises. Even tangential involvement is as dangerous as playing with matches in a gasoline refinery.

Illegal Actions

Lawsuits can arise when a bodyguard overreaches himself, exceeds his instructions or breaks the law. A photographer brought suit against a rock performer, claiming that he was attacked by the performer and his bodyguard when he tried to photograph the singer at an MTV Awards show.[7]

Another singer's bodyguard was found guilty of raping a 15-year-old girl at a hotel in Minneapolis after a concert. Performer David James Parker and stage technician Gary Chris Saunders were found innocent, but the bodyguard, Christopher Tsipouras, got a ten-year sentence.[8]

"Don't Let Them Take Me Alive"

Some clients may be very afraid of being captured by their enemies. This may be because they're criminals or political extremists. A former organized crime figure may fear reprisals from former associates. In such a case, it's very believable that his enemies may not want to kill him quickly and cleanly, but intend instead to torture him to death. In another instance, a foreign political leader may fear severe mistreatment at the hands of the opposition. This sort of client may tell you categorically that if his capture seems imminent, you are to take all steps to ensure that he's not taken alive.

If you're the bodyguard, this puts you on the spot. Your conscience may be clear if you kill the client at his own request in certain extreme situations, but there may be unacceptable legal ramifications. In the United States and most other countries, a member of any conspiracy which results in anyone's death is vulnerable to prosecution for murder. The victim's consent does not get you off the hook. Taking a human life is illegal because the law does not allow a person to consent to his or her own death. Even though you may have the most noble motives, you can be prosecuted. There have been successful prosecutions of people who have put terminal cancer patients out of their misery at their own request. It's still murder under the law.

What do you do? Your action will depend on many circumstances. One is the country in which you work. A lot depends on how much political influence your client has, and whether or not he can make arrangements to have you exonerated before the event.

Another factor is your escape. If you can walk away from the scene and not fear reprisals, you may be tempted to comply with your client's wish. "Walking away" means just that. If the attack upon your client takes place in a remote area where there are no witnesses and you can escape cleanly, you can bring your involvement to an end with your client's death. If such is the case, make sure that your client pays you a couple of weeks' salary in advance.

A third possibility is fudging the evidence so that it appears that the protectee was killed by the attackers. This is tricky because it always involves improvisation under pressure, and the uncertainties that it brings.

The fourth, and certainly the safest, possibility is to refuse this condition and risk being dismissed. This is simply saving your skin, the only one you have. There will always be other clients. Probably the deciding factor will be that if the client is so concerned about not being taken alive, it's his responsibility to do something about it himself. Sloughing off the task onto another is a very wimpy act.

Proactive Operations

From the viewpoint of pure logic, the preemptive strike makes sense. Anyone fearing an attack is well-advised to eliminate the attacker first. Some protectees think exactly along those lines, and if they know the party intending to attack them they will seek to hire a killer to hit the enemy first.

In other instances, there have been rumors that some swashbuckling protective outfits follow a policy of reprisal. Anyone sponsoring an attack upon their clients will have a "contract" put out on him.[9] A few maverick bodyguards have committed illegal violence for their clients.

We got an excellent example of the type of activity to avoid from the incident in which Shawn Eckardt, bodyguard for Tonya Harding, set up an attack on rival skater Nancy Kerrigan with an expandable baton. Eckardt and his co-conspirators planned to incapacitate Kerrigan and knock her out of the running for Olympic medals. Eckardt showed his unprofessionalism by committing an illegal act. The aftermath of this mistake destroyed several careers.

Unfortunately, the law does not legitimize a preemptive strike or a reprisal killing. If someone cancels your client's birth certificate, you're never allowed to tear his up in retaliation. In such a situation, your best course is to advise your client that

there are specialists available for these tasks. If he seeks a preemptive attack or a reprisal to avenge his death if he's killed, he should deal with a contract killer, not a bodyguard. Your job is to defend him from a deadly attack, not to commit an aggression.

Take Prisoners or Not?

Normally, this decision is not the bodyguard's concern. As we've seen, his job is to evacuate the protectee and not even to engage the attacker in combat unless this is the only way to ensure the client's safety. Dealing with attackers is the job of the outer screen or the local police. There are occasions, however, when the bodyguard or his team has to deal with the attacker themselves, and he must face the decision.

Most of us have a prejudice, inspired by our system of laws, to use only "minimal force" to stop the attack and to effect the arrest. This is perhaps the humane thing to do when dealing with an attack by a deranged person, if we can be sure that the attacker is deranged by making the diagnosis on the spot and in a split second.

Often, the quickest way of dealing with the close-in attack is by "swarming," which leaves the bodyguard team with a live captive. Whether to turn him over to the local police or execute him on the spot is a critical question, one that depends on practicalities, not on any vengeful or cruel impulses by the bodyguard or his principal. As with most of these questions, there is more than one viewpoint:

The first is that if the attacker is a "terrorist," he should not be taken prisoner. A terrorist in prison is the focus of further attempts at kidnapping or killing.[10] There have been many such instances.

The hijacking of an El Al airliner in 1968 resulted in the release of Palestinian prisoners from Israeli jails. This is an important point to remember when one hears the claim that the Israelis never negotiate with terrorists.

In 1976, Germans and Palestinians hijacked an Air France craft bound from Israel with many Jewish passengers on board. This aircraft wound up at Entebbe, in Uganda, and again the demand was the release of prisoners. This time the Israeli government did negotiate, but it simultaneously was exploring the prospect of solving the problem by force. The Israeli attitude had hardened after the previous experience. The result was the well executed and widely publicized raid at Entebbe by Israeli commandos to release the hostages.

The kidnapping of Hans-Martin Schleyer was an effort to obtain the release of terrorists held in German prisons.[11] The sequel to that incident was the hijacking of a Lufthansa airliner, which eventually wound up in Mogadishu, where the hostages were rescued by the troopers of GSG-9.[12] Again, the demand was the release of imprisoned terrorists.

There is an unpublicized side to this story. After the Schleyer and Lufthansa incidents, it was crystal clear that terrorist prisoners were liabilities because they almost certainly would inspire rescue attempts. The sequence of events in the Lufthansa hijacking is very interesting and suggestive. The aircraft was hijacked on October 13, 1977. On October 18, German troopers assaulted the aircraft and liberated the hostages. At the same time, in the Stammheim high security prison in Germany, four of the most prominent terrorist prisoners "attempted suicide," and three succeeded. A few hours after that news broke, Schleyer's captors killed him and left his body where police would find it.

Apparently Schleyer's kidnappers did not accept the official version regarding the "suicides." There is cause to question it, simply because of the clearly evident fact that prisoners are liabilities.

These events brought about a widely accepted change in attitudes towards the taking of terrorist prisoners. Special police units charged with hostage rescue started looking more closely at the doctrine of "shoot on sight."[13] For once, this doctrine could be justified in the eyes of the law, because the law in most Western countries allows the use of deadly force to stop a felony in progress and/or to save a human life. In a hostage rescue, the lives of the hostages are obviously at stake.

Hostage rescue teams have, therefore, developed tactics exactly for this. One is the "failure drill," firing two shots into the chest and one in the head to ensure that a hostage taker does not survive the experience, even if he's wearing body armor. The other is the two-man team, which has the lead man firing at the suspect's chest to put him down, and the back-up member placing one shot into the suspect's head to make sure he never gets up again.

From this, it's easy to see that taking a prisoner during an attempt on a protectee may lead to further attempts. This line of logic fails to take into account that further attempts are likely to happen anyway, but

the purpose will be kidnapping for money, not for the release of a prisoner.

The other viewpoint is that the prisoner's life should be preserved, because he may yield valuable information during interrogation. This is true whether the plan is to turn him over to the police or conduct a rigorous interrogation on the premises. In some instances, it's possible to satisfy both needs. If the attack takes place in an area remote enough that the authorities are unaware of it, it becomes possible to take a captive, interrogate him and then dispose of him to avoid any embarrassing aftermath. If the protectee owns an island, for example, access is so limited that anything can happen.

From all this, we see that the fate of a prisoner depends not on the kindness and sense of justice of the bodyguard, but on the realities of the everyday world. A rational decision must take all possible consequences into account, and the decision maker must thread his way through several possible courses of action to find the best one for his client.

Be Flexible!

All told, you may run into some unusual problems in protective work. It'll be necessary to be both flexible and innovative. It'll also be necessary to have decided in advance how far you're prepared to go for an employer. As with other types of clients, some can be very demanding indeed, and occasionally it's better to give up a client than to let one drag you down into an unhealthy "no-win" situation.

Notes:

1. *Executive Protection*, Mares, Benny, Boulder, CO, Paladin Press, 1994, p. 70.
2. *Ibid.,* p. 71.
3. Trebbe, Ann, "Love Blooms With Bodyguards," *USA Today*, June 2, 1992, p. 2D.
4. *The Executive Protection Bible*, Martha J. Braunig, Basalt, CO, Executive Protection International, 1992, p. 326. Libbers please note that this quotation is from a female protector's essay on the role of women in protection.
5. *Ibid.,* p. 326.
6. Personal communication from Richard Ryan, martial arts and executive protection trainer.
7. Landis, David, "Guns N' Lawsuits," *USA Today*, September 6, 1990, p. 1D.

8. Gliatto, Tom, "It's A Rap," *USA Today*, February 6, 1990, p. 1D.
9. *Dead Clients Don't Pay*, Leroy Thompson, Boulder, CO, Paladin Press, 1984, p. 9.
10. *The War Against The Terrorists*, Gayle Rivers, NY, Stein and Day, 1986, pp. 210-211.
11. *Terrorism and Personal Protection*, Brian Jenkins, Editor, NY, Butterworth Publishers, 1985, pp. 51-54.
12. *Ibid.*, p. 54.
13. Discussions between the author and members of elite police units who wish to remain anonymous.

23

How To Bodyguard Yourself

After reviewing the techniques described in this book, you have a better idea than before of how to assess, forestall and cope with personal threats. In your own best interests, you'll want to protect yourself and your family with at least the diligence you'd expend on a client.

If you are the client, this book will help you to understand your bodyguard's viewpoint, the whys and hows of the way he goes about protecting you. Your bodyguard may not have been expressive enough, or detailed enough, in explaining your role to you.

You also have to face another fact: your bodyguard may not always be available to protect you, and you have to know how to protect yourself during his absence. Unless you're a government official, or very wealthy, you may not have a large team of agents looking after you around the clock. What do you do when your bodyguard's off duty, or ill, or on vacation? If you hired him through an agency, they may supply a replacement, but there's another and more sinister possibility.

Your bodyguard may have been "taken out" by attackers, leaving you on your own. This is quite likely, because attackers generally go for the bodyguard first. Eliminating the bodyguard frees them to kill or kidnap their target.

Also, many clients have budgets that allow only part-time bodyguards to accompany them while commuting or traveling. At home they either feel relatively safe or are prepared to attend to their own safety. Others may not have any budgets to pay for bodyguards. Corporate downsizing has led to cuts in security budgets, because security is not a profit center, and corporate security directors have to cover the same responsibilities with fewer people.[1]

Guarding yourself and your family is for the most part an intelligent adaptation of some of the methods described herein. Simple and everyday security measures help avoid danger.[2]

Some companies offer security awareness training for their executives.[3] This training may also be available for family members. The spouse is a key figure, because, in the case of kidnapping, the spouse is usually the first person the abductors contact. This type of program typically covers home and office security, physical safeguards, security while traveling and hostage precautions.

Security at Home

With the country's crime rate still very high, despite a slight decline in recent years, you need to use basic physical security at home. We've already skimmed over locks and alarms. You probably have that knowledge under your belt already. If not, have a competent person install solid locks and an alarm system. It's worth the expense.

No lock or security system is perfect, and the most for which you can hope is to deter the majority of the bad guys, and send them to prey on your less well protected neighbor. You also may encounter a persistent burglar, or one who doesn't mind running risks. In that case, resign yourself to being ripped off, and be thankful he didn't take your life.

If an intruder comes in while you and your family are home, the situation suddenly becomes deadly serious. You probably can tolerate losing some of your property, but your life and those of your family are not expendable. Coping with this problem requires a higher order of preparedness.

Home Defense Preparations

To start, you need a plan. You also need to work this plan out with your family, and rehearse it with them. For the purposes of this discussion, let's assume that you have a wife and two school age children. If you're single, your problem's much simpler.

Start by surveying your home with the eye of a security specialist. Where are the likely points of entry? Can you reinforce some of them, to channel the attack? "Channeling" the attack means directing it into a certain direction. This is vital because one person can't carry on an all round defense. If you can channel the attack to come from a direction where you can set up a defense, your chances of surviving are greatly improved.

Placing solid iron bars over bedroom windows helps avoid the problem of an intruder coming right in on you. Of course, the bars have to open quickly from the inside in case of fire. If you live in a high-rise, you won't have this problem, and most likely there's only one door leading into your apartment. This "channels" any invasion, making it easier for the defender.

Some people recommend the building of a "safe room," an inside room with no windows that you can reinforce, as a last ditch refuge.[4] Some go as far as to suggest that you stockpile food and water, much like in a fallout shelter. The theory is that in case of a civil war, insurrection or mob attack, this will be a safe place for you to retreat with your family. This isn't necessarily so, as a gasoline bomb will make a "safe room" very hot, very quickly.

There should be a defensive core, a room or section of hallway where the family can stay and be protected from some gunfire. The bathroom often has metal fixtures which provide some protection, and placing steel paneling inside some of the cabinets is a quick way to build in additional protection. This need not be armor plate, as light weight is not important. Simple, half-inch thick "boiler plate" will provide protection against any pistol bullets and some rifle fire.

An important feature of your home's defensive core is communication. This can be a cordless or a cellular phone. Designate one member of your family to telephone the police in case of emergency, and to remain on the line until the emergency ends. The point is to inform responding police officers of the nature of the threat, the location of the intruders and, most importantly, your location and description, so that they won't mistake you for the intruder.

Discuss your basic defense plan with your family. Make sure each knows his or her role by rehearsing the defense plan. One crucial factor is knowing where everyone is in a crisis. There have been instances of people shooting family members after mistaking them for intruders. A common way this happens is when the householder hears a noise at night, and doesn't stop to think that a family member may have gone to the kitchen or bathroom.

Tactics

Tactics make it or break it, because the best hardware is useless if used ineffectively. Good tactics help you make the best use of what you've got.

Early warning is important. A solidly built home, with stout doors and securely locked windows, ensures that an intruder will make noise in forcing an entry. Another possibility is a dog. This doesn't necessarily mean a guard dog. Even the tame family pooch has hearing more sensitive than that of humans, and can often alert you to intruders.

Using light defensively is important. As a start, you should have outside lighting, as discussed previously. This isn't only a deterrent. It lets you observe who's scratching at your door lock. You can observe your intruder, his weapon and any accomplices.

Another technical aid is closed-circuit TV, which is today very affordable. Popular electronic outlets, such as Radio Shack, have CCTV sets for home security, and prices are low enough to allow placing several cameras to cover all approaches.

Inside your home, you should have the unoccupied rooms lit. A small night light in each is enough. The purpose is to have the intruder illuminated while you remain in the shadows. You should be able to find your way around your own home without the use of light. Light enables you to direct your gunfire more precisely, and staying in the shadows handicaps the intruder when you decide to open fire.

An important point is not to use a flashlight to locate an intruder at night. This only tells an intruder where you are. Obviously, he'll see you long before you see him.

One tactic is to make use of surprise. This means not letting an intruder know that you're observing him until you open fire. This requires remaining concealed. Also important is remaining silent. Some people think that the sound of a racking shotgun is intimidating, and will frighten any intruder into surrendering. Don't bet your life on this. The intruder may panic and open fire, or may run. If he runs toward the exit, this provides a satisfactory outcome, but if he runs towards where other family members are hiding, shooting at anything he sees, this causes more problems than you can handle.

Staying concealed and observing carefully buys you time. You need time, because time means safety. You can observe whether the intruder is alone, or if he has companions. This can make the difference between life and death. If he's got a partner, listen to any conversation, which may alert you to the presence of a third party out of sight.

Staying in place has another advantage. It lets the intruder come to you, exposing himself over terrain that is familiar to you.

Think of cover. Concealment is not cover. Cover is protection from gunfire as well as from view. If the intruder has a chance to return fire, you'll need to be behind cover.

The moment to open fire is when you're sure that you know where the intruders are, and when you're sure of scoring hits. Generally, you'll also want to have the intruders in an open area, where they can't easily drop behind cover or concealment. The middle of a room will be the best you can hope for.

The point of defensive fire is fire control, not firepower. It's not important how many shots you fire. All that counts is how many shots hit. At all costs, you don't want a protracted gun battle in your home, unless you live alone and are far from any neighbors. An exchange of shots is dangerous for all within range. You will, of course, be careful to direct your shots so that you don't endanger innocent people, but don't expect the same consideration from the intruder. Your best course of action is to put him down before he can open fire and endanger your family.

If you can, avoid shooting in the direction of your family. Try to direct your shots outward and away from them. This means, among other things, never allowing an intruder to get between you and your family, because any shots you miss will go flying in their direction. Face the prospect that you might miss. Most shots in a gunfight do miss.

Admit to yourself that fright may give you the shakes. Why not? It's normal to be frightened. Courage is acting effectively in spite of your fear. When you open fire, be prepared to support your shooting hand. If you can, grip the weapon with both hands. You may lean against a wall or rest the weapon on a chair arm or back.

Fire at least two shots into each intruder. Despite all of the verbiage we read about "stopping power," you can't be confident that the suspect will go down and stay down with only one shot. You may even miss the first time. More likely, you won't hit a vital spot to cause an instant drop. It's very unlikely that you'll be able to hit the brain or spine in poor light. Aim at the center of the body and depend on normal shot dispersion to hit vital spots. Continue firing until the intruder goes down and stays down.

Coming Home

If you arrive home and notice signs that there's been a forced entry, don't try to be a hero or macho man — just clear the premises. If you're a target for assassination or kidnapping, there may be someone waiting inside for you to show up. Your best bet is to call the police and let them handle the problem. If for some reason the police can't respond, it's better to sleep in the car or at a hotel than to try to enter your home.

Security While Traveling

Where are you going? Is this trip necessary? Always remember that the protection of anonymity goes only so far. Don't think that nobody's after you because you're "only the bodyguard." You are a prime target, even when off duty, because an attacker may decide to take you out while you're less alert.

When driving your car, remain alert, instead of letting the miles slide by while you think of other things. If you're in the habit of day dreaming, you're surrendering a prime advantage to an ambusher or kidnapper. Always be aware of vehicles around you, and give each a quick look. Try to see if you spot the same vehicle behind you during a trip. Whenever you make a turn, watch for who follows you.

Make it a habit to drive ahead of your car, instead of keeping your focus only on the car ahead. Look several hundred yards down the road to spot any unusual activity on the sides of the road. This may save you from an ambush, but more likely it will help you spot that radar cop waiting for you to come within range. With more police departments using speed traps to gain revenue for city and county governments, alertness may save your money and driver's license, if not your life.

Take a cellular phone with you, both to ensure communication with your employer and to be able to dial "911" in case of emergency. Today, cellular phones are so commonplace and inexpensive that there's no excuse for remaining out of touch.

Kidnapping

You may be abducted by a kidnapper, or taken hostage as a trading piece by political terrorists. Your abductors may be one of four types: novice kidnappers; religious or politically motivated ideologues; emotionally disturbed persons; and skilled professional criminals.[5]

The degree of danger you face depends on the mind sets of those who kidnapped you, and on the responses of those they contact. The most dangerous types of kidnappers are the mentally disturbed and the ideologues, because of their emotional volatility. Amateur criminals may harm you out of ineptness, but professional criminals understand that the main goal is obtaining the ransom, not proving a point. They also know that a murder charge is more serious than a kidnapping count. Most of all, professional criminals understand that a dead victim is useless as a bargaining tool. Only a live victim can be ransomed.

Forget about any show of dignity, machismo or iron will. If you're a kidnap victim, you're totally in your abductors' power, and it's best not to do anything to antagonize them. Your chances of survival may well be directly tied to how faithfully you obey their orders. An example is not trying to remove a blindfold or sneak a peek at the kidnappers. It's a rule of thumb that if the kidnappers plan on eventually releasing you, they don't want you to be able to identify them, but if you do get a look at them, your release then becomes a threat to them.

On the other hand, if the kidnappers don't appear to care if you see their faces, they're probably not planning to release you. In such a case, you can take greater risks in planning an escape on your own.

Weighing the risks is a vital preliminary step. You have to judge whether you're better off waiting to be ransomed or rescued, or whether you're truly on your own. If you work for a company with a "no ransom" policy, it's clear that your employer is prepared to write you off. If the demand is political, and the government to which your captors make their demand has a policy of never negotiating with terrorists, you're likewise abandoned and expendable. Your only hopes, then, are to escape on your own or to wait for rescue.

The chances of escape are very slim, but they occasionally come. Not all terrorists are experts, and they often make tactical errors. Five percent of victims escaped, in one study.[6] This might not be the best tactic for you, in some situations. You may not want to try to escape if you're traveling with your family and escaping means leaving them behind.

What are your odds in case you're kidnapped? In this country, of 759 people kidnapped between October, 1990 and April, 1992, 669 were released. 86 were killed in some way, and 90 were never found. The international picture isn't as encouraging, though. Of 2,090 kidnappings between January, 1987, and June, 1992, 56 percent of the victims were recovered after payment of a ransom.[7]

When a kidnapping takes place, negotiations usually begin between the kidnappers on one side, and the victim's family or the police on the other. It's important for you to know that negotiators follow different agendas, because they may well have different priorities.

The family's main concern is to recover the victim unharmed. To this end, they're usually willing to pay any price, go any place and meet any demands. Private security managers and consultants may have other priorities, and in some countries police have priorities squarely opposed to those of the family. In some countries, it's illegal to pay ransom to a kidnapper, so a family has to avoid contacting the police to get their victim back.

A private security consultant or manager has his priorities dictated by the party paying his salary or fee. The family's security manager will make the victim's welfare his first priority. However, a corporate security director may be influenced to negotiate for as little ransom as possible, to minimize the financial loss to the company. Likewise, if the family has kidnap insurance, the insurance company's representative will try to keep the amount of the ransom down, protecting his company's interests. Finally, a police agent may be more concerned with deterring future kidnappers than rescuing the present victim, and may take a very hard line during negotiations.

From a strictly rational point of view, refusing to pay any ransom in all cases is an effective way to deter prospective kidnappers. A corporation taking this hard line will eventually acquire the reputation of being kidnap proof among professional and amateur criminals. However, enforcing this policy usually takes a few dead bodies before potential kidnappers begin to believe that the policy is serious and inviolable. This is very hard on the kidnap victims.

A no-ransom policy is useless when the object is not monetary gain. Political objectives are less tangible, and can be very hard to negotiate. It becomes especially difficult when the kidnapping results in a three-cornered negotiation. The kidnappers abduct a private citizen or foreign corporate executive to impose a demand, such as the release of political prisoners, on the local government. Government agents are necessarily involved, and they may not be inclined to make concessions to criminals for the sake of a foreign citizen. In such cases, negotiations become very delicate, and the victim's survival becomes very chancy.

Finally, we have to look at the emotional component. The negotiations may degenerate into a macho contest between the kidnappers and a negotiator whose main agenda is not recovering the victim, but defending his reputation as a tough negotiator. The victim's well being takes a definite second place when this happens. On the other side, the kidnappers may lose face if they back down at all, or they may feel that they have nothing to lose by killing the victim. A terrorist group trying to score points may feel it necessary to kill the victim to prove that they're serious.

Hostage

There's little valid advice for those taken hostage. We read of various cautions, such as not making eye contact with the terrorists and speaking only when addressed. These are valid as far as they go, but in reality there's not much a hostage can do except to not "rock the boat," to remain watchful, and wait for rescue or an opportunity to escape. As a hostage, you must hope that luck will be on your side.

A popular myth is that "The primary goal of hostage negotiations is the safe release of the hostages, and the secondary goal is the safe capture of the hostage taker(s)."[8] Not necessarily, unless you're such an important person that the government considers your personal safety paramount above all else. If they let your captors go in order to save your life as a result of political pressure, sooner or later they'll face the same problem once more. From the police viewpoint, it's preferable to capture or kill the hostage takers, so that further occurrences are prevented. That's the abrasive edge of reality, and you should be aware of it if you're ever taken hostage.

One vital point is to know what to expect during a commando raid to rescue you. Victims are rescued about 23 percent of the time during international kidnappings.[9] If a commando raid does occur, be prepared for the worst. The terrorists may be prepared to kill the hostages upon the arrival of rescue forces. The wide publicity given to the Entebbe, Mogadishu and Iranian Embassy rescues has ensured that anyone interested knows that there are specially trained and equipped rescue teams in most countries. If a rescue attempt comes, and the terrorists don't blow you all away with explosives, stay on the floor. The rescue team will be storming in, and the only warning you're likely to have is the noise and blinding flash of "stun grenades." The rescuers will be keyed up, and will fire at anyone or anything that appears to be a threat or even moves, so stay down. Don't even lift your head or say anything. Play dead. It's safer.

Also expect to be treated like a terrorist, handcuffed and hog tied with a black hood over your head until the rescuers can get the situation sorted out and everyone's identity verified.

Be Responsible For Yourself

Always remember that your bodyguard may or may not be able to cope with the threat. He may, or may not, keep you out of trouble. He may, or may not, be available when the problem strikes. This is why you must be prepared to look after your own skin. It's the only one you have.

Notes:

1. Flores, Thomas V., and Nudell, Mayer, Executive, "Protect Thyself," *Security Management*, January, 1993, p. 41.
2. *Terrorism and Personal Protection*, Brian Jenkins, editor, New York, Butterworth Publishers, 1985, pp. 369-386. This chapter, written by James R. Jarrett, is a hardcore, realistic appraisal of the reasons for the protectee's learning to do something for himself. In reality, no protective ring can be foolproof and invulnerable, as several American presidents have found out the hard way. The meager security systems the rest of the protectees can afford leave many gaps which need filling.
3. Flores, Thomas V., and Nudell, Mayer, Executive, "Protect Thyself," *Security Management*, January, 1993, pp. 39-41.
4. *Executive Protection Manual*, Reber, Jan, and Shaw, Paul, Schiller Park, IL, MTI Teleprograms, 1976, p. 148.
5. Van Zandt, Clinton R., "Hostage Survival Strategies," *Security Management*, January, 1993, pp. 33-38.
6. *Ibid.,* p. 34.
7. *Ibid.*
8. Braunig, Martha J., *The Executive Protection Bible*, Basalt, CO, Executive Protection International, 1992, p. 273.
9. Van Zandt, Clinton R., "Hostage Survival Strategies," *Security Management*, January, 1993, p. 34.

24
For Further Reading

Braver Men Walk Away, Peter Gurney, London, Harper Collins Publishers, 1993. Paperback. His autobiographical book tells the story of one of the world's top bomb disposal officers, who began his career in the British Army, where he neutralized bombs in Northern Ireland, and ended up on the London Metropolitan Police's Bomb Squad. The author traces the development of terrorist bombs during the past 40 years, and sketches various terrorist campaigns. His descriptions of anti-handling devices included in improvised explosive devices are persuasive arguments for leaving discovered bombs alone and calling in the experts. Peter Gurney's value as an eyewitness is excellent, because he was on the scene during the Harrod's bombing, the attempted bombing of an El-Al airliner, and many other bombings that took place in Britain during the last several decades.

The Executive Protection Bible, Martha J. Braunig, Basalt, CO, Executive Protection International, 1992. This large, soft cover book contains 486 pages of text and about another 100 pages of appendices and checklists. Written in a conversational style, this book covers many practical aspects of executive protection neglected by other texts. Among these are dressing for the part, and how to handle a client's illegal activity.

Executive Protection, Benny Mares, Boulder, CO, Paladin Press, 1994. This 108-page soft cover book is a quick introduction to bodyguarding, and serves as a primer for the person interested in entering the field.

Executive Protection Manual, Jan Reber, and Paul Shaw, Schiller Park IL, MTI Teleprograms, 1976. This huge book is an encyclopedic collection of data, checklists, and other information regarding executive protection. It provides a comprehensive discussion of the details of providing executive protection. A bonus is a series of extensive checklists for the bodyguard to follow in ensuring the safety of his client. Although old, this book is not dated.

Federal Bomb Intelligence, U. S. Government Guide to Terrorist Explosives, Boulder, CO, Paladin Press, 1991, Commercial Reprint. This is a high-quality reprint of a federal manual describing an assortment of homemade bombs used for assassinations. This book provides explicit information, including drawings and photographs, on a variety of bombs used by terrorists. This is a good reference and training volume, because it helps the bodyguard recognize explosive devices, even when they're disguised, and to seek them out when they're concealed. Well illustrated, this book depicts improvised explosive devices, hoax devices, suitcase bombs, and even describes some disarming procedures. Note: It's best to leave disarming to the specialist, even though this volume provides clear instructions for one type of bomb.

Living In Troubled Lands, Patrick Collins, Boulder, CO, Paladin Press, 1981. This paperback book is a good guide for the American who travels or lives outside his country. The author covers the low profile, threat analysis, residential security, security while on the move, hostages and other related topics. This is a thorough guide to coping with terrorist attacks abroad. Although dated, this book is very valuable because it's oriented towards the executive living abroad, explaining what he can do to protect himself.

On Assassination, H.H.A. Cooper, Boulder, CO, Paladin Press, 1984. This book is a good overview on assassination. Cooper deals with details as well as painting with a broad brush.

Prime Target, Bruce L. Danto, M. D., Philadelphia, The Charles Press, 1990. This book, written by a psychiatrist, includes several guest chapters written by protection specialists. These chapters are the best in the book. However, Chapter 23, "Written Threats and Fan Letters: Linguistic Analysis," covers a topic rarely seen in print and provides several examples of extreme crank mail a protectee might receive. Also included in this book is a chapter on terminated employees and workplace violence, as well as chapters dealing with body armor, business security, terrorists and terrorist organizations, and hostage taking. Overall, this is a comprehensive guide to how an executive can protect himself from threats at home and abroad.

Privacy For Sale, Jeffrey Rothfeder, NY, Simon & Schuster, 1992. Rothfeder's book concentrates on computerized records, and shows how it's possible to obtain a great deal of information about almost anyone by gaining access to the right computer database. Databases are crucial to stalkers, and to private investigators whom stalkers may employ under a pretext.

Protecting the President, Dennis V. N. McCarthy, NY, William Morrow & Company, 1985. McCarthy is the man who was there, the first Secret Service Agent to jump on John Hinckley after he'd opened fire at President Ronald Reagan and injured four people. McCarthy provides valuable insights into what it's like to work protective details, including the trivial details that tax the agent's patience.

Protective Services, Field Circular 19-136, U.S. Army Military Police School, reprinted by Loompanics Unlimited. This manual promotes the official U.S. Government views on protective operations, including a protective team, and copious back-up and logistical support. This makes it worthwhile for the bodyguard who has a team at his disposal, but it's also worth reading by the agent running a one-man operation who can adapt its techniques to his constrained situation.

Providing Executive Protection, Edited by Dr. Richard W. Kobetz, Berryville, Virginia, Executive Protection Institute, 1991. This volume, compiled by the major figure in American executive protection training, contains chapters written by experts. Some topics covered are: threat assessment, team dynamics, interviewing unwanted visitors, dining, etiquette, protocol and legal considerations. The value of this volume is that it covers some topics not discussed elsewhere.

Providing Protective Services, A Practical Guide For Police, James A. King, San Diego, CA, EPS International, 1990. This is an excellent manual for executive protection. The author concentrates on practical techniques as well as on equipment. This volume contains many checklists and information on their application to personal protection.

Seven Steps to Personal Safety, Richard B. Isaacs, M. A., and Tim Powers. NY, Center for Personal Defense Studies, 1993. This is a basic book on personal safety for people who need an entry level discussion of personal protection. It's suitable for an executive's or bodyguard's family members, because it deals with easy to understand concepts and tactics. It will be necessary to supplement this book with some additional instruction covering the family's special situation, especially if stationed abroad.

Terrorism and Personal Protection, Brian Jenkins, Editor, NY, Butterworth Publishers, 1985. This collection of essays by some of the top people on executive protection and terrorism provides various viewpoints and valuable information on the nuts and bolts of protection. Jenkins has gathered a group of experts to provide chapters in their areas of expertise. This collection will probably never go out of date.

You're The Target, Theodore G. Shackley, Robert L. Oatman, and Richard A. Finney, New World Publishing, Inc., 1989. Available from Paladin Press. This book is an overview of the dangers from terrorists and kidnappers at home and abroad. It provides copious information on terrorist attack methods and how to cope with them, citing many cases as examples. It's also valuable for its nuts-and-bolts discussion of terrorist tactics, such as ambushes and car bombings.

Appendix I
Threat Assessment Worksheet

This is for use regarding every identifiable individual who is a threat to the protectee. Do not omit starting a file just because not all of the information is available. Try to obtain the subject's photograph, handwriting exemplar, and fingerprints.

Name_____ S/S#_____

Aliases _____

Address _____

Date of Birth _____Telephone number _____

Driver's license state & number _____

Make, model, and color of vehicle owned _____

Motor vehicle license number _____

Height_____ Weight_____

Hair color_____ Eye color_____

General health_____ Drug use_____

Scars and tattoos _____

Psychiatric history _____

Sexual perversions _____

Military service _____

Rank_____ Discharged _____

Skills attained in firearms _____

Explosives _____

Criminal history _____

Prison history _____

Marital status _____

Relatives and addresses _____

_____

_____

_____

_____

_____

Threats Made _____

Interview date and time _____

Interview summary _____

_____

_____

_____

_____

_____

_____

_____

_____

Appendix II
Building Security
Checklist

This form applies both to the client's dwelling and workplace.

Address _____

Building owner/manager _____

Resident manager?_____

Building type _____

Construction_____

Number of floors _____

Building entrances _____

Windows _____

Stairs _____

Elevators _____

Roof access _____

Fire alarms _____

Access control _____

Security guards_____

Parking lot _____

Perimeter fence _____

Gates _____

Patrol plan _____

Building area occupied by client _____

Security quarters _____

Neighbors_____

_____

Special problems _____

_____

_____

Appendix III
Advance Security Checklist

This form is for completion before the client sets out on a trip. Completing all applicable sections is essential.

Contact police officials _____

Name of Police Chief or watch commander _____

Telephone number _____

Client's accommodations _____

Interviewed hotel manager _____

Address of nearest police station _____

Nearest fire station _____

Telephone number _____

Nearest hospital _____

Trauma level # _____

Telephone number _____

Arranged for extra security _____

Local security agency _____

Number assigned _____

Distributed lapel pins _____

Arranged for vehicle rentals _____

Arranged unattended vehicle security _____

Surveyed route from airport to site _____

Surveyed routes inside buildings _____

Inspected rooms, stairs, and elevators _____

Arranged for occupation of surrounding rooms _____

Laid out protective assignments _____

_____

_____

Security Team Leader _____

Selected restaurants _____

Appendix IV
Airport Security Checklist

Note: This form also serves for railway stations and seaports.

Airport location _____

Airport manager's telephone_____

Surveyed route from airport _____

Nearest hospital _____

Surveyed curbside facilities _____

Surveyed baggage handling _____

Surveyed airport fire/ambulance _____

Surveyed route to departure/arrival gate_____

Arranged for VIP lounge _____

Arranged security with airport manager_____

Arranged security with airline company_____

Airline company manager's telephone _____

Special boarding?_____

Parking for private aircraft_____

Fueling for private aircraft _____

Security for private aircraft _____

Lodgings for aircrew _____

Lodgings for security force_____

Lodgings for client_____

Special problems _____

_____

_____

_____

_____

Appendix V
Protectee Personal File

Name _____ S/S # _____

Date of birth _____ Title _____

 Home address _____

Telephone number _____

Other address _____

Telephone number _____

Business address _____

Telephone number _____ ._____

Club/organization name _____

Address _____

Telephone number _____

Club/organization name _____

Address _____

Telephone number _____

Club/organization name _____

Address _____

Telephone number _____

Height _____ Weight_____

Hair Color _____ Eye Color _____

Facial Hair _____

Eyeglasses/Contact lenses _____

Scars or tattoos_____

Personal physician _____

Address _____

Telephone number _____

Blood type _____ Prostheses _____

Surgical History _____

_____

_____

Current medical problems _____

_____

_____

Prescription drugs _____

_____

_____

Dentist _____

Address _____

Telephone number _____

False Teeth/implants _____

Spouse _____ S/S # _____

Date of birth_____

Other address_____

Telephone number _____

Business address _____

Telephone number _____

Height _____ Weight _____

Hair Color _____ Eye Color_____

Facial Hair _____

Eyeglasses/Contact lenses _____

Scars or tattoos_____

False Teeth/implants _____

Blood type _____ Prostheses_____

Child _____ S/S#_____

Date of birth _____ School _____

Height _____ Weight _____

Hair Color _____ Eye Color _____

Facial Hair _____

Eyeglasses/Contact lenses _____

Scars or tattoos_____

Blood type _____ Prostheses _____

Child _____ S/S#_____

Date of birth _____ School _____

Height _____ Weight _____

Hair Color _____ Eye Color _____

Facial Hair _____

Eyeglasses/Contact lenses _____

Scars or tattoos _____

Blood type _____ Prostheses _____

Child _____ S/S# _____

Date of birth _____ School _____

Height _____ Weight _____

Hair Color _____ Eye Color _____

Facial Hair _____

Eyeglasses/Contact lenses _____

Scars or tattoos _____

Blood type _____ Prostheses _____

Comments: _____

_____

_____

_____

_____

Include fingerprints, photographs and dental charts of each family member.

Appendix VI
Bomb Threat Checklist

NOTE: Work straight down this form. Ask questions on checklist, if possible, in order given. Try to keep caller on the line as long as possible, using supplementary questions to fill time. Signal to someone else to try to trace call. If you have Caller I. D. and a list of nearby pay phones, you may be able to pinpoint the caller's location to allow apprehension by security or police officers.

Date_____ Time_____

Person reporting_____

Received: Mail _____ Return address _____

_____

Type of envelope or package _____

Telephone # and extension where received _____

Telephone originating call (from Caller I. D.) _____

Caller:

Male_____ Female_____ Young _____ Old _____ Child _____ Accent_____

Caller's words_____

_____

_____

Characteristic or repetitious words or phrases _____

_____

_____

Describe caller's mood:

Calm _____ Excited _____ Logical _____ Irrational _____ Angry _____

Was voice familiar?_____ Whom recognized?_____

Describe any background noises _____

_____

_____

Time call ended _____ Was call taped?_____

Ask caller critical questions in this order:

Where is the bomb? _____

What does it look like? _____

When will it go off? _____

Why did you do it? _____

What is your name? _____

Where are you calling from? _____

Time-filling questions:

Did you ever work here? _____

For how long? _____

What was your job? _____

Did you enjoy your job? _____

Did you feel the pay was fair? _____

Who was your supervisor? _____

Was your supervisor fair to you? _____

Do you know anyone who works here? _____

What are you going to do now? _____

Where did you get the idea for your bomb? _____

How did you make it? _____

What explosive did you use? _____

NOTE: At this point, fill more time by inserting compliments, such as: "That's very clever," etc.

What do you look like? _____

How old are you? _____

What are you wearing? _____

Ever do this before? _____

Where? _____

When? _____

What happened? _____

Have you ever been arrested? _____

How did you avoid being arrested? _____

Index

kidnap teams, 2
kidnapping groups, 14
Kidnap/Ransom Insurance, 145, 164
Kilburn, Peter, 145
killing zone, 127, 128, 135
King, Martin Luther, 11
King, Rodney, 8

Landon, Michael, 14
lapel pins, 33
Latin America, 11
Lay off bomb 19, 129, 140, 141, 142
Ledbetter, Tina Marie, 13
Lennon, John, 7, 14
Letter bomb, 31, 137, 138, 141
liability insurance, 44
limpet bomb, 141
linguistic analysis, 14
local police, 117, 129, 153, 158
local police agencies, 35, 38, 39
local police officers, 39, 152
local threat patterns, 13
London Metropolis Police's Bomb Squad, 167
Lone assassin, 12

metal detectors, 10
Mexican politician Jose Francisco Ruiz Massieu, 95
microwave detectors, 55
Middle East, 7, 9
Middle East terrorists, 28
Moawad, Rene, 140
Moore, Sarah Jane, 37
Moriarity, Michael, 15
Moro kidnapping, 21, 129
Mossberg 500, 69
motion detector, 121
motorcade routes, 33
motorcycle attacks, 127, 128
moving targets, 82
Murphy's Law, 51

Native American extremists, 11
Neave, Airey, 137
New York City Police Department, 62
No-ranson policy, 165

N.A.A.C.P. President Willye Dennis, 12

off duty police officers, 151
off post agents, 98
oil slick, 120
Oleoresin Capsicum (OC) aerosols, 85, 88, 89
Oregon Police Officer Frank Ward, 89
Organization de L'Armee Secrete, (O.A.S.), 2, 10, 34, 35
Oswald, Lee Harvey, 1
outside lighting, 50
Overseas Security Advisory Council, 13

Palme, Olaf, 107
panic button, 32, 55
paramedic certification, 23
Parton, Dolly, 155
Penn, Sean, 14
personal attacks, 9
personal relationships, 155
personal threats, 161
photos of crowds, 15
physical location, 13
physical search, 114
physical size or strength, 1
Pinochet, Augusto, 119
Platt, Michael, 70
PLO Security Chief Hayel Abdel-Hamid, 42
pocket pistol, 64
Police Officer Thomas Delehanty, 34
police officers, 23, 24, 28, 37, 81, 91, 108, 114, 150, 155
political assassins, 10
political figure, 9
political unrest, 9
Posse Comitatus, 11, 32
post office, 10
potential threats, 5
President Bush, 34, 109
President Clinton, 107
President Eisenhower, 68
President Gerald Ford, 1, 37, 38, 109

President Harry Truman, 3, 41, 107
President Kennedy, 1, 117, 118, 133
President Nixon, 9
President Ronald Reagan, 1, 5, 34, 37, 66, 71, 92
President Roosevelt, 33, 41
presidential protection, 31
Presidential Protection Corps. 2, 35
pre-emptive strike, 158
Princess Diana, 155
Princess Stephanie of Monaco, 155
private academies, 25
private bodyguards, 35, 39, 97, 122, 156
private detective agencies, 42, 43, 149
private investigators, 37, 40
private investigator's license, 5
private protective agents, 40, 142
professional criminals, 10, 164
property damage, 11
Prosecutor Paoloa Borsellino, 140
Protective Research Section, 32
protective rings, 9
protective screen, 21, 31
Provisional Wing of the Irish Republican Army, "Provos," 2
proximity cards, 53, 55
psychotic employees, 10
psychotic stalker, 15
public figures, 2
Pulido, Jorge, 127

Rabbi Meir Kahane, 11
radiator shield, 119
radio controlled bomb, 122
Raven MP-25, 66, 76
reinforced bumpers, 120
Remington Model 700 Police Sniper Special, 71
Remington Model 788, 71
remote control bombs, 140

YOU WILL ALSO WANT TO READ: